Diverse and Creative Voices

Diverse and Creative Voices
Theological Essays from the Majority World

EDITED BY
DIEUMEME NOELLISTE
AND
SUNG WOOK CHUNG

FOREWORD BY
SAMUEL ESCOBAR

☙PICKWICK *Publications* · Eugene, Oregon

DIVERSE AND CREATIVE VOICES
Theological Essays from the Majority World

Copyright © 2015 Wipf and Stock Publishers. All rights reserved. Except for brief quotations in critical publications or reviews, no part of this book may be reproduced in any manner without prior written permission from the publisher. Write: Permissions. Wipf and Stock Publishers, 199 W. 8th Ave., Suite 3, Eugene, OR 97401.

Pickwick Publications
An Imprint of Wipf and Stock Publishers
199 W. 8th Ave., Suite 3
Eugene, OR 97401

www.wipfandstock.com

ISBN 13: 978-1-61097-978-8

Cataloguing-in-Publication Data

Diverse and creative voices : theological essays from the majority world / edited by Dieumeme Noelliste and Sung Wook Chung, with a foreword by Samuel Escobar.

xxiv + 254 p. ; 23 cm. Includes bibliographical references.

ISBN 13: 978-1-61097-978-8

1. Christianity and culture. 2. Theology—Developing countries. 3. Jesus Christ—Person and offices. 4. Salvation—Christianity. 5. Holy Spirit. 6. Church. 7. Missions. I. Chung, Sung Wook, 1966–. II. Noelliste, Dieumeme. III. Escobar, Samuel, 1934–. IV. Title.

BT80 C49 2015

Manufactured in the U.S.A.

Dedicated to the Memory of

Dr Isaac Zokoué (1944–2014)
Pastor and leader in theological education in Africa and leader of the Evangelical movement in Francophone Africa

and

Emilio Antonio Núñez (1923–2015)
Pioneer and Dean of Latin American Evangelical Theology.

Contents

List of Contributors | vii
Foreword by Samuel Escobar | ix
Acknowledgments | xv
Introduction | xvii

PART 1 **GOD AND HUMANITY**

1. God and Humanity in African Religious Beliefs and Christianity | 3
   Abel Ndjérareou

2. God and Humanity in Islam and Christianity | 24
   Ng Kam Weng

3. The Self-Revealing God and the Human Predicament | 48
   Burchell Taylor

PART 2 **CHRIST AND SALVATION**

4. Redeemer and Transformer: The Relevance of Christ for China's Cultural Renewal and Liberation | 67
   Carver Yu

5. Christ and Liberation: Toward a Messianic Christology for a Postcolonial Society | 84
   Delano Palmer and Dieumeme Noelliste

6. The Promise of a Trinitarian Christology for the Latin American Evangelical Church | 102
   David del Salto

PART 3 THE HOLY SPIRIT AND THE CHURCH

7. The Church as Pneumatic Community:
Toward an Ecclesiology for the African Context | 143
   Isaac Zokoué

8. The Church as Liberated and Liberating Community:
A Primer for a Latin American Ecclesiology. | 160
   Dario Lopez

PART 4 ESCHATOLOGY AND MISSION

9. An Eschatologically Driven Missiology for
Holistic Engagement with African Realities | 181
   Abel Ngarsoulede

10. Prophecy and Preaching in the Last Days in John's Revelation:
A Reflection on the Ministry and Mission of the Church in South-East Asia | 198
    Tony Siew

11. Sino-Theology: Recapitulation and Prospect | 216
    Wu Dongri and Chen Yuehua

Bibliography | 239
Index | 251

List of Contributors

Abel Ngarsoulede (PhD, Faculté de Théologie Evangélique de Bangui) is Chadian. He is director of Studies at the Ecole Supérieure de Théologie Evangélique Shalom in N'Djamena, Chad.

Abel Ndjérareou (PhD, Dallas Theological Seminary) from Chad in Central Africa, is a former President of the Faculté de Théologie Evangélique de Bangui (FATEB) in Bangui, Central African Republic, and former coordinator of the Conseil des Institutions Théologiques d'Afrique Francophone (CITAF). He has written the commentary on "Exodus," the "Introduction to the Pentateuch," and "Yahweh and the Other gods" for the *Africa Bible Commentary*, as well as the monograph *De Quelle Tribu Es-Tu?*, a book that seeks to contribute to the resolution of tribal conflicts in the African churches.

Burchell K. Taylor (PhD, University of Leeds, UK) from Jamaica is Pastor of Bethel Baptist Church in Kingston, Jamaica, and Lecturer in Ethics and Biblical Studies at the United Theological College of the West Indies, also in Kingston, Jamaica. He is the author *Saying No to Babylon*, *The Church Taking Sides*, *Free For All?*, and *What Does the Lord Require of You?*

Carver Yu (DPhil, Oxford University, UK) from China is President and Professor of Dogmatic Theology at the China Graduate School of Theology in Hong Kong. Among his many publications in the area of systematic theology is the book, *The Cross in Asia Today*.

Dario Lopez Rodriguez (PhD, Oxford Center for Mission Studies/ Open University, UK) is Peruvian. He is a former President of the National Evangelical Council of Peru, and Pastor of the Mount Sinai Church of God in Lima, Peru. Among other subjects, he has taught religion and politics, missiology and human rights, in theological institutions throughout Latin America.

David del Salto (PhD, Lutheran School of Theology) from Ecuador serves at Communidad Nueva Creacion in Chicago and teaches theology in that city and in several places in Latin America.

Delano Vincent Palmer (ThD, University of South Africa) from Jamaica is a senior lecturer at Jamaica Theological Seminary, Kingston Jamaica. He is the author of *New Testament Theology in Context* and *Messianic "I" and Rastafari in New Testament Dialogue*.

Dongri Wu (PhD, Yonsei University, Seoul, South Korea) from Malaysia is executive director of the International Center for Innovative Thinking in the Department of Philosophy at Tsinghua University in Beijing, China. His doctoral thesis is entitled *Sino-Theology in China: An Evaluation from the Perspective of Christian Ethics*.

Isaac Zokoué (1944–2014) (PhD, Université des Sciences Humaines, Strasbourg, France) was a former President of the Alliance of Evangelicals of Central Africa, Pastor of Kina Baptist Church, and Professor and Coordinator of the doctoral program at the Faculté de Théologie Evangélique de Bangui (FATEB), in Bangui Central African Republic. Sadly Isaac died before this book came out. The essay contained in this volume was his last written contribution.

Ng Kam Weng (DPhil, University of Cambridge, UK) from Malaysia is Research Director at Kairos Research Centre, Malaysia. He has published widely in the area of systematic theology. His primary interest lies in explicating other world religions, especially Islam, in relation to Christian theology.

Tony Siew (PhD, University of Otago, New Zealand) from Singapore is Lecturer in New Testament Theology at Trinity Theological College, Singapore. His publications have focused on the New Testament, particularly the book of Revelation. His major work is entitled *The War between the Two Beasts and the Two Witnesses: A Chiastic Reading Revelation 11:1—14:5*.

Yuehua Chen (PhD, Tsinghua University in Beijing, China) from China is Assistant Professor at the Institute of Religious Studies in Zhejiang University in Hangzhou, China. Beside his work in Neo-Platonism and Sino-Theology, he is the Chinese translator of Boethius's *Consolation of Philosophy*.

Foreword

DURING THE THREE MORE recent decades theological reflection has become a global enterprise. It is not anymore simply the efficient transmission of an intellectual product developed in Germany, the British Isles, or the United States of America. During the twentieth century, and with God's blessing on the missionary activity of a myriad of individuals and organizations, new churches rose around the world, and as they grew up in size and maturity men and women started to reflect about their faith and delve into the biblical sources in order to respond to the questions that their context posed.

In Latin America we have come to define Theology as the reflection of the people of God on their Christian practice in light of God's Word. So theological *reflection* is not just the intellectual activity of specialists in University departments or Bible schools. It has become closely connected with what churches *are doing* in countries around the world in all six continents.

This book is a representative expression of this new reality and I feel honored by the request of its editors to write a foreword for it. As I read it I have come to appreciate the good compiling and editorial work of Sung Wook Chung and Dieumeme Noelliste. We have contributors from Asia, Africa, Latin America, and the Caribbean, all of them part of what has come to be known as "the majority world." I have had the privilege of becoming acquainted with several of these writers in Evangelical student work, in the Lausanne movement, and in the theological conferences organized by the International Fellowship of Evangelical Mission Theologians (INFEMIT). In several cases we have experienced together the joy and the anguish of posing burning questions coming from our ministries and entering together in a communal exploration into the richness of God's Word and the wealth of the Evangelical tradition.

As the table of contents shows the chapters of this book have been arranged following a selection of themes from classical theology. However, as you read each chapter you will find new ways of dealing with classical issues, and new questions posed as each issue is approached. In some chapters it is clear that the reflection points finally to the application of the truth expounded in the daily life of churches. These authors are active in pastoral and teaching positions.

Several of the essays in this book call our attention to the liberating dimension of the gospel and to Jesus Christ as a Liberator. In order to better understand the direction of this reflection you have to take into account what Dieumeme Noelliste and Delano Palmer say about their own Caribbean context, which is also characteristic of other contexts in the majority world: "This thirst for emancipation in a freedom-denying context is one of the factors that explain the pull that many dwellers of the Caribbean Basin have felt toward Jesus and his message of liberation that the New Testament writers, particularly the authors of the Gospels have written about."

This liberating thrust of the person and the message of Jesus is more evident on the chapters about Christology that come from China, the English speaking Caribbean, and Latin America. The Christological questions are definitely posed from the perspective of evangelism and mission. Besides that, the chapter by David del Salto is representative of a younger generation of Latin American theologians that can now benefit from the pioneer work of the earlier generation of Evangelicals that related to the Lausanne movement and were the founders of INFEMIT.

Some of the essays from Asia and Africa reflect the fact that Christians in those regions have to come to terms with the pervasive influence of Islam, Buddhism, Confucianism, or African religions. The early missionary approaches have to give way to a fresh understanding of other religions that pose difficult questions for Christians and churches in a post colonial atmosphere. A fresh reading of what Scripture teaches about religion is high in today's theological agenda. This task has become more difficult because of the change of approach towards religion in the academic world, moving from an expectation of a triumphant secularizing process to an acknowledgement that religion is back and will stay, even in modern societies. Lutheran sociologist Peter Berger points to that process and calls it "desecularization," and theologian Harvey Cox has moved from his classic *The Secular City* to his more recent *Fire from Heaven*.

The bibliographies of this valuable collection of essays allow us to see that though the reflection is contextual it is not provincial in any way. By their academic formation and up-to-date acquaintance with theological activity in Europe and North America, these authors make good use of definitions and insights of well-known Western theologians. In their work with the Bible they also make good use of tools developed in a long Western tradition, mainly Protestant, of biblical scholarship.

The readers of this volume will find it challenging and stretching, but never boring. As I was reading it one of my conclusions was that for the future of theology around the world it would be highly desirable that opportunities for a global theological dialogue will continue to be fostered by Evangelical bodies.

Samuel Escobar
Valencia Spain, July 2013

Acknowledgments

WE ARE PLEASED THAT this book has finally seen the light of day. It has been in the making for the past six years, and, at times, we wondered if it would ever reach the finish line.

As is well known, the completion of a project of this sort is rarely, if ever, the product of the effort of a solitary person, or a small circle of persons. Things are no different in the case of this book. Its coming into being is the result of the labor of a fairly large group of persons to whom we'll be forever indebted.

Our gratitude goes first to our friends and colleagues in the Majority World who believed that this project was important enough that they gave of their time to contribute to it. Without their participation, the book could not be produced. We are particularly grateful to the late Isaac Zokoué who prepared his chapter while battling cancer. Sadly, Isaac went to meet his Lord before the book was published. We gladly dedicate the volume to his memory as well as the memory of another pioneer and giant of Majority World theology—Emilio A. Núñez of El Salvador and Guatemala who passed way just weeks before the book went to press.

As can be seen, the contributors to the book come from different regions of the Majority World. Although they all speak English, some elected to write their chapters in their native tongues, which, of course, necessitated the translation of their work into English. We are grateful to our friends and colleagues who offered their time and expertise to help us with this task. Our thanks go to Tim Erdel of Bethel of Bethel College (Indiana) for the translation of Darío Lopez's chapter from Spanish; Rony Joseph for his translation of Isaac Zokoué's chapter from French; Killick and Néhémie Aristide for their translation of Abel Ngarsoulede's chapter also from French.

Beside these, several others have provided invaluable help without which the project could not be completed. They include: Lindy Scott, editor of the Journal of Latin American Theology, who gave us permission to reproduce David del Salto's chapter in the book; Samuel Escobar, who contributes the forward to the book; our colleagues at Denver Seminary, Danny Carroll Rodas, who encouraged us all along and provided helpful suggestions regarding the way the project could be reconfigured when we ran into difficulty with our original plan, Alex Mekonnen and David Buschart who lent us their sympathetic ears when we encountered seemingly unsurmountable roadblocks; and our students, Andrew Chun and Ahnna Ellie Cho Park, who did the painstaking work of preparing the manuscript for publication; and Robin Parry, our editor at Wipf and Stock, for his patience and generosity in extending the deadline for the submission of the manuscript more than once.

Lastly, we would like to express sincere gratitude to our wives Gloria (Dieumeme's) and In-Kyung (Sung Wook's) for their moral support along this arduous journey. Most of all, we thank our God for his sustaining grace during this long process. To Him be the glory.

Introduction

IT HAS BEEN WELL established that the centers of Christianity have moved to the parts of the world known as the Majority World or the global South. Whereas up to the first half of the twentieth century, the main theaters of the global Christian movement were European and North American cities such as London, Geneva, and New York, today they are found in southern metropolises such as Seoul, Buenos Aires, Nairobi, and Sao Paulo. As historians of missions have been reminding us of late, after some four hundred years of Western dominance, Christianity has entered a period of Western retrenchment and non-Western advancement.[1]

This historic change in the landscape of global Christianity has already begun to be felt in various areas of the life of the worldwide church, including theology. As recently as the middle of the twentieth century, the theological reflection that was produced in Europe and the United States enjoyed virtually total hegemony over the rest of the world. Following the early period of the Christian movement, when many of the leading figures of Christian thought came from North Africa, theology essentially flowed from North to South.[2] For this reason, Majority World theologians were educated and trained in Europe and North America, and, in the main, their theological endeavors consisted in importing European and American theologies to their lands of origin. But as time elapsed, this foreign theological diet proved less and less satisfying to the inhabitants of the non-Western regions of the globe. While Christians in the global South have undeni-

---

1. See for example Walls, *The Missionary Movement in Christian History*; Walls, "Christian Scholarship and the Demographic Transformation of the Church," 173, 174; Sanneh, *Whose Religion is Christianity?*

2. In his book entitled *How Africa Shaped the Christian Mind*, Thomas Oden has shown that Christian thought began to develop in Africa centuries before it penetrated Europe and America.

ably learned much from mainstream European and American theologies, they have found them lacking in many ways. Increasingly, they see in these theologies features that are merely reflective of their own geographical and cultural contexts. As a consequence, they find them inadequate to address the burning realities of other regions of the globe. Some even argue that aspects of the theology produced in the West are less than faithful to the biblical witness about the reality of the triune God and the gospel.

As the twentieth century passed its midpoint and was rushing toward its end, a growing number of Majority World theologians came to realize that they could, in fact, do theology in their own contexts for the benefit of their own people. Thus, from the 1960s onward, theologians in the global South have embarked on a form of theological reflection which has some time been described as "contextual" reflection or "contextualized theology."

The first major modern attempt at the formulation of a homegrown Majority World theology occurred in Latin America and was called "liberation theology." This theology purported to be a theology of liberating praxis that speaks from the viewpoint of those who live at the margins of the dominant social structures.[3] From its very inception Liberation Theology has generated a great deal of controversy, both on the Latin American scene and abroad. But despite the concerns it evoked, it is undeniable that liberation theology did provide a platform and an impetus for Majority World theologians in various parts of the globe to raise their own voices for a genuinely global theological engagement. One should not lose sight of the fact that it was in the aftermath of the launch of liberation theology that a body such as the Ecumenical Association of Third World Theologians (EATWOT) emerged. Also, following the launch of LT, social groups in various parts of the world, who became conscious of their own condition of disenfranchisement, have found in the new theology a way to interpret Christian faith and a channel to press for the redress of their situations. Of the many examples that could be cited one thinks of Dalit theology in India, African liberation theology, particularly the anti-apartheid theology of South Africa, *Minjung* theology of South Korea, and feminist theology in its various forms and expressions. And besides these theologies that lean toward a liberation perspective, there are others that were motivated by a search for cultural identity and anthropological affirmation.[4]

It has been pointed out that some of these theologies have shown the influence of philosophical underpinnings considered extrinsic to biblical

---

3. Gutierrez, *A Theology of Liberation Revised Edition*, xxix.

4. This is by and large true for instance of the theological thought that developed in Sub Saharan Africa.

revelation, either because they allegedly reflect the influence of Marxist sociopolitical and economic analysis, which is grounded in the notion of an ongoing class struggle, or because they are deemed too bound to the cultural contexts from which they emerged. Based on this critique, some doubt that these theologies can pass the test of orthodox Christian theology.

It is very important to appreciate, however, that since the 1970s, theologians in various parts of the Majority World have sought to conduct the theological task in a manner that has endeavored to be faithful to Scripture and responsive to the needs of their own cultural and social contexts. A prime example of this is the International Fellowship of Evangelical Missions Theologians (INFEMIT), which has endeavored to articulate an evangelical missiology in the context of the majority world that accords prime place to the features of holism and transformation.[5] These efforts have resulted in a theological reflection which, we believe, would be beneficial for Christians in other parts of the world to know about. It is this conviction that motivates the production of this book. Convinced of the importance of the theological reflection that is now taking place in the Majority World, the editors of this book have invited a group of Majority World theologians to share their reflections on several themes of Christian faith from their own socio historical perspectives but with an unswerving commitment to the authority of Scripture. We hope that this modest effort will be used by Christians in the West to engage the perspectives of fellow believers in the global South and benefit from their reflections on our common faith.

The book consists of four parts, each dealing with a set of theological themes. The themes selected for treatment are: God and Humanity, Christ and Salvation, the Holy Spirit and the Church, and Eschatology and Mission. Each set of themes is addressed from a variety of perspectives. For example, Part I, which focuses on the twin themes of God and humanity, explores these foci from an African perspective (Abel Ndjérareou), a Caribbean vantage point (Burchell Taylor), and an Asian perspective (Ng Kam Weng). Part II zeroes in on the themes of Christ and salvation and explores them from the lenses of an Asian theologian (Carver Yu), a Latin American thinker (David del Salto), and two Caribbean theologians (Delano Palmer and Dieumeme Noelliste). Part III discusses the themes of the Holy Spirit and the Church and broaches these loci from an African vantage point (Isaac

---

5. INFEMIT was established in 1987 and embraces three continental evangelical movements from the majority world, namely, the Latin American Evangelical Theological Fraternity, the African Theological Fraternity and Partnership in Mission Asia. See Tizon, *Transformation After Lausanne*, especially chapter 4; Yung, *Mangoes or Bananas?* 196; and Samuel and Sugden, *Mission as Transformation: A Theology of the Whole Gospel*.

xx   *introduction*

Zokoué) and a Latin American perspective (Dario Lopez). Finally, Part IV focuses on eschatology and mission and offers the reader an African view and two Asian perspectives on these themes. The African understanding is provided by Abel Ngarsoulede of Chad and the two Asian perspectives are offered by Tony Siew of Singapore and Dongri Wu and Yuehua Chen from mainland China.

In Part I, Abel Ndjérareou of Chad tackles the themes of God and humanity and seeks to bring to the fore the relationship that exists between the two. It is Ndjérareou's view that African theologians should discuss these theological themes against the backdrop of African Traditional Religions (ATR). He deems this important because, as he sees it, it is impossible to formulate a genuine and authentic African theology without a proper appreciation for the perspective provided by the ATR. For Ndjérareou, Africans learned from African traditional religions that there is a Supreme Being which they identify with the God of Christianity. Furthermore, these religions teach that humans were created by the Supreme Being. It is this background that enables African Christians to resonate with the biblical account of creation without difficulty and to view the God of the Bible as their Creator. With respect to humanity, African traditional religions have emphasized that humans are essentially communal beings. Thus, in the context of African traditional religions, family and community play a decisive role in the formation of human identity. This communitarian orientation of African traditional religions is resonant with the Christian view of God who is a triune communion.

Speaking from an Asian perspective, Ng Kam Weng embarks on a comparative study of Christianity's concept of God and humanity and Islam's view of Allah and humanity. In his study, Weng found that while Christianity and Islam are both monotheistic faiths, there are fundamental differences between them with respect to their views of God and his relationship to human beings. For example, while Islam stresses Allah's transcendence and fatalistic predestination and human beings' nonnegotiable responsibility to submit to Allah's absolute sovereignty, Christianity emphasizes the possibility and reality of a personal and mutually loving relationship and fellowship between God and human beings, without compromising God's transcendence. Weng's comparative discussion of the idea of God can prove helpful to Euro-American theologians and Christians who are interested in detecting convergences and divergences between Christianity and Islam.

Addressing these loci from the vantage point of the Caribbean, Jamaican theologian and churchman, Burchell K. Taylor, launches on a search for a view of God that can help humans face the existential problems of life, particularly the vexing issues of pain and suffering. In his exploration,

Taylor argues that neither the dismissive posture of the New Atheism nor the transcendence-skewed perspective of traditional theism can provide such a concept. For him, the solution lies in the biblically sanctioned notion of God as the "Ultimate Self-Revealing Subject" who is actively engaged in the historical domain for its redemption and liberation. This God, Taylor argues, exhibits his liberating power eminently in Jesus Christ, his ultimate self-expression, who both endured and conquered suffering and pain. In him, God presents himself as the hope of all suffering humanity.

In Part II, Carver Yu, a theologian and theological educator from Hong Kong, engages with the theme of Christ and salvation from a Chinese perspective. In particular, given the current crisis and disintegration of Chinese culture, Yu focuses his discussion on the relationship between Christ and culture, arguing that the gospel of Christ can make a significant contribution to the transformation of Chinese culture. Yu endorses the Reformed model of Christ as Transformer, contending that Christ should be regarded as the fulfiller and judge of culture as well as the restorer of full humanity. In the process of his argumentation, Yu offers insightful comments on the comparison between Confucianism, Daoism, and Christianity in the area of truth claims.

Moving across the seas to the Caribbean region with its history of slavery, colonization, and neocolonialism, theologians Delano Palmer of Jamaica and Dieumeme Noelliste of Haiti offer a perspective on Christ and salvation that, they believe, might respond to the aspiration of the Caribbean people for the experience of complete freedom. With a focus on aspects of the writings of Luke and Paul, they argue for a perspective that views Jesus Christ as the bearer of a multifaceted salvation which persons experience when they come under the sway of the life transforming Spirit that the risen Lord poured out at the conclusion of his messianic mission. Such an experience sets the believer on a course toward full transformation into the likeness of Christ which is the essence of full liberation. But because both the messianic salvation and the transformation that it unleashes share the eschatological tension of the "already" and the "not yet," they argue that the experience of full liberation, at both the personal and social level, will remain an eschatological hope.

Still on the same themes, but with a clear stress on the doctrine of Christ, Latin American theologian David del Salto of Ecuador introduces the reader to the Christology of Rene Padilla and Orlando Costas, two pioneering thinkers of an earlier generation of Latin American evangelical theologians who conducted their reflection on the platform provided by the Latin American Theological Fraternity in the last quarter of the twentieth century. Proceeding comparatively, del Salto found that the motivation for

Padilla's Christology is, among other things, ethical and pastoral. Del Salto interprets Padilla as being particularly concerned with challenge that Latin American Christians face when it comes to relating their faith to social, economic, and political matters "due to a lack of an adequate Christological foundation for action and thought." Padilla, he argues, seeks to fill this void by underscoring the importance for Christology of the historical rootedness of Jesus and the message of the kingdom that he came to inaugurate and proclaim. For his part, while appreciating the need to recover the historical Jesus for Latin America, Costas' main concern was to search for a Christology that puts on a firm footing a theology of mission and evangelization. He finds the linchpin for that Christology in the cross.

Tackling the themes of the Holy Spirit and the Church, African theologian Isaac Zokoué of the Central African Republic directs the reader's attention squarely to the Bible. Speaking specifically from the standpoint of Francophone Africa, Zokoué argues for a perspective that is scripturally anchored and consciously integrative. According to him, since there can be no church without the Holy Spirit, a robust ecclesiology needs to be forged with a constant gaze on pneumatology. Conversely, because the church is the sphere where the promise of the Spirit found its fulfillment, and the primary domain of the Spirit's activity, Zokoué is convinced that, to be enriching and substantive, a doctrine of the Spirit must be formulated in close connection with the church. Such an approach, he avers, necessitates a parting of the ways with the fragmentary and atomizing methodology which, under the influence of modernity, has characterized much of Western theology.

Writing from the vantage point of Latin America, Peruvian theologian Dario Lopez agrees with Zokoué on the need for "an intimate relation between the Holy Spirit and the church." But his treatment of the themes is avowedly missiological. Taking his departure from the missionary praxis of Jesus (which he sees reflected in the early Christian communities), Lopez sees the church as a "liberated and liberating community" that is entrusted with the mission of loving and defending life—particularly the life of the poor and the excluded. It carries that mission in the power and fullness of the Spirit. The church then is a missional and pneumatic community that represents a radical alternative to the dominant culture. Her uniqueness, Lopez contends, stems from her kerygmatic nature which incorporates the values of inclusiveness, equality, empowerment, subversiveness, and prophetic critique. In the view of Lopez, when measured by these yardsticks, the Latin American evangelical church fares well with the first three criteria, and badly in the latter two. For according to him, the Latin American church's "destabilizing" and "prophetic" witness vis a vis the sociopolitical order still remains weak.

Part IV, which focuses on the themes of eschatology and mission, opens up with a contribution by Abel Ngarsoulede of Chad. With a sharp focus on the African continent, Ngarsoulede begins with a challenge and endorsement. He challenges John Mbiti's denial of the presence of any futuristic element in the African understanding of eschatology and endorses Byang Kato's position that the African popular view is akin to the biblical perspective on the subject. Having said this, however, Ngarsoulede goes on to bemoan the fact that missiologically this feature of the African culture, which could be an asset in the establishment of a robust Christianity on the continent, has not been put to good use. He argues that while the notion of a *postmortem* existence in a world beyond the present one is very much part of the belief system of most Africans, the manner in which the gospel was communicated to the Africans by the Western missionaries did not sufficiently exploit that cultural asset for the emergence of a vibrant Christianity on the continent. He believes that, combined with the arrival of secularism and the posture of skepticism regarding the relevance of the gospel for the here and now, this initial missionary *faux pas* has contributed to the rise of enormous challenges for the conduct of the missionary task in the African milieu. According to Ngarsoulede, the answer to this problem lies in an eschatologically driven missiology which, while endeavoring to be attentive to the realities of the transient world, seeks to elevate the minds and hearts of Africans to the world beyond and to Christ whose lordship encompasses both domains.

With feet firmly planted in South East Asia, Tony Siew of Singapore broaches the themes of Eschatology and Mission exegetically and contextually. In his study of various passages of the book of Revelation, Siew argues that the proclamation of the gospel will be part of the mission of the church during the final stage of the end times—a task which will grow more and more difficult as the End approaches. Applying this understanding to his region, Siew challenges the church in South East Asia to summon the courage to preach the eternal gospel despite the constraints and opposition that it is likely to encounter. To carry out this mandate effectively, Siew argues that the church needs to make full use of modern technological advances, particularly social media, in addition to working collaboratively, and employing the dominant language of the region—Malay—as the medium to communicate the gospel.

While not delving into a discussion of eschatology, Dongri Wu and Yuehua Chen from mainland China introduce us to the new field of Sino-theology. They define Sino-theology as "an academic movement committed to the investigation and research on the Christian faith in the Chinese language." Alongside their discussion of the emergence, development, the current state, methodology, and major characteristics of this fairly new discipline, the authors highlight the potential that Sino-theology holds for a pertinent missional engagement in the Chinese context. They argue that Sino-theology should facilitate a dialogue between Christianity and Chinese native religions in an effort to forge a public theology that could serve as a missional tool to stir the interest of the Chinese people in the Christian faith and its contribution to larger Chinese society. At a time when Chinese Christianity is gaining in public attention and Chinese churches are becoming more and more cognizant of the responsibility to develop a homegrown theology that is faithful to the Word of God, Wu's and Chen's article represents a timely and welcome contribution.

From our survey of the content of the chapters that constitute the book, it is clear that our authors take a variety of approaches to the themes they chose to address. While some adopt a strictly exegetical approach, others prefer to frame their reflection more in the systematic theology fashion, while still others proceed by way of comparative religions. Also, it should not escape our notice that our authors did not feel bound to devote equal attention to the set of themes covered in their essays. This, to us, is not insignificant. For in our view, both their choice of methodology and the particular theme(s) they deem worthy of emphasis contribute to the perspective they bring to their treatment. Theologically, this speaks of their concern to scratch where their particular context itches. Their reflections clearly show that the theology that is currently being done in the majority world is by no means monolithic. Far from being homogeneous, these essays show that it is expressed in various and, dare we say creative, voices. We hope that Christians in the West will find their perspective beneficial and enriching.

Dieumeme Noelliste and Sung Wook Chung

PART 1
God and Humanity

1

God and Humanity in African Religious Beliefs and Christianity

Abel Ndjérareou (Chad)

INTRODUCTION

A STUDY OF GOD and humanity in an African perspective cannot be done without referring to the findings of the basic elements of the African religious system known as African Traditional Religions (hereafter ATR). In recent times this has become even more true with the resurgence of the ATR that occurred in the aftermath of the African independence movement of the 1950s, and the explosion of the African cultural revolution movement of the 1970s. These developments have inspired a search for an African Christianity that takes into serious account the African religious experience. This has resulted in the production of a body of literature that has focused for the most part on the phenomenological study of the ATR.

Yet, concomitant with this resurgence of the ATR which African theologians regard as "a contemporary living reality"[1] is an explosion of

---

1. Idowu, "The Study of Religion with Special Reference to Africa Traditional

Christianity on African soil. Richard Gehman observes that "within a little more than a century Africa has turned away from ATR to embrace the Christian faith."[2] To many, Christianity appears to pose a mortal threat to the ATR. But more serious than the question of religious competition is the dilemma the encounter of Christianity with the ATR poses for African Christians. Put bluntly, the issue is how to live the Christian life with the haunting legacy of a religious past.

While we have admitted that we cannot study God and humanity in an African perspective without an adequate understanding of the ATR, we also know that the identity and the acts of what that religious system refers to as Supreme Being have been a puzzle for Africans in their search for the truth about God and his relationship to humanity. In light of this, the purpose of this chapter is to explore what it means to be human, how Africans can come to know God and thus have a genuine relationship with him, and what it means to experience an identity that embraces both their cultural heritage and their faith in Christ.

Our inquiry will follow a threefold approach encapsulated by the following questions: How do Africans view God and humanity? How does the Bible describe what Africans conceive as God? And what are the implications for Christianity in Africa today of the encounter of the traditional African view of God with the biblical perspective. Although we are aware of the danger of syncretism that African Christianity faces, our inquiry will, nonetheless, take into serious account Africa's pre-Christian religious experience as an important step toward the knowledge of the true God and his relationship to humankind.

Yusufu Turaki, to whom I am indebted for the perspective that I will share in this chapter, warns that the interpretation of the concepts and attributes of God in the ATR should be measured by the traditional religion itself. He goes on to state that, "They cannot be interpreted by using Christian categories, for then, they lose their traditional meanings and import."[3] In other words, according to Turaki, in order to accurately understand the African concept of God, our interpretation needs to be undertaken in the framework of the African religious worldview itself. But, since Turaki himself acknowledges that, "the traditional concepts of God as stated by . . . African . . . scholars are comparable with those of Christianity,"[4] we will not seek to interpret the ATR as a religion. Instead, we will highlight those areas

Religion," 1.
    2. Gehman, *African Religion in Biblical Perspective*, 3.
    3. Turaki, *Christianity and African Gods: Methods in Theology*, 28.
    4. Ibid.

that it shares with Christian faith in order to come to an understanding of what it means to be an African believer in Jesus Christ. In light of this, our description of the ATR will be limited to the categories which bear on the themes of God and humanity.

Before considering the questions mentioned above, we will describe briefly the religious context in which the biblical revelation of God to humanity through Jesus Christ took place. This is extremely important for our purpose here. For the people to whom God revealed his plan of salvation came out of their own religious experiences just as the Africans. Yet, they were challenged to embrace the new message of salvation through Jesus Christ just as the Africans are challenged to do.

SETTING THE BIBLICAL RELIGIOUS BACKGROUND

The Bible shows that people of traditional religions were confronted by the revelation of the God of Israel as the true God who claimed the whole human race to himself by right of creation (Gen 1:1; Exod 19:5; Ps 100:1). From Abraham to the Jews, to the Africans via the Athenians, the challenge has always been to reflect critically on the original religions of the nations in light of the new revelation of the true God and his relationship to humanity. Abraham left his pagan family to respond to the call and mission of God to become a source of blessings to "all the families of the earth" (Gen 12:1–3). Later on, Joshua will refer to his pagan ancestors as idol worshippers, and choose, along with his family, to abandon their "foreign gods" and serve Yahweh alone (Josh 24:14–24). Paul, likewise, challenged Jews, Gentiles, and pagans alike to establish a proper relationship with God which requires a drastic adjustment of their previous concept of God and humanity (Acts 14:8–18; 17:16–34).

In his discourse to the Athenians, Paul rehearses the basic doctrines of Christian faith and challenges his hearers to re-examine the tenets of their religious systems in light the biblical view, and to respond accordingly. This comes out with particular clarity in his exposition of the doctrines of God and humanity. Paul states:

> The God who made the world and everything in it, being Lord of heaven and earth, does not live in temples made by man, nor is he served by human hands, as though he needed anything, since he himself gives to all mankind life and breath and everything. And he made from one man every nation of mankind to live on all the face of the earth, having determined allotted periods

and the boundaries of their dwelling place, that they should seek God, and perhaps feel their way toward him and find him.

In light of Paul's discourse, we contend that the Supreme Being of ATR can be identified with the "Unknown God" of the Athenians. Hence, adherents of the ATR, like the Athenians, are challenged to respond to the new message. What kind of knowledge of God and humanity do Africans have outside God's revelation of himself through Jesus-Christ? How do we integrate the revelation about the true God and his will for humanity into our African traditional religious beliefs? We argue that the search must begin with the Africans' own religious awareness and proceed with a spiritual journey that leads to a proper relationship with the true God.

THE MEANING OF THE KNOWLEDGE OF GOD AND HUMANKIND IN THE ATR

How do Africans view or know God? The biblical worldview through which traditional religions are assessed is quite different from the African religious worldview. In this latter worldview, the concept of God is composed of three mains elements: the Supreme Being, the spirit world, and the mystical powers which are subordinated to the Supreme Being. Most African traditional religions, while emphasizing one or the other of these divine powers, hold the existence of a Supreme Being as a common basis for spiritual and social reality. These powers operate either directly or indirectly under the power of the Supreme Being.

The Supreme Being in the ATR

Through myths, legends, and stories, Africans came to an awareness of God as the Supreme Being. In Yoruba belief he is depicted in terms that are similar to the Christian description of God. According to Opoku, the Yoruba views God as follows:

> He is credited with omnipresence, omniscience, and omnipotence. He is the just and impartial Judge, sometimes meting out judgment in the next world. He is Olurun Adakedajo, God the silent but active Judge. He is Olarun Olore, God the Benefactor. He is Olorun Alamu, the Merciful God. The creation of the universe is attributed to Him, and He therefore bears the title of Eleda, Creator. Other titles given to Him are significant. He is Alaye, the Living one, Elemi, Owner of Spirit, that is, spirit

given to human beings, and Oga-ogo, the High One or the Lord of Glory.⁵

But more amazingly, a pygmy considered primitive and untutored, celebrates the Supreme Being as changeless and bodiless, from his remote forest:

> In the beginning was God,
>
> Today is God
>
> Tomorrow will be God.
>
> Who can make an image of God?
>
> He has no body
>
> He is as a word which comes out of your mouth
>
> That word! it is no more,
>
> It is past, and still it lives!
>
> So is God.⁶

Typically, Western observers regard the African concept of the Supreme Being as primitive. Some, however, in agreement with African thinkers, view him quite differently. Richard Gehman, for instance, echoes Asare Kofi Opoku when he says that "Many of the African statements about God are startling in their splendor."⁷ On this basis, he confesses being "impressed with the many 'truths' which Africans held before the coming of the Gospel."⁸ And for him this phenomenon is cause for praise stating that: "Since all truth is God's truth, we readily acknowledge with gratitude the gracious work that God has done in Africa by his Spirit before the preaching of the gospel."⁹

The ATR's traditional concept of God is variously assessed by Africans themselves. Given the complexity of the African traditional worldview, which includes the Supreme Being, the spirit world, and magical powers, it is difficult to single out specifically the activities of Supreme Being. Because he is viewed as remote, God does not seem to be actively involved in everyday life. The task of attending to the daily needs of humans is the purview of the divine intermediaries such as gods, divinities, and ancestors.¹⁰ Although

---

5. Opoku, *West African Traditional Religion*, 27.
6. Mbiti, *Concept of God in Africa*, 23.
7. Gehman, *African Religion in Biblical Perspective*, 360.
8. Ibid., 357.
9. Ibid.
10. Turaki, *Foundations of African Traditional Religion and Worldview*, 56.

there might be an effort to single out the Supreme Being and understand who he is, the prominent role that these lesser agents play renders the inquiry difficult. This explains why African theologians assess differently the concept of God in relation to the overall fabric of the African religious worldview. Turaki sums up this complexity with an elaboration on what he calls "the holistic or organic worldview":

> In the traditional worldview, the Supreme Being appears to be ontologically transcendent. He occupies a hierarchical position in the pantheon of the spirit beings and may assign roles and functions to the lesser beings. He himself is inactive or does not get involved in daily communal affairs. However, this transcendence and aloofness must not be interpreted in absolute terms. He is also present in the community and in the hierarchy. Sometimes the gods, divinities, spirits and ancestors are seen as mediators acting with the sanction and knowledge of God himself although at other times they act as independent agents.[11]

Contrary to the conclusions of thinkers of an earlier period, in recent times, studies of the ATR have led Africans to believe in the universality of the Supreme Being revealed therein. Furthermore, modern thinkers tend to see appreciable similarities between the views of God found in the ATR and the Bible respectively. For instance, just as the Bible does not discuss the question of the existence of God, but simply assumes it, so the ATR merely affirms God's existence on the basis of his acts in creation. Insights such as this, lead us to agree with Gehman's conclusion "that there is a lot of divine truth revealed by God through nature and conscience, so that African peoples knew some true things about God, albeit, limited and corrupted. The minds of Africans were not void of divine truth when missionaries first came."[12] If this is true, it seems that the question that needs to be addressed concerns the identity of the universal God of the ATR when viewed from the perspective of biblical revelation.

Humanity in the ATR

How do Africans understand humanity? We've already observed that in the African popular conception, there are hundreds of myths and stories about the concept of God. The same is true of the origin of humankind. These stories yield a view of humanity which includes the creation of humans by

---

11. Ibid.
12. Gehman, *African Religion in Biblical Perspective*, 358.

God, their original relationship with him, the subsequent loss of that communion with God, and his relation to community. We will consider each of these in turn.

In the perspective of the ATR, human beings are created by God. Mbiti reports that among the people of the Nile Valle, the general idea is that God created humans in the heavenly realms and then lowered them into this world.[13] Because of their divine origin, humans are seen as spiritual beings; however, they are endowed with bodies which are subject to decay, and a soul which is immortal. These parts of the human person are ascribed various functions in life or in death. In relation to God, the Igbo of Nigeria believe that the soul of each human being, called *Chi*, is derived from *Chukwu*, the Creator God.[14] Ikenga-Metuh highlights three prominent features of the human person. First is the vital breath which is a life force that links humans with other life forces in the universe and ensures vital relationship with them. The second feature is the soul which is an emanation of the Creator. And the third is the bodily representation of the human person.[15] As can be seen, most of the myths and stories, emphasize the direct origin of humans from God, either as a divine part of God himself (i.e., *Chi*), or an act of divine creation from another matter.

Turning to the issue of humanity's original relationship with God, we find that in the view of the ATR, in their original state, humans lived in happiness and peace with God. But something happened that resulted in the loss of that relationship and the idyllic life that stemmed from it. Various reasons are advanced for this unhappy turn of events, including humans' disobedience to God, God's annoyance with them, and the distance that exists between heaven and earth.

Because God became distant and remote, humans tried through religious activities to re-establish a relationship by drawing God closer to themselves. Thus, according to Idowu, religion "results from man's spontaneous awareness of a Living Power, 'Wholly Other' who is infinitely greater than himself, a power of mystery because unseen, yet a present and urgent reality, seeking to bring man into communion with Himself."[16] If Idowu is correct, it appears that it is God who is seeking to bring humans into communion with himself. However, others observed that in the ATR the search is initiated by humans and is done for their benefit. Turaki, for instance avers that in the

---

13. Mbiti, *Africa Religions and Philosophy*, 92.

14. Ilogu, *Christianity and Igbo Culture*, 34.

15. Ikenga-Metuth, *God and Man in African Religion*, 108, and Turaki, *Foundations of African Traditional Religion and Worldview*, 56.

16. Idowu, *Africa Traditional Religion*, 75.

ATR "beliefs, practices, rituals, offerings, sacrifices, and ceremonies seem to suggest that Africans are preoccupied with their security, needs, and well-being in their dealings with the spirit beings and the mystical, mysterious, and unseen powers which surround them."[17] As we will see below, we have here a utilitarian view of God which poses a serious problem to a genuine relationship with him. For as Mbiti observes:

> when communities get satisfactory amounts of food, children, rain, health and prosperity, they have approached something of original state. At such times they do not generally turn to God in the utilitarian acts of worship as much as they do when these items are at stake.[18]

But despite this obvious utilitarian use of religion, there is still a hidden longing for the original communion that existed between God and humankind. Yet, as we intimated before, the ATR seems devoid of an avenue to satisfy such longing. As Mbiti observes, "out of these many myths concerning primeval man and the loss of his original state, there is no single myth, . . . which attempts to suggest a solution or reversal of this great loss. Man accepted the separation between him and God."[19] Here lies one of the blatant shortcomings of the ATR. The search for a solution to the problem of humanity's separation from God cannot be conducted inside the system but outside it. Here then is a clear entry point for the presentation of the gospel to Africans who are in search of "lost paradise."

What about humans' relationship to community? On this point Turaki echoes the thinking of many scholars when he asserts that "it is impossible to think of a human being in isolation. Humans are always conceived of in relationship with others: those who are alive, those who inhabit the spirit world and the mysterious powers of nature."[20] In similar vein, Ikenga-Metuth asserts:

> The African doctrine of man strikes a balance between the social and individual dimensions of man. Man is essentially seen as a member of a community of beings as well as a uniquely individual person. He is a force in a universe of living forces, a member of the community of men and at the same time a unique individual endowed with a unique destiny which only he himself can realize."[21]

17. Turaki, *Foundations of African Traditional Religion and Worldview*, 17.
18. Mbiti, *Africa Religions and Philosophy*, 96.
19. Ibid.
20. Turaki, *Foundations of African Traditional Religion and Worldview*, 109.
21. Ikenga-Metuth, quoted in *Trinity of Sin*, Yusufu Turaki; 66.

According to Ikenga-Metuth, humanity's social nature is aptly encapsulated in the Bantu word "Ubuntu." Ubuntu describes, "what it means to be a member of humankind.... It applies to all human beings and describes humans as created by God."[22] Based on this social understanding of the human person, some African thinkers suggest that the African response to the Cartesian "I think therefore I am," is "We are therefore I am."[23] Another popular dictum goes like this: "I am because we are, and since we are, therefore I am." The fundamental value of humanity and a high esteem for interpersonal relationships are opposed to anything else, particularly material possessions.

What is the theological value of the ATR for an understanding of God and humanity? We note two responses. First, based primarily on a phenomenological study of the ATR, some African theologians conclude that the traditional religious system provides a sufficient avenue for a full knowledge of God and the experience of a satisfying relationship with him. This assessment, which some see as an overrating of the ATR's theological cash value is detected by Kwame Bediako in the following comments by Archbishop Desmond Tutu:

> It is reassuring to know that we have had a genuine knowledge of God and that we have had our own ways of communicating with deity, ways which meant that we were able to speak authentically as ourselves and not as pale imitators of others.[24]

It is, of course, reassuring that the ATR has helped to discover the African ways of communication with God. But is this, indeed, a "genuine knowledge of God"? This question seems to call for a re-examination of the value of ATR in relation to humankind's knowledge of a transcendent God, the restoration of relationship with him, and the meaning of life as Mbiti so painfully observed above.[25] This is what characterizes the second response to the theological value of the ATR.

The theologians who represent this approach seek not merely to describe ATR but to engage in a theological reflection on ATR in light of the Bible. This latter approach seems to be what the apostles adopted as they engaged contemporary pagan worshippers in light of God's plan and way of salvation. Thus, Turaki pleads for a theological approach that can

22. Kapolyo, *The Human Condition. Christian Perspectives through African Eyes*, 34.
23. Ibid., 21.
24. Bediako, "Understanding African Theology in the 20th Century," 50.
25. See also Ndjérareou, "Theology as the Hermeneutic of Identity" (paper presented at a colloquium sponsored by LES AMIS DE LA THEOLOGIE, Abidjan, Fateac, March 1999).

"takes the valuable knowledge available and weave it into a theological and methodological framework to guide the study of traditional religions and cultures from a biblical perspective."[26] Such an approach, we believe, allows us to remain true to the biblical teaching while being sufficiently attentive to African culture. We need to make full use of the biblical word if we are to evaluate more accurately the ATR.

THE BIBLICAL DESCRIPTION OF THE RELATIONSHIP BETWEEN GOD AND HUMANITY

How does the Bible describe what nations (including Africans) outside the Christian faith believe regarding God and his relationship to mankind?

The Bible's view of the religions that fall outside the purview of Christian faith is essential to our assessment of these faiths. When we search the biblical text we encounter two important insights. On the one hand, Scripture concurs that these religions do contain nuggets of truths that are parts God's general revelation, and as such, can be useful in leading people to the fuller truths of special revelation. On the other hand, the Bible describes the beliefs of these religions as the imagination of the human mind which is devoid of the full truth concerning the divine being. For instance, while the Bible clearly states that God "did not leave himself without witness" (Acts 14:17), it challenges the people to "turn from these vain things to a living God who made the heaven and the earth and the sea and all that is in them" (Acts 14:15). Furthermore, while it teaches that the nations have a general awareness or knowledge of God, they desperately lack the proper knowledge of the true God (Rom 1:18; 1 Cor 8:1–6). These affirmations are based on other biblical passages which make a good case for an accurate assessment of the ATR's knowledge of God and humankind (Gen 1:26–28, 12; Josh 24:14–24; Acts 14:8–18; 17:16–34; Rom 1:19–32; 1 Cor 8:1–6; 10:18–21).

For instance, to the Corinthians Paul stated they might imagine knowing God but they do not know as they ought to know (1 Cor 8:2). He says: "If anyone imagines that he knows something, he does not yet know as he ought to know." So the issue is not "knowing" as such, but the *proper way to know* the true God and his will for humankind and the world. Likewise, we submit that the ATR lacks the "proper way" to know God. Jesus told the Samaritan woman that both Jews and Samaritans miss the proper way of knowing and worshipping God. That is, "God is spirit, and those who worship him must worship in spirit and truth" (John 4:24). Furthermore, since God is spirit, no location is allocated to him, "neither on this mountain nor

---

26. Turaki, *Foundations of African Traditional Religion and Worldview*, 9.

in Jerusalem" (John 4:21). Because the nations lack the proper knowledge of God and the proper way of worship, "what they sacrifice, they offer to demons and not to God." (1 Cor 10:20). Paul did not want the believers in Corinth "to be participants with demons" (1 Cor 10:20).

Prior to the Aeropagus discourse, the Gentiles and Jews in Lystra took Paul and Barnabas as divinities and likened them to Zeus and Hermes, their local divinities, because of the healing they had performed (Acts 14:8–16). The temptation to worship human beings and to represent divinities in human forms seems inherent to most non-Christian religions as described in the Bible (Rom 1:18; Acts 14:15; Rev 21:8–9). Scripture consistently maintains the distinction between humanity and God, and establishes proper relationship between humans and God—the creature and the Creator.

Romans 1:18—3:20 is a clear description of the lack of a proper knowledge of God on the part of people. It is also a demonstration of the truth that all have fallen short of the righteousness of God. Because of such deficiency, they fail to discern God's general revelation in creation. Paul goes on to highlight the universal depravation which is the predicament of all people (Rom 1:18–32; 2:1—3:8; 3:9–20). The core depravation of all is that, "although they knew God, they did not honor him as God, an give thanks to him, but they became futile in their thinking, and their foolish heart were darkened. Claiming to be wise, they became fools, and exchanged the glory the immortal God for images resembling mortal man and birds and animals and creeping things" (1:21–23). Likewise, the psalmist echoed the golden calf event (Exod 32) when he recalled Israel's history that "they exchanged the glory of God for the image of an ox that eats grass" (Ps 106:20), stressing the first of the ten commandments to be violated shortly after they were given to establish the terms of covenant relationship between God and Israel. The consequences of these idolatrous acts were disastrous in the Old Testament as well as in the New Testament. Israel and the nations were brought under God's judgment.

Although there are elements of truth in religions outside of Christ, Paul stated that, "in past generations he [(God)] allowed all nations to walk in their own ways. Yet he did not leave himself without witness, for he did good by giving you rains from heaven and fruit seasons, satisfying your hearts with food and gladness" (Acts 14:17). As our brief survey shows, the biblical story focuses on the opportunity that general revelation provides to proclaim the gospel, which is centered in the life and work of Jesus Christ. The gospel is a new message that challenges the way humans have sought to relate to the true God. The gospel clearly challenges people to "turn from these vain things to a living God who made the heaven and the earth and the sea and all that is in them" (Acts 14:15; 1 Thess 1:10).

With regard to the complex religious systems of the world, including the ATR, Turaki rightly asserts that, "The Bible clearly categorizes all the traditional religions of the world as idolatry. The numerous lesser gods, divinities, powers, and spirits who receive worship fall under biblical category of unclean spirits, demons, idols, and the 'gods of the nations.'"[27] He further challenges Christians to ensure that their understanding of the various aspects of traditional religion within their cultural contexts is "brought under the authority of the Bible." In keeping with this, we highlight four basic claims that the Bible makes about God and humanity. They pertain to the uniqueness of God, the nature of the creation, the locus of salvation, and the necessity of humanity's proper response to God.

As we do so we will bear in mind Turaki's warning's that while there are theological ideas that the ATR shares with Christianity, "it is important to stress that the commonality of the theological framework does not mean that the theological foundations are the same or that the two religions have the same theological message or meaning."[28]

God Alone is the Living God

As we saw earlier, Joshua denounced the religious practices of his ancestors as idolatry and challenged the Israelites to choose to "serve Yahweh alone" (Josh 24:14–24). Though the ATR is a living reality today, the Supreme Being, like the deity Joshua's ancestors worshiped, may not be the living and God of biblical revelation. He cannot be fully identified with Yahweh owing to the difference that obtains between the biblical worldview and the worldview of the ATR. As in the case of Joshua, the Supreme Being of the ATR may well be a "foreign god" to Yahweh. As prophet Jeremiah declares to the worshippers of the gods of the other nations "Yahweh alone is the living God" (Jer 10:1–16, ESV)

Creation

The creation motif frames the biblical narrative. The Bible begins with the creation of "the heavens and the earth" and concludes with the creation of a "new heaven and a new earth" (Rev 21:1). There are two basic truths that we must always bear in mind when we think of the creation. First, God is the creator of everything that exists, and he remains distinct from his creation

---

27. Turaki, *Foundations of African Traditional Religion and Worldview*, 71.
28. Ibid., 53.

(Gen 1:1). Secondly, after God created humanity, he gave them a mandate (Gen 1:26–28).

He Is the Creator of Everything.

On this first point, the ATR concurs with the biblical assertion that God (the Supreme Being) is the creator of everything. This is a fundamental belief that is common throughout Africa. However, the creation stories that permeate African popular culture fall short of the biblical portrayal the living God and his purpose for humankind. Just like the Athenians, the view of God and the creation that these creation stories embody reveal a distortion of the truth about both (Acts 17:22–15; Rom 1:18). The most one can acknowledge is that they are points of contact to teach the biblical account of creation.

As Creator, God Gave Humanity a Mandate.

Just like the creation motif, the note of a fulfilled humanity enjoying the presence of God frames the entire Bible. The Bible begins with the creation of man in the image of God in a condition of bliss in the Garden (Gen 1:26–28), and concludes with human beings in worship before God's throne (Rev 22:8–9). God's decision to create humankind was a sovereign decision which establishes his ownership of humanity. In keeping with this the Bible likens God to a potter who does what he likes with the clay in his hand. Humanity therefore is a vessel made by God, the potter. One of the ways God shows his sovereignty over humanity is in delegating to them responsibility for the rest of the creation (Gen 1:26–28). But this mandate was not a license given by God for the abuse of the rest of the creation as it has been interpreted in many cultures of the world including African culture. As Joe Kapolyo rightly observes:

> Human beings . . . are the pinnacle of God's creative activities. [But] this is a position of responsibility rather than anthropocentric indulgence abusing the rest of creation" (Kapolyo 2005:25). Most cultures in the world fall short of this noble responsibility, by oppressing destroying other human beings community particularly in man and woman relationship. Women are not only subordinate to men in society; they are inferior too

and as a result suffer all manner of deprivation, disrespect, and sometimes humiliation.[29]

Only the right biblical understanding of Genesis 1:26–28 can limit humankind's mistreatment of other human beings who bear the same image as them. For as Kapolyo comments:

> Unlike these derogatory statements about women and womanhood, the Scriptures unequivocally give men and women dignity and an exalted but equal status. Men and women bear the image of God in equal proportions. . . . Since the image is described as "male and female" it must mean at least that femininity is represented in God the Creator. . . . The mandate to represent God on earth was given to men and women together, not just man. Genesis 1:28 is very inclusive indeed. God gives both man and woman the same tasks: there is no differentiation based on biological make-up. . . . As recipients of the salvation Jesus offers, there is neither male nor female (Gal 3:28).[30]

Now we turn to the salvation of humankind.

Salvation

We stated in the introduction that the African search for truth about God and humanity in light of ATR has been a puzzle, especially when it comes to the appraisal of what it means to be African and Christian. While ATR has clarified many religious issues for the Africans' own understanding of their religious past, it has not provided a solution to the question of humanity's relationship with God. The ATR's inability on this front is well expressed by John Mbiti:

> Yet behind these fleeting glimpses of the original state and bliss of man, whether they are rich or shadowy, there lie the tantalizing and unattained gift of the resurrection, the loss of human immortality and the monster of death. Here African religions and philosophy must admit a defeat; they have supplied no solution. This remains the most serious cul-de-sac in the otherwise rich thought and sensitive religious feeling of our peoples. It is perhaps here then, that we find the greatest weakness and poverty of our traditional religions.[31]

29. Kapolyo, *The Human Condition. Christian Perspectives through African Eyes*, 70.
30. Ibid., 71–72, 86.
31. Mbiti, *African Religions and Philosophy*, 99.

Mbiti uses strong terms to express the shortcomings of the ATR. He sees some glaring lacks in the ATR system. Its redemptive deficiency includes "unattained gift of resurrection," "the loss of human immortality," powerlessness in the face of the "monster of death," its "weakness and poverty" as a "traditional religion," etc. Here the ATR reveals the same salvific impotency that besets all the other non-Christian faiths. Like them, it is incapable to offer redemption because, as Paul stresses, genuine redemption is a transcendental provision that is made by God himself and hence cannot be found anywhere else: "the righteousness of God through faith in Jesus Christ for all who believe. For there is no distinction: for all have sinned and fall short of the glory of God, and are justified by his grace as a gift, through the redemption that is in Christ Jesus, whom God put forward as a propitiation by his blood, to be received by faith. That is to show Go's righteousness because in his divine forbearance he had passed over former sins" (Rom 3:22–25, ESV).

It is interesting to observe that although the law and the prophets bear witness to the righteousness of God (Rom 3:21, ESV), it has been manifested in a unique way in Jesus Christ, beyond the expectations of these witnesses. Likewise, by analogy, one may say that the ATR bore a witness to general revelation in a pedagogical function similar to the law, to lead Africans to the full and unique manifestation of God's provision of salvation. God filled the vacuum of all expectations in a very drastic and original way: an innocent man was crucified in order to reestablish the lost relation between God and humanity. The cross, then, is a nonnegotiable "area of Christian belief." For as Kwesi Dikson puts it:

> No matter what the cultural perspective of the Christian might be, the matter of Christ's death and its significance cannot but be considered more central; Christians everywhere, from whatever cultural background, must react to this central belief.[32]

Africans often liken death to going on a journey on the other side of life. This concept can help to deepen the faith of the African Christian about the death and resurrection of Jesus Christ. Death does not end life in African thought, says again Dickson; it "leads to life." In Africans, the resurrection of Jesus Christ has ready listening ears.

But more than that, in embracing the cross, Africans can find a solution to the ATR dilemma regarding the gulf that separates God and humanity due to the latter's sin. If this is understood by Africans, African Christianity can become rooted in what God himself has accomplished for

---

32. Dickson, *Theology in Africa*, 185.

them, not what a system of religion, such as the ATR offers. In so doing the knowledge of the ATR as a pre-Christian experience can to be taken into account; but its contribution and shortcomings will come under the searchlight of Scripture. When this is done, the African Christian can affirm: "I know where I have come from" (religious past), "I know what I believe" (the new revelation of God in a new person), and "I know whom I believe" (Jesus Christ, the way of reconciliation to God). Unless the African believer becomes cognizant of the gaps and shortcomings pointed out by John Mbiti as a part of his religious pre-Christian heritage (or religious identity according to Bediako), he will embrace Christianity just as another system of religion that does not provide any solution to problem of salvation that he faces.

The cross is a unique link between God and humanity. As Gehman stated so well, "ATR stands in solidarity with mankind as a whole outside Christ"[33] and thus needs salvation. Those who feel that vacuum in the ATR system will see that they need salvation through Jesus Christ just as any other people of traditional beliefs.

Human's Response in Worship

Humanity's most important response to God is first and foremost to worship God, their Maker. In agreement with the psalmist (Ps 95:6; Acts 14:15), Erik Thoennes says that, "Human beings are intended to live as God's created analogy for his own glory. God did not create humans because of any need within himself (Job 41:11, Ps 50:9–12, Acts 17:24–25) but primarily so that he would be glorified in them as they delight in him and reflect his character. We were created primarily to be in relation with our Creator and find our greatest joy in him."[34]

Mbiti is concerned about the lack of the pursuit of God in worship in the ATR. According to him, "the African image of the happy life is one in which God is among the people, His presence supplying them with food, shelter, peace, immortality or gift of the resurrection, and moral code."[35] It seems that this awareness of God's presence should naturally drive the African to worship. However, it appears that the utilitarian use of religion inhibits the worship of God simply for his presence! There is a lack of a thirst to worship God for his own sake. Aware of this feature of the ATR, Mbiti wonders: "would it be legitimate to suggest, perhaps, that African acts of worship are basically utilitarian, searching primarily for the lost

---

33. Gehman, *African Religion in Biblical Perspective*, xii.
34. Thoennes, "Biblical Doctrine: An Overview (Mankind)," 2527.
35. Mbiti, *Africa Religions and Philosophy*, 96

paradise rather than for God himself?"[36] The call is to worship God for his own sake and with the legitimate requests for the many human needs that God can provide.

According the Christian faith, therefore, the salvation that God provides in Jesus Christ is more than a recovery of "African identity, historical consciousness, or cultural salvation."[37] It is the way of the cross which provides forgiveness and restores fellowship between God and humankind. Certainly, a forgiven and a transformed African can influence positively his cultural environment and advocate for human dignity as he or she fulfills the cultural mandate entrusted to them by their Creator (Gen 1:26–28). African Christians must particularly reflect God's character in all their undertakings. As the Bible declares: "So, whether you eat or drink, or whatever you do, do all to the glory of God" (1 Cor 10:31).

WHAT ARE THE IMPLICATIONS FOR CHRISTIANITY IN AFRICA TODAY.

Elisabeth Isichei says that "Christianity in Africa is of global significance, and the directions it takes are of importance to Christians everywhere."[38] What does this mean? I see four areas where the African church can share the global significance of Christian faith with believers everywhere.

The Pre-Christian Experience

At the eve of cultural and religious revolutions that swept Africa in the 1970s Renato Berger wrote, "before colonialism and missionary activity African religion was lived as an absolute truth and undisputed belief."[39] Based in this, many African theologians advocate the continuity of some ATR beliefs with the new Christian life. Some feel that to overlook the pre-Christian experience is to experience a painful discontinuity which renders Christian faith artificial, shallow, and readily dismissible as a foreign religion.

As we have already shown, although the ATR reflects the religious nature of the human race which has the law of God written in their heart, it lacks the provision of "redemption from sin."[40] This evokes the question

---

36. Ibid.
37. Musopole, *Being Human in Africa*, 6.
38. Isichei, *A History of Christianity in Africa*, 1.
39. Berger, "Is Traditional Religion Still Relevant?" 15.
40. Gehman, *African Religion in Biblical Perspective*, 367.

of the value of Africa's religious past in relation to Christianity. With John Mbiti, Kwame Bediako, and several other African theologians, I hold that answer is found in an approach that affirms both continuity and discontinuity between the ATR and Christian faith. Mbiti displays great insight when he says: "ATR was a valuable and indispensable lamp on the spiritual path . . . but it cannot be made a substitute for the eternal Gospel which is like the sun that brilliantly illuminates that path."[41] For his part, Bediako who labored hard to integrate responsibly Africa's pre Christian experience with Christian faith asserts forcefully that "theological consciousness presupposes religious tradition and tradition requires memory and memory is integral to identity: without memory we have no past and if we have no past, then we lose our identity."[42]

Bediako's stress on African identity has caused some misunderstandings as he seems to elevate African identity over Christian identity. But the critics seem to have misread him for elsewhere he makes plain that our common identity in Christ takes precedence over our cultural identity. He says:

> But the primary history that gives fundamental dignity and self worth to every Christian is our history rooted in God through Christ. Jesus Christ is at the heart of our identity as Christians, whatever our nationality may be. Our joy and pride is not in ATR but in Christ. Paul said, "May I never boast except in the cross of our Lord Jesus Christ . . ." Gal 6:14.[43]

However controversial Bediako's plea may be, the point is that African pre-Christian experience constitutes a starting point for religious consciousness for the knowledge of the true God in his revelation through Jesus Christ. The church in African can become more vibrant when believers understand where they have come from and critically integrate in their lives, the useful insights contained in their traditional religions with the truths of their newly found faith. The challenge is to examine our traditional beliefs biblically and theologically, and "to hold fast what is good, and abstain from every form of evil" (1 Thess 5:21–22). This seems to be an effective way to avoid syncretism, on the one hand, and to progress in Christian maturity on the other. This process to Christian maturity was tested in several countries in Africa (e.g., Chad) when believers were persecuted for their faith as they refused to bow down in idol worship in the name of cultural revolution which wrongly depicted Christianity as a white man's religion. Those who stood firm and were ready to die were those who knew where they have

---

41. Mbiti, "Christianity and Africa Religion," 282.
42. Bediako, *Christianity in Africa*, 16.
43. Ibid.

from with regard to their pre-Christian life enlightened by the new revelation of Christ for mankind (not for one single nation nor ethnic group).

African Spirituality as a Driving Force against Secularism and Human-centeredness.

The invasion of Africa by Western values seems for a time to have done away with belief in a supernatural power—a belief which has been basic to African life. At one point, the leaders of the newly independent nations seemed to think that they could improve the life of their people without God's help. They took this stance notwithstanding the fact that Africans, on the whole, have always been sensitive to a sense of God's presence, as is evident in the numerous references to God in the national anthems of the new nations.

However, faced with the reality of economic stagnation that continues to plague many of these nations after some fifty years of independence, surprisingly, some of the same leaders are now calling for a return to God. This about-face seems to argue against Gehman's suggestion that the attitude that these leaders previously exhibited toward God represented a denial of his existence.[44]

It seems that in spite of an intruding secularism, which for a moment, seemed to threaten belief in the existence and power of God in some sectors of African societies, the positive elements of the pre-Christian religious experience that are embedded in the ATR helped to maintain alive an atmosphere of belief in the supernatural which serves as a source of sustenance for social and political life.

Humanity as Family and Community

It was stated above that for Africans, humans discover their full personality in group relationships such as family and community as expressed by the concept of Ubuntu. This means that God places human beings in families, communities, people-groups or tribes, and in nations. In the family, since children ensure a link between generations, the life of the child, both the born and the unborn, is protected. Here the African concept of Ubuntu upholds the sanctity of life in order to ensure continuity and leave a legacy to the community.

---

44. Gehman, *African Religion in Biblical Perspective*, 386.

With regard to community, the African meaning of life is understood in terms of kinship. But at times, the ATR seems to take the role of the community too far. As Turaki has pointed out:

> The community makes life and gives purpose and meaning to life. It is both the lawgiver and the judge. Outside of the community, there is no life, no hope, no identity, no destiny and no existence, in short no salvation"[45]

There is, here, a sort of "personification" of the community which does not seem to make room for an identifiable individual to incarnate the values of the community. At this point, the life and work of Jesus Christ for our salvation is needed to correct the misguided views which are inherent in the African concept of community. Jesus Christ is the one who has been building the ideal community. This new community consists of family, Church, and the Kingdom and includes all those who respond to the gospel that he incarnates. He is the one who provides life, hope, peace, identity, destiny and existence. He is the one who establishes a covenant relationship with the individual and the community of which he or she is a member—be it the Church or a particular social group. Here Mbiti is correct when he invites us to "understand the world and African humanity from his viewpoint of his identity with Christ who is the embodiment of the new humanity . . . As culture is preparatory to the Gospel, so the philosophical and cultural understanding of humanity is preparatory to the new humanity in Christ."[46]

CONCLUSION

This chapter may seem to be a comparative study of ATR and Christianity about God and humanity. The African perspective might give this impression. But it is really an effort by an African to understand the biblical claims about God and humanity by taking into account our spiritual milieu and cultural heritage. I would like to conclude my argument by highlighting three key elements:

1. African Traditional Religion is still a live religion in Africa today. We appreciate the abundant literature that has been produced on it by many pioneering African theologians and missionaries. Their work has paved the way for further theological reflection in Africa. The Supreme Being of the ATR religious system can be likened

---

45. Turaki, *Foundations of African Traditional Religion and Worldview*, 118.

46. Musopole, *Being Human in Africa. Toward an African Christian Anthropology*, 6–7.

to the "Unknown God" of the general revelation, worshiped by the Athenians. The African Supreme Being cannot, however, adequately represent Yahweh, the Creator of heaven and the earth and humankind. There is no doubt that the biblical view of humanity, as God's unique creation, and the African communal understanding of humans can foster a better perspective on the meaning of social, national and church life. Having said this, however, because God created human beings in his image, their primary identity, though disfigured by sin, remains the starting point for religious consciousness and the apprehension of biblical truths.

2. This means that the difference in worldview between the ATR and Christianity needs to be taken into account in theological dialogue about God and humanity. The value of common theological themes is that they provide contact points for fruitful interaction among contending perspectives with a view to arriving at a more accurate knowledge of God and his relationship to humanity as revealed in Scripture.

3. Above all, from whichever perspective we seek to approach God and humanity, Genesis 1:26–28 remains foundational. There has been no other religious system which has fully claimed nor developed the truth that God created man and woman in his image and gave them responsibility over the creation as his representatives. Because of sin which perverted our identity shortly after our creation, God himself provided a way to re-create humankind through the new man (Adam), Jesus-Christ. Thus, the uniqueness of Jesus Christ, his death on the Cross and his resurrection for the salvation of the world is foundational for the African's Christian faith and identity. The uniqueness of the Christian faith is "to love God and to be known by God" 1 Co 8:2–3. It is worth quoting Mbiti to conclude:

> The only identity that counts and has full meaning is the identity with Christ and not with any given cultures. Cultural identities are temporary, serving to yield us as Christians to the fullness of our identity with Christ.[47]

---

47. Mbiti, "African Indigenous Culture in Relation to Evangelism and Church Development," 79.

2

God and Humanity in Islam and Christianity

Kam Weng Ng (Malaysia)

COMMON ROOTS: RADICAL CHALLENGE

God is most great, God is most great,
I bear witness that there is no god except Allah:
I bear witness that Muhammad is the Apostle of God.
Come ye unto prayer. Come ye unto good. Prayer is a better thing than sleep. Come ye to the best deed.
God is most great. God is most great. There is no god except Allah.

EVERY DAY ACROSS THE Muslim world, the call of the muezzin breaks the silence of dawn with sudden forcefulness as it summons the faithful to prayer. One cannot help but sense a note of compulsion as the call intrudes into the half-awakened mind. Wake up from your slumber! I bear witness to God Almighty and Muhammad as his prophet! The call, loudly amplified by speakers these days, serves as a strident message in contrast to the rolling tunes of church bells which gently invite believers to prayer and worship. On the other hand, the minaret call assertively declares Islam's uncompromising self-referential demands that insist on being taken on its own terms.

"*La ilaha illallah* (There is no God but Allah)." Thus asserts the Muslim his belief in a unique God who is absolute unity (*tawhid*). Islam as an inclusive religion has an aggressive quality. One may describe it as zeal for the glory and unity of God. Islam is uncompromising to the point of being militant in rejecting any comparison or association between God and his creatures. As the Quran asserts, all sins may be forgiven except this sin of *shirk*.

The Christian faith shares similarities with the monotheism and Semitic ethos of the Quran, especially with the latter's acknowledgment of the faith of Abraham. The similarities are well reflected in the first chapter of the Quran, *Al-Fatiha,* the gateway or essence of the Quran.

> In the name of Allah, Most Gracious, Most Merciful.
> Praise be to Allah, the Cherisher and Sustainer of the worlds;
> Most Gracious, Most Merciful;
> Master of the Day of Judgment.
> Thee do we worship, and Thine aid we seek.
> Show us the straight way,
> The way of those on whom Thou hast bestowed Thy Grace,
> those whose (portion) is not wrath, and who go not astray.

I suspect that the recitation of this verse at a Christian Sunday meeting might just be acceptable if the word "Allah" is replaced with the English equivalent of "God" and the congregation is not told that the verse is taken from the Quran. Nonetheless, the word "Allah," especially when uttered in its Semitic guttural tone, is a fitting carrier for the forceful and dynamic vitality of incomparable Divinity.

The Quran asserts that Allah is the source and the final destiny of all creatures. His attributes, aptly captured in the traditional list of the ninety-nine names, include the Guardian (*wakil*), the Great (*kabir*), the Lifegiver (*muhyi*), the Seer (*basir*) and omniscient Knower (*sami, alim*), the Reckoner of all things (*hasib*), and hence he is the Powerful (*qadir*) who compels all things by his will (*jabbar*).

> Surah 2:163: "And your Allah is One Allah. There is no god but He, Most Gracious, Most Merciful."

> Surah 112:1–3. "Say: He is Allah, the One and Only; 2. Allah, the Eternal, Absolute; 3. He begetteth not, nor is He begotten."[1]

---

1. Yusuf Ali's translation of the Quran elaborates: "The nature of Allah is here indicated to us in a few words, such as we can understand. The qualities of Allah are described in numerous places elsewhere, e.g., in 59: 22–24, 62:1, and 2:255. Here we are

26   PART 1—god and humanity

The Christian reader easily resonates with those Quranic passages which proclaim in concrete imageries, the God of justice and judgment and the God of compassion who is concerned for widows and the social underclass. Can any Christian disagree with Islam's insistence on the oneness of God, the sovereign Creator, the God who reveals because of his mercy toward wayward humans? Should not the Christian be grateful for the Muslim's stubborn insistence regarding our final accountability to the "Master of the Day of Judgment"? In Islam we are confronted with a magnificent vision of ethical monotheism comparable to that of Isaiah's vision. However, despite obvious spiritual affinities between Christianity and Islam, it cannot be denied that there exist fundamental theological differences on the idea of God and salvation of humankind.

Uncompromising Zeal for the Glory of God

Islam is synonymous with submission to the righteous demands of God. Many Christians in the West today simply presume on the grace and forgiveness of the loving God and are hesitant to preach a sovereign God who demands exclusive allegiance. In the process of trying to avoid offending the wider culture, many Western theologians speak of the limited God of process theology and open theism and echo the post-modern Dionysian dance of primeval playfulness recently embodied by volatile Deconstructionists and Nietzchean nihilists. In contrast, Muslims remain unwavering in their insisting on *Islam* (submission to God).

Islam entertains no concession to any suggestion that may compromise the idea that God is sovereign and absolutely transcendent. While there are Quranic passages that point to God's work in creation, for example, that he is closer to humans than humans are to their own jugular veins, nonetheless

---

specially taught to avoid the pitfalls into which men and nations have fallen at various times in trying to understand Allah. The first thing we have to note is that His nature is so sublime, so far beyond our limited conceptions, that the best way in which we can realise Him is to feel that He is a Personality, 'He,' and not a mere abstract conception of philosophy. He is near us; He cares for us; we owe our existence to Him. Secondly, He is the One and Only God, the Only One to Whom worship is due; all other things or beings that we can think of are His creatures and in no way comparable to Him. Thirdly, He is Eternal, without beginning or end, Absolute, not limited by time or place or circumstance, the Reality before which all other things or places are mere shadows or reflections. Fourthly, we must not think of Him as having a son or a father, for that would be to import animal qualities into our conception of Him. Fifthly, He is not like any other person or thing that we know or can imagine: His qualities and nature are unique." Ali, *The Meaning of the Holy Quran*, 1429.

the thrust in Islam is to accentuate the transcendence (*tanzih*) of God.[2] Allah creates and decrees everything at all times—the assertion of Allah's continuous creative activity that directly and immediately causes everything leads inexorably to the doctrine of Islamic ocassionalism. Islam's resolute insistence on God as absolutely transcendent and unconditioned power can only mean submission. In this regard, Muslims are remarkable in their piety expressed in utter submission to the will of Allah, a submission that sometimes borders on fatalism, most evident when Muslims stoically respond to misfortune in life with passive resignation—it is predestination (*qadar*)!

Islamic Predestination

Not surprisingly, belief in the predestination of God features significantly in the tenets of Islamic beliefs. H. W. Stanton explains the decree of God,

> The determinism of the Quran is summed up in the word *qadar*, i.e. measuring. The well-known word *qismat* is not used in this sense in the Quran, but its meaning is the same, viz., apportionment. *Qadar* expresses the divine act or decree which determines the apportionment of the lot of all things, animate or inanimate, and all events in life as well as its limits. . . . Allah do all beings in the heavens and in the earth adore, whether they will or no (S13: 6). Had He pleased there would have been no idolatry. Allah is the Creator of everything; He is the One, the Dominant (S13:17).[3]

Islam's emphasis on the absolute and unconditioned power of God gives rise to the corollary doctrine of *shirk*. In the Quran *shirk* describes the sin of associating Allah with other deities (S25:3). The punishment for these idolaters will be judgment (S28:62–74).

Even when a person commits the sin of *shirk* it is the consequence of determinism by Allah. If Allah willed, all men would be believers (S6:107; 10:99f), and all men would be "one," but he leads astray or guides aright as

---

2. In my view, the existence of Islamic mystical movements does not invalidate the preeminence of the teaching of the absolute transcendence of God in Islam. See Schimmel, *Mystical Dimensions of Islam* and Chittick's two books, *The Sufi Path of Love* and *The Sufi Path of Knowledge*. Indeed, prominent mystical theologians of Islam influenced Ibn Al-Arabi represented by Hanzah Fansuri in South-East Asia who taught the Unity of Being (*Waḥdat al-Wujud*) have been accused of promulgating pantheism. See Bousfield, "Islamic Philosophy in South—East Asia;" Al-Attas, *The Mysticism of Hamzah Fansuri*, and Lubis, *The Ocean of Unity, Waḥdat al-Wujūd in Persian, Turkish and Malay Poetry*.

3. Stanton, *The Teaching of the Quran*, 54–55.

he wills (S16:95). The debate between God's sovereignty and human free-will rages in Christianity, but for Islam Allah's action is not conditioned in any way by humans. In contrast to James 2:13, which says no one when tempted may blame God, the Quran unapologetically declares that Allah does as he pleases. There are verses that say that Allah leads astray only evil doers (S2:24; 14:32). S6:39—God leaves whoever he will to stray, and sets whoever he will on a straight path (S6:39, cf. 7:154; 17:77; 14:4; 16:39) and there is no guidance for those whom Allah misleads (S4:90, 142; 7:185; 13:35). Indeed, Allah is the creator of people's thoughts, intentions, and acts, whether good or evil. At best, a person can only "appropriate" (*iktisab*) what God has created for him. Even then this "appropriation" is not an act of free will, but an inescapable compliance to Allah's decree. Allah even "drives the sinners to Hell, like thirsty cattle driven down to water" (S19:86ff).

Finally, such sin cannot affect Allah. It is not appropriate to depict human sin grieving Allah who transcends all creation. Naturally, such unqualified transcendence explains why Muslims cannot accept the Christian testimony to being drawn into a personal relationship with the Savior God through the grace manifested through Jesus Christ. Much less can the Muslim comprehend the suggestion that Allah's wounded love calls forth a self-sacrifice to save humankind.

On the other hand, the Christian insists that it is precisely because God initiates his love to undeserving humans that it is appropriate for believers to go beyond submission to God and to loving God. Indeed, as the Epistle of John says, "We love because God first loved us" (1 John 4:19). The contrast between the Christian God and Allah of Islam is most telling in the traditional list of the names of Allah. The word *Allahu Muhibba* or "God is love" is not found among the 99 names of God given in Islam. There is, however, the name *Al-Wadud* or "the Loving One," which is found in Surah 11:90 as well as Surah 85:14 though it should be noted that the common translation for the word is "full of loving kindness."

To be fair, modern Islamic theologians attempt to soften the traditional austere image of the absolutely transcendent God who provides little consolation to the believing longing for his care and love. Fazlur Rahman links both the Lordship of God and the Giver of Mercy (S2:255; S59:22–24; Q27:60–64). Thus Fazlur Rahman comments,

> While these passages emphasize God's lordship and power, they equally underline His infinite mercy. As these five verses make clear, God's lordship is *expressed through* His creation; His sustenance and provision of that creation, particularly and centrally of man; and, finally, through re-creation in new

forms. His creation of nature and man and of nature *for* man is the most primordial mercy of God. His power, creation, and mercy are, therefore, not only fully co-extensive but fully interpenetrating and fully identical: "He has imposed the law of mercy upon Himself" (6:12), and "My mercy comprehends all" (7:156). His very infinitude implies not a one-sided transcendence but equally His being "with" His creation; note that He is nearer to man than is man's jugular vein (50:16). Whenever a person commits a lapse and then sincerely regrets it and "seeks God's pardon," God quickly returns to him—indeed, among His often-mentioned attributes besides the "Merciful" and the "Compassionate" are the "Returner" (as the opposite of "forsaker": S2:37, 54, 160, 128; 5:39, 71; 9:117, 118; 20:122, etc) and the "Forgiver" (S40.3; 2:173, 182, 192, 199, 218, 225, 226, 235; and about 116 other occurrences), which are almost invariably followed by "Compassionate." For those who genuinely repent, God transmutes their very lapses into goodness (S25:70).[4]

It seems that at this point modern Islamic theologians like Fazlur Rahman are trading on the semantic ambiguity of "love." It may be noted that mercy and compassion are benevolent attitudes that Allah, the superior, extends to suffering humans, especially when they are in a position of dire need. But, in no way does Allah allow himself to be (even potentially) affected by his creatures. In this regard, the final relational category (if the word relational is applicable to Allah) remains one of unconditioned power. The use of words like "mercy," "compassion" must be qualified as a figure of speech used to describe Allah's benevolent attitude toward humans and are not descriptive of the inherent nature of Allah.

In contrast, the biblical God condescends to the level of making himself vulnerable to rejection by man. When Christians talk about the love of God found in Christ they are merely elucidating the profound insight into the pathos of God so poignantly captured by the Old Testament prophets.[5] Abraham Heschel notes that in contrast to the god of the Greek philosophers who thinks but does not speak and is conscious of himself but oblivious to the world, the biblical God is deeply involved with his people, "Pathos denotes, not an idea of goodness, but a loving care . . . a dynamic relation

---

4. Rahman, *Major Themes of the Quran*, 6.

5. Abraham Heschel elaborates, "It is not a passion, an unreasoned emotion, but an act formed with intention, rooted in decision and determination . . . its essential meaning is not to be seen in its psychological denotation, as standing for a state of the soul, but in its theological connotation, signifying God as involved in history, as intimately affected by events in history, as living care." Heschel, *The Prophets*, 11.

between God and man . . . no mere contemplative survey of the world but a passionate summons." Herschel adds,

> The theology of pathos brings about a shift in the understanding of man's ultimate problems. The prophet does not see the human situation in and by itself. The predicament of man is a predicament of God who has a stake in the human situation. Sin, guilt, suffering, cannot be separated from the divine situation. The life of sin is more than a failure of man; it is a frustration of God. Thus man's alienation from God is not the ultimate fact by which to measure man's situation. The divine pathos, the fact of God's participation in the predicament of man, is the elemental fact.[6]

> The idea of divine pathos has also anthropological significance. It is man's being relevant to God. To the biblical mind the denial of man's relevance to God is inconceivable as the denial of God's relevance to man. This principle leads to the basic affirmation of God's participation in human history, to the certainty that the events in the world concern Him and arouse His reaction. It finds its deepest expression in the fact that God can actually suffer. At the heart of the prophetic affirmation is the certainty that God is concerned about the world.[7]

However, these words should be taken with a measure of caution so that we do not pose a dichotomy between the transcendence and pathos of God. After all, Hershel himself qualified the pathos of God by saying that pathos describes the relationship of God with humanity and creation, but not his essence. But there is no doubt that traditional Islamic theology places exceeding emphasis on the transcendence of God that precludes talk about the pathos, much less the love of God.

Disturbing Concerns and Unsettled Questions

It should be noted that human language is stretched to the limits when one talks about the pathos or love of God. The fragility and limitation of language is easily exploited by *avant-garde* theologians ready to recast doctrine to suit the dominant "spirit of the age" (*zeitgeist*). As a defensive posture, traditional Islamic theologians consistently go far to insist that all language that "refers" to God be qualified so as to avoid any association (*shirk*) between Allah and creation. However, some quarters allow for the doctrine of

---

6. Ibid., 6.
7. Ibid., 39.

Al-Mukhalafah, which is the idea that terms derived from human meanings may be applied to God "with a difference." Kenneth Cragg explains,

> Classical Muslim theology developed a form of compromise solution in effect inclining to the negative answer. There developed the idea of *Al-Mukhālafah*, "The Difference." Terms taken from human meanings—and there are of course no others—were said to be used of God with a difference. They did not convey the human connotation but were used in those senses feasible of God. When the further question was pressed: What then do they convey as applied to God? No precise answer was capable of being formulated. Islam here falls back upon a final agnosticism. Terms must be used if there is to be religion at all. But only God knows what they signify. Muslim theology coined the related phrases *Bilā kaif* and *Bilā Tashbih*. We use these names "without knowing how" they apply and without implying any human similarity.[8]

Nevertheless, the concession assumes that only God can specify wherein lies the difference. But would not such a move reduce religious (Islamic) discourse to reverent agnosticism, if not empty talk? In this regard, despite claims of divine revelation, the Muslim knowledge of God amounts to an awareness of the Unknown who remains inscrutable and inaccessible to knowledge. If the non-Muslim expresses puzzlement about the theological difference between language and the transcendent One, the Muslim assures him that it is enough and proper for God's creature to accept his limitation. Only God knows.

The difference between Christianity and Islam's idea of God and revelation becomes all too clear. For Islam, God is hidden with a sense of mystery. Christianity disagrees with Islam and allows for positive statements about the revelation of God without compromising God's transcendence. In this regard, Christians are mindful of the cautions given in Deuteronomy 29:29 or Isaiah 55:8–9. The mysteriousness of a God robed in unapproachable light is, after all, also familiar to the prophets of the Old Testament. But, Kenneth Cragg cautions that one must not confuse transcendence with transcendental isolation. He warns that a purely negative theology may emphasize the surpassing mystery rather than annul the reality of revelation in the theatre of creation. "To find *only* enigma in God is to find only jest in the universe. Revelation becomes a sorry joke if its claims are no more than a tantalizing stance, an 'as-if' which derides us when it most enjoins. 'We have not created the heaven and the earth and all they hold together as if We

---

8. Cragg, *The Call of the Minaret*, 55.

jested' (S21:16, 44:37). We must not equate the fragility of language with the futility of faith."[9] This misunderstanding leads one down the slippery slide of post-modern linguistic nihilism and deconstruction.

It is natural that Islam concludes that humans cannot plumb the personality of God (even with the aid of divine revelation). It suffices that God's will is made known and that his revelation is inscribed in a revealed book, the Quran. Islamic transcendence of God precludes any possibility of personal revelation epitomized by the Christian belief that "God was in Christ." But the Christian asks, "Does not an all-transcending God isolated from his creation render him irrelevant to creation?" Indeed, one may argue that any theology bereft of a genuine anchor in creation becomes an abstraction.[10] Conversely, an unmitigated transcendence would rob creation of its integrity. The meaning of a created world that is continually dependent on the sustenance of God is undermined. The words used to describe God's mercy, compassion, and revelation towards humankind would be robbed of their personal and moral significance. In other words, if nothing can be related to God then the unity of all things under God becomes problematic.[11]

To overcome this formidable predicament, Kenneth Cragg suggests that *shirk* should not be understood as "association." It should be translated as "idolatry"—the act to deify earthly realities or to rank creation alongside the Creator.[12] To insist on absolute dissociation of the divine and the human would also preclude prophethood and thus the very office of prophet Muhammad. Some Muslims, to be sure, insist on the total passivity of prophet Muhammad as the bearer of Quranic revelation. But this is to ignore history, even the early biographies of Muhammad (*Sirat rasul 'Allah*) who portrayed Muhammad as one struggling for a sense of certitude in proclaiming his message and subsequently became a forceful activist. Was Muhammad not admired precisely because of his creative leadership in the midst of conflicting contests of the poets? Were not his military victories evidence of his strategic genius? Such abilities to be sure, presume the full engagement of

---

9. Cragg, *Jesus and the Muslim*, 200.

10. Torrance, *Reality and Evangelical Theology*, 25.

11. For a Christian contrast, see Hendrikus Berkhof who provided an instructive contrast when he admirably described the plurality and unity of creation. "The createdness of the world implies the fundamental unity of the world. More basic than the diversity of nations, races and cultures, is their unity. And more basic than the difference in matter of spirit, body and soul, nature and existence, is their oneness. . . . [C]reation means that all phenomena are irreducible, because the world has its ground outside itself in its creator. Everything forms a unity, but within it everything also has its own place and character." Cf. Berkhof, *Christian Faith* 2nd ed., 167.

12. Cragg, *Muhammad and the Christian*, 111.

his critical faculties, however enhanced they might have been in his mystical experiences.

The Christian argument is that when Islam accepts prophets as bearers of divine revelation, it has accepted that divine transcendence is not merely divine isolation. Divine participation in the contingencies of creation is inevitable regardless of whether Islam acknowledges it or not. In this regard, the veto of *shirk* is unjustifiable. To the extent that participation need not compromise divine transcendence, we have an opening to the possibility of the Incarnation.

Regardless of these strictures, Islamic theologians remain insistent that as creatures we can never ever know the personality of God. For Christianity, God has revealed his personality through the Incarnation; for Islam, revelation ended in a book detailing the will of God rather than the personality of God.

We arrive at the question concerning which attribute of God is preeminent in his dealings with humanity. Is the final word on God "power" or "love?" If God is transcendent in the sense of being above relationships, then power is the obvious answer. God is then to be admired, honored, and worshipped but only from a distance. But if God's nature allows for the possibility of relationship, then the attribute of love becomes primary. In any case, it is misleading for the Christian to pit these two categories against one another. It is precisely because God is Almighty that he has the capacity and willingness to reach out to his creatures. He is not just the God who sends warnings and exhortations (through the prophets). He is also the God who comes (in Jesus Christ). Gregory of Nyssa has given us a beautiful resolution to the problem between power and love.

> That the omnipotence of God's nature should have had the strength to descend to the lowliness of humanity furnishes a more manifest proof of power. . . . It is not the vastness of the heavens . . . and the unbroken administration over all existence, that so manifestly displays the transcendent power of God as the condescension to the weakness of our nature, in the way the sublimity is seen in the lowliness and yet the loftiness descends not.[13]

These considerations lead to the Christian doctrine of Trinity, an ingenious (more properly, revealed) insight into how God is transcendent (immanent Trinity) and yet works out his purposes in human history (economic Trinity). Obviously, this insight is not acceptable from the perspective of Islamic transcendence—if God does not care to be involved in human history in a manner that is significant to him, there will be no possibility of the

13. Cragg, *Jesus and the Muslim*, 207.

Incarnation. Not surprisingly, the rejection of the Trinity has been a battle cry among Islamic theologians.

Muhammad's Misconception of the Trinity

Islam's rejection of the Trinity arose from two sources. Historically it began with Muhammad's misconception of the Christian teaching of the Trinity. Later, when Islam spread beyond Arabia and its Semitic ethos (where God is depicted in concrete imageries in his dealings with human history), Islamic philosophers followed the Greeks in taking flight from history and concluded that Allah cannot be involved, or rather be contaminated through his involvement in history. That is to say, the logic of the absolute transcendent God of Islam found a suitable intellectual apparatus to rationalize its decisive rejection of the possibility of the Trinity and the Incarnation of God in Christ.

Historical Sources of Misunderstanding

The rejection of the Trinity flows logically from the concept of Islamic *Tawhid* (Oneness of God). First, Muhammad emphasized that God is self-subsisting, and sufficient.

> S5:75 They do blaspheme who say: "Allah is Christ the son of Mary." But said Christ: "O children of Israel! Worship Allah my Lord and your Lord." Whoever joins other gods with Allah Allah will forbid him the garden and the Fire will be his abode. There will for the wrong-doers be no one to help.

> S5:76. They do blaspheme who say: Allah is one of three in a Trinity: for there is no god except One Allah. If they desist not from their word (of blasphemy) verily a grievous penalty will befall the blasphemers among them.

Obviously this God cannot have partners or offspring

> S23:91–92—No son did Allah beget nor is there any god along with Him: (if there were many gods) behold each god would have taken away what he had created and some would have lorded it over others! Glory to Allah (He is free) from the (sort of) things they attribute to Him! He knows what is hidden and what is open: too high is He for the partners they attribute to Him!

> S19:35—It is not befitting to (the majesty of) Allah that He should beget a son. Glory be to Him! When He determines a matter He only says to it "Be" and it is.

It appears that Muhammad erroneously equated the Christian Trinity with the teaching of surrounding pagan polytheism and wrongly believed that the idea of sonship suggests God has a partner (c.f. S4:171–172 and S19:35:wherein the gods engaged in sexual union and reproduction). This is a far cry from what Christianity *actually* teaches about the Trinity and the eternal Sonship of Christ.

Second, Muhammad rebuked Christians for describing God as a threesome, "And say not 'three'" (S4:171),

> S4:171. O People of the Book! Commit no excesses in your religion: Nor say of Allah aught but the truth. Christ Jesus the son of Mary was (no more than) an apostle of Allah, and His Word, which He bestowed on Mary, and a spirit proceeding from Him: so believe in Allah and His apostles. Say not "Trinity": desist: it will be better for you: for Allah is one Allah. Glory be to Him: (far exalted is He) above having a son. To Him belong all things in the heavens and on earth. And enough is Allah as a Disposer of affairs.

> S4:172. Christ disdaineth not to serve and worship Allah, nor do the angels, those nearest (to Allah): those who disdain His worship and are arrogant, He will gather them all together unto Himself to (answer).

It should be pointed out that Muslim commentators such as Yusuf Ali, try to hide this Quranic misunderstanding by translating the word *thalauthah* as "Trinity," when in the nineteen occurrences of the word elsewhere in the Quran, it simply means the number three. In contrast, A. J. Arberry keeps the proper meaning, "They are unbelievers who say 'God is the Third of Three.' No god is there but the One God" S5:76 (A. J. Arberry).[14]

Classical Islam was less defensive. For example, the famous commentator Zamakhshari suggests that the word *thalaathah* in Surah 4:171 confirms that the Quran was attacking tritheism.

> According to the evidence of the Quran, the Christians maintain that God, Christ, and Mary are three gods, and that Christ is the child of God by Mary, as God says (in the Quran): "O Jesus son of Mary, didst thou say unto men: 'Take me and my

---

14. Arberry, *The Koran Interpreted*, 140.

mother as gods, apart from God'?" (S5:116), or: "The Christians say: 'The Messiah is the Son of God'" (S9:30).[15]

It should be intriguing to speculate how Muhammad came upon the idea that Mary was believed to be one of the three persons the Christians held to be divine. Most probably, what gave rise to this idea was the veneration given to Mary by heretical sects around Arabia at that time. Hence, Muhammad strongly rebuked these sects:

> They do blaspheme who say: Allah is one of three in a Trinity: for there is no god except One Allah. If they desist not from their word (of blasphemy), verily a grievous penalty will befall the blasphemers among them. Why turn they not to Allah, and seek His forgiveness? For Allah is Oft-forgiving, Most Merciful. Christ the son of Mary was no more than an apostle; many were the apostles that passed away before him. His mother was a woman of truth. They had both to eat their (daily) food. See how Allah doth make His signs clear to them; yet see in what ways they are deluded away from the truth! Say: "Will ye worship, besides Allah, something which hath no power either to harm or benefit you? But Allah,—He it is that heareth and knoweth all things." (S5:73–76).

These verses teach that Christ the son of Mary is not God but only a prophet: God is not one of three. Thomas Hughes elaborates on the expression "they both ate food":

> [H]istorians tell us that there existed in Arabia a sect called Collyridians, who considered the Virgin Mary a divine person, and offered in worship to her a cake called Collyris; it is, therefore, not improbable that Muhammad obtained his perverted notion of the Holy Trinity from the existence of this sect. From the expression "they both ate food," we must conclude that Muhammad had but a sensuous idea of the Trinity in Unity, and had never been instructed in the orthodox faith with reference to this dogma.[16]

In summary, Muhammad completely misconstrued the Christian Trinity in concluding that Christians are either advocating three gods, or that the Trinity consists of God, Mary, and Jesus—Surah 5:116: "And behold! Allah will say 'O Jesus the son of Mary! didst thou say unto men "Worship me and my mother as gods in derogation of Allah"?'"

---

15. Gatje, *The Quran and its Exegesis*, 126.
16. Hughes, *Notes on Muhammadanism*, 265.

Theological Consequences

Regardless how the misunderstanding of the Trinity arose from the contingencies of history, it is important to keep in mind the underlying theological presuppositions that continue to (mis)inform Muslims concerning the Trinity. Such a misunderstanding remains very much alive today as we often come across Muslim apologists who rehash old arguments framed by early polemics against Christianity.

First, Muslim theologians assert that it is inappropriate, if not blasphemous, to apply human concepts like "Father" and "Son" to God. After all, these words imply the idea of physical procreation that contradicts the sublime spirituality of transcendent monotheism.[17] In response, the Christian assures the Muslim that these terms are only used analogically, a literary form that is also used in the Quran.

Second, Muslim theologians argue that the Trinity suggests a God who is a compounded being, that he is divisible. God becomes a three-some, if not polytheistic. The Christian notes that this objection rests on a faulty analogy taken from the physical realm. At the human level we reason from an abstract unity concept like "Man" (a species/genus) and observe it can comprise three particular members such as Abdul, Ahmad, and Anwar. Applying the same reasoning, the Muslim concludes the term "Trinity" functions as a genus and includes three gods.

The Christian responds by noting that divisibility applies only to physical entities and the objection fails since God is spiritual. God is not a generalization from empirical observations in the way "Man" is a generalization of many human individuals, an intellectual construct. The genus "Man" as a relative category with limitations of physical existence should not be applied to an absolute being like the Triune God. But it is the suggestion that there can be inner differentiations or modes of Being relating to one another within the Triune God that Islam rejects. Islam is contented merely to assert the oneness of God without any relationship.

But how could a bare unrelated and undifferentiated Being be the highest existing Being? The Christian contends that the Perfect Being would

---

17. Ismail Faruqi writes, "Islam charged Christianity with extending the nontranscendent concept of God's 'fatherhood of the Jewish kings' to Jesus and giving it . . . the de-transcendentalizing ontological connotation of unity of substance between God and Jesus. . . . Although Christians never ceased to claim that God is transcendent, they spoke of Him as a real man who walked on earth. . . . When pinned down, every Christian will have to admit that his God is both transcendent and immanent. But his claim of transcendence is *ipso facto* devoid of grounds. To maintain the contrary, one has to give up the laws of logic." See Faruqi, *Al Tawhid: Its Implications for Thought and Life*, 20–23.

not be compromised by the quality of relatedness. Being perfect means possessing varied distinctions internally and being plenipotentiarily rich suggests the ability to impart relative existence to subsidiary beings. How else is God the first cause and the ground of all beings? Kenneth Cragg makes a pertinent observation in this regard:

> [T]o elevate the Unity of God so as to be removed from experiential relevance would be religiously barren. "A bare unity, philosophically understood, is a barren one. . . . We cannot say that 'God is Love' and also say that 'God is solitary' or, in this solitary sense, that 'God is One.' Entire transcendence is in the end a blank agnosticism."[18]

Finally, internal differentiations (but not divisibility) point to a richer concept of unity. For example, a human being is more complex and differentiated than an octopus. By the same token he is a higher form of unity. The great Muslim theologian, Al-Ghazali himself perceived the possibility of conceiving distinctions within identity and acknowledged that plurality does not necessarily contradict unity. He offers the following analogy:

> How can the many be one? Know that this is the goal of all revelations. And the secrets of this science should not be penned down in a book, for the people of knowledge said: The unveiling of the secret of Lordship is blasphemy. . . . The thing can be many in one sense, but also can be one in another sense. And so, as man is many in one sense if you look at his spirit and body and limbs and blood vessels and bones and members, but in another sense he is one man.[19]

The Christian concludes, then, that the highest and richest Unity of all, the Divine, exists in the indivisible but real internal differentiation of three Consciousnesses. Hence the Trinity.

The Incarnation

It should be stressed that the Trinity is not a deduction of abstract analysis that is irrelevant to religious devotion and spiritual vitality. On the contrary, the doctrine of Trinity actually arises from the Christian experience of God's personal revelation and salvific acts in human history. That is to say,

---

18. Cragg, *Call of the Minaret*, 317.

19. Ghazali, *Ihya' 'Ulumed-Din*, vol. 4, 263, quoted by Anderson, *The Trinity*, 32–33. The full English text of Ghazali's classic work is available in four volumes, *Ihya Ulumud-Din* 4 vols. (Lahore: Kazi Publication, no date).

the Trinity is the correlate of the Incarnation of God in Jesus Christ. Islamic theologians vaguely sense the vital connection between the Trinity and the Incarnation, and yet offer a list of objections.

Objection 1: "The Word became flesh" suggests that God is transmuted into physical flesh, that is to say, the eternal became saddled with the world of contingency.

Response: A key passage which will answer this objection can be found in Philippians 2:5–11. In particular, verse 7 describes the Incarnation as the process whereby God in Christ "made himself nothing" (emptying) and "taking the form of a servant." It should be noted that the participles "made himself nothing" and "taking" suggest the act of "making himself nothing" is simultaneous with the "taking."[20] In other words, "made himself nothing" means adding humanity to deity rather than subtracting deity from the person Christ. As such, the Incarnation is not a dilution of God's divine power, nor a transmutation of God into flesh. The more accurate understanding of the Incarnation is that it is not the case that God was transformed into flesh, but that God took on human nature for his earthly existence as Jesus Christ. Theologically, in the Incarnation, God assumed flesh and veiled his divine glory in his earthly existence.

Objection 2: The Incarnation imposes the limitations of space-time on to God and thus dilutes his deity.

Response: Admittedly, if the Incarnation is a transformation (an exchange between deity to humanity) then it would amount to a dilution of God. But in reality the doctrine of the Incarnation affirms that God remains both God and man in Jesus Christ. As the Chalcedonian Creed declares, Christ is both God and man at the same time. The implication of this statement is that God remains omnipresent and omnipotent throughout the universe, while presenting himself in a particular locality of the Universe. Surely there is no logical impediment to the ability of the omnipresent God sustaining

---

20. See R. P. Martin, Martin, *Philippians* 2nd ed., 118: "μορφὴν δούλου λαβών, 'by taking the form of a slave.' The expression ἑαυτὸν ἐκένωσεν, 'he poured himself out,' is now defined more precisely by the participial phrases that follow: 'taking [λαβών] the form of a slave,' 'being born [γενόμενος] in the likeness of human beings,' and 'being recognized [εὑρεθείς] as a human.' These participles, although aorists, are nevertheless participles of simultaneous action (c.f. Blass Debrunner Funk §339[1]) and express the means by which the action of the verb ἐκένωσεν, 'poured out,' was effected. Paradoxically, then, Christ's self-giving was accomplished by taking, his self-emptying was achieved by becoming what he was not before, his kenosis not by subtracting from but by adding to, if some literal sense is intended."

the universe while giving special attention to a local region of the universe. The objection of dilution of the deity cannot be upheld.

Objection 3: The Incarnation is conceptually incoherent.

Response: It is a sign of intellectual decline among the Islamic intelligentsia that Muslim theologians today hardly exploit the sophisticated polemics against the Incarnation based on classical Islamic (Aristotelian) philosophical categories in medieval times.[21] But there are signs of rediscovery of this heritage with recent republication of classical critiques of the Trinity and Incarnation.[22] One popular rehash of this polemical tradition is *Al-Ghazali's Criticism of Christians' Theological Doctrines (Al-Radd Al-Jamil)*.[23]

The author displays firsthand knowledge of the Gospels although he reads them strictly within his Islamic terms of reference. I shall only focus on Al-Ghazali's objection to the Incarnation as a failed attempt to explain the two natures of Christ. Al-Ghazali first critiqued the Jacobites' position as it results in a third being that is a composition of both the divine and human natures.[24] In turn, this composition presupposes the prior existence and the complementary qualities of the two components. By definition, each part cannot be perfect. That is to say, there is human nature distinct from divine nature. As such, Al-Ghazali asserts that if God could be united with the human nature this would mean that God was not perfect before the union. If that be the case, the Christian Incarnation suggests that God needs the human nature to realize fully his own existence. Al-Ghazali refuted the Melkites for relying on an abstract human nature which Christ supposedly assumed as no more than a figment of human imagination.

---

21. On the other hand, it should be noted that Christian theological scholarship on Islam did not make much progress in the last fifty years. The most comprehensive philosophical study that consciously compares Christianity and Islam with respect to their Neo-Platonic and Aristotelian heritage remains the four volume work by James W. Sweetman written from 1945–67. See Sweetman, *Islam and Christian Theology*.

22. See books by Abu 'Isá al-Warraq, *Against the Trinity* and *Against the Incarnation*. See also ibn Tamiyyah, *Al-Jawab Al-Sahih. A Muslim Theologian Response to Christianity*.

23. See English translation by Razali Nawawi, *Al Ghazali's Criticism of Christians' Theological Doctrines*. For convenience, I shall refer to Al-Ghazali as the author, since there is considerable debates on whether Ghazali is the actual author. See "Al-Radd Al Jamil: Ghazali's or Pseudo-Ghazali" by Maha El-Kaisy Friemuth in David Thomas ed. *The Bible and Arab Christianity*, 275–94. The philosophical critique by al-Warraq is more robust, but Ghazali's book is more accessible and is more influential among popular Islamic polemists.

24. The Melkites were the Byzantine Christians who supported the Chalcedonian Creed (AD 451) but the Jacobites opposed the creed.

More importantly, regardless of the teaching of both Jacobites and Melkites as to whether the Messiah's supposed two natures were mixed or separate, Al-Ghazali found their teaching of the crucifixion of the Messiah to be self-refuting. The contradiction of their position can easily be demonstrated by a simple syllogism:

The Messiah was crucified;
Nothing that was ever crucified is God.
Therefore, nothing of the Messiah is God.

Finally, Al-Ghazzali addressed the Nestorians by asking how they understood the oneness of wills in Christ. He argued that if the Nestorians referred the will to the "Five Judgments"—that is, what is obligatory, what is forbidden, what is approved, what is disapproved, and what is permissible—then it should not be uniquely applied to Christ since the same oneness of wills could be applied to all the prophets and to saints who do not have the status of prophets. For full measure, Al-Ghazali further retorted and noted that one may doubt this "oneness of wills" since Christ's will differed from God's will as is evident when Christ asked that the cup to be passed at Gethsemane.

In summary, Al-Ghazali found all three major Christian theological traditions wanting and proceeded to offer his own Islamic understanding of the Incarnation as the Indwelling (*hulul*) of the Divine in Christ. Al-Ghazali was prepared to grant the term Son of God only a metaphorical meaning. For him, the unity between Jesus and God arises not because God dwells in the body of Christ, since such a concession would require the same indwelling of God in the bodies of the disciples who were one with Christ. Rather, for Al-Ghazali, the unity refers to a *moral* union—Christ perfectly conformed to the will of God.

Denial of the Cross

Objection: If there is no Incarnation, there is no divine atonement at the cross. The locus classicus is found in Surah 4. It begins with a list of the many sins of the Jews: they worshipped the calf (S4:153); they broke the covenant made at Sinai; disbelieved the revelations of God; killed his prophets (S4:155); and spoke against the Virgin Mary—"a tremendous calumny" (S4:156). The passage continues:

> That they said (in boast), "We killed Christ Jesus the son of Mary, the Messenger of Allah";—but they killed him not, nor

> crucified him, but so it was made to appear to them, and those who differ therein are full of doubts, with no (certain) knowledge, but only conjecture to follow, for of a surety they killed him not:—Nay, Allah raised him up unto Himself; and Allah is Exalted in Power, Wise ;—And there is none of the People of the Book but must believe in him before his death; and on the Day of Judgment he will be a witness against them. (S4:157–159).

The majority of Islamic theologians say this passage refers to God substituting Jesus with someone who looked like him on the cross. The real Jesus was raised up to heaven. This teaching suggests that Muhammad was influenced by Gnostic sects in the Arabian Peninsula.

It is more important to understand the presuppositions underlying the Quranic rejection of the crucifixion—i.e., allowing the Messiah to be crucified suggests that God not only allowed failure to beset his divine mission, but worse still, God abandoned his prophet, who ended up being executed. But surely this is unbefitting of the divine Lord since even earthly kings do their utmost to protect their ambassadors.

The Christian needs to help the Muslim appreciate the deeper logic of salvation. First, God may not have prevented the crucifixion, but he did vindicate Christ by raising him from the dead and glorifying him in heaven. God allowed the crucifixion in order to deal with the problem of sin—sin according to the Bible being rebellion and not just forgetfulness as taught in Islam. As such, forgiveness cannot be simply set aside by a decree (that would be indulgence rather than forgiveness). In effect, forgiveness without punishment undermines the integrity of divine law that governs the cosmos. The necessity of atonement that was foreshadowed in the Old Testament sacrificial system explains when Jesus died on the cross.

AN ADEQUATE REVELATION THAT CREATES RESPONSIBLE RELATIONSHIPS

It is imperative that Christians not only answer Islamic objections but offer positive arguments to defend the Christian concept of revelation. To begin with, the Christian argues that divine revelation must be personal. It is granted that religious faith expresses a willing submission to the will of God. But divine exhortation must go beyond an abstract list of duties and restrictions. A list of "dos and don'ts" will lead to despair on the part of the believer, who is weighed down by a sense of moral inability (sin). Despair arises because when command does not grant the power to obey, it can only result in condemnation for both sins of omission and sins of commission.

Rebellion results because abstract commands are seen as restrictions to one's freedom imposed by an unsympathetic external power.

Therefore, the demand for a righteous life requires that divine commands be exemplified by personal role model(s). The Christian insight into moral psychology is that character formation and moral action is best nurtured in the context of relationships; as such, the goal of revelation is not abstract moral knowledge but alleviation of moral inability concomitant with the restoration of relationship through a personal revelation of God in the person of Jesus Christ.

EXCURSUS: HELPFUL INSIGHTS FROM SPEECH ACT PHILOSOPHY

I also want to argue that the concept of revelation of divine commands as a list of "dos and don'ts" alone sees language as primarily a carrier of information. However, this view of language is inadequate especially given the insights of speech-act theory which was pioneered by J. L. Austin. For Austin, language is multi-dimensional. The use of language can be analyzed in terms of the "locution" (the act of saying—*what* is said), the "illocutionary" aspect of the words (the purpose of the utterance—*why* it is said), and the "perlocutionary" effect (the actual results of the speech act). In other words, speech is a form of action. Brummer notes that in speaking we go beyond proposing a picture of reality (expressives). We also express convictions and attitudes (constatives), we express convictions and attitudes (expressives), we commit ourselves before our hearers to some specific future act(s) (commisives), and we finally accept an obligation before our hearer(s).[25]

Believers who restrict revelation to a holy book operate with a view of language that postulates a duality which separates the speaker from reality and from the persons he wishes to communicate with. In contrast speech-act theory emphasizes that when a person uses language he projects himself into reality with the intention to change it. Speech also creates a relationship between the speaker and the hearer. There is, therefore, no dichotomy between language (thought) and action (reality and relationship). Speech then is more than a cognitive intent; it involves the whole person. Jerry Gill emphasizes that the speaker gives his personal backing to his speech. "Thus *truth is a function of personal commitment*. There is a sense in which every

---

25. Brummer, *Theology and Philosophical Inquiry*, 10–12.

statement must necessarily participate in both the factual and valuational dimensions simultaneously. Technically speaking, each statement should be prefaced by the phrase, 'I say,' thereby indicating the speaker's responsibility for making it."[26]

The purpose of communication is certainly more that just to convey information; it is to establish a relationship between the speaker and the hearer. In the light of recently gained philosophical insights into the nature of language we see the cogency of the Christian understanding of revelation which makes the chief purpose of divine revelation the establishment of fellowship and eliciting of a human response in the form of worship of a personal God.

We cannot simply expect to read off God's personal intention statements from a book filled with statements in abstraction. Revelation creates an ontic relationship which places the recipient into a concrete relationship with God. Revelation creates a dialogical relationship through God's word. Human beings are affirmed in a dialogical relationship. Ray Anderson writes, "In concrete social situations, only relationships which have the character of placing person into the truth of relation with God are considered normative, and is the standard by which all other concepts of personality are measured."[27] The Christian then sees a person as affirmed in the context of community. A person is only totally a person in community. The Christian rejects any atomistic concept of persons which isolates them from a larger community. Revelation is appropriated in the context of involvement, response, integration, that is to say, in the context of relationship.

We are again forced back to the issue regarding the fundamental nature of God's revelation. Here Kenneth Cragg reiterates that God is by nature revealing, and given his righteousness and mercy, his revelation also redeems:

> This revelation is finally personal and consummates all its words into a Word that lives and moves and has its being in our ken. But further, this revelation—if it is of a living God—intends fellowship. God will not simply tell us what, but show us Who He is. Revelation bringing God to us and us to God in knowledge means communion. The end of the law is obedience; the end

---

26. Gill, *The Possibility of Religious Knowledge*, 115.
27. Anderson, *Historical Transcendence and the Reality of God*, 82.

of education, understanding; the end of revelation, knowledge. God is not an idea; nor can He be obeyed, understood, or known merely as an idea. God as Muslims and Christians suppose Him, in their common if contrasted traditions, is a God Who seeks worship and intends fellowship. Revelation overcomes not merely darkness, but distance.[28]

Many Muslims wonder if the centrality of the cross has softened Christians to the point of being unable to transform society. Perhaps such a conclusion arises from an inappropriate criterion of judgment. Marshall Hodgson helpfully distinguished Christian and Islamic views in his magisterial work, *The Venture of Islam*.

For Christians, being based on revelation means being in response to redemptive love as it is confronted through the presence of a divine-human life and the sacramental fellowship of that which is the source. For Muslims, being based on revelation means being in response to the total moral challenge as it is confronted in an explicit divine message handed on through a loyal human community. The two senses of revelation not only contrast to one another: they exclude one another categorically.[29]

Herein lies the parting of ways between Islam and Christianity. Islam rejects the message of the cross since divine self-humiliation at the cross undermines the weightiness of truth and undermines confidence in the efficacy of God's law to regulate social life. For Islam God's truth will certainly confirm itself and will triumph over untruth and godless powers. In operational terms, Islamic revelation offers a blueprint of God's perfect and perfectible society. What is revealed is achievable and therefore to be followed through. The present deficiencies of society must not be excused by appealing to eventual eschatological fulfillment resulting from direct divine intervention. There is no break or gap between the history of God's action and the history of the Islamic enterprise.

Kenneth Cragg elaborates on Ibn Khaldun's concept of *asabiyyah*, or group solidarity: "God sent no prophet except that he should be obeyed" (S4:64). This obedience goes beyond mental assent or even ethical discipleship. It is, rather, a reciprocal bond of prestige and protection that exists between the leader and his adherents. The outcome is an organized community to protect their interest. Khaldun concluded that Christianity is therefore not a "missionary religion" precisely because it has no Jihad. Religion

---

28. Cragg, *The Christ and The Faiths*, 310–11.
29. Hodgson, *The Venture of Islam. Vol. 1 The Classical Age of Islam*, 29.

in this regard "must enjoy the benefit of power as proof both of its own sincerity and of its competence to be effectively sincere. Verbal propagation is not only incomplete: it compromises, if not corroborated by the power-form of group solidarity politically operative."[30] Truth is confirmed by the power and deliverance of his people from injustice, or shall we say, conquest by the Ummah? The historical success of the Muslim community confirms the veracity of the authority of Muhammad as the seal or final prophet.

But is Islam justified in having this confidence? Has history not time and again proven itself not amenable to human ventures, and that includes the Islamic community itself? One calls to mind G. K. Chesterton's dictum that the one empirically verifiable doctrine is the doctrine of original sin. In contrast, Islam views human sin not so much as rebellion but as forgetfulness. Human beings, in its view, are born pure (*fitrah*). All that is needed for the transformation of the human heart is to heed the call to remember the laws of God. All that is required for attaining a righteous society is education and legislation of morality and religion.

Islam takes pride in its possession of an allegedly final revelation that serves as a blueprint for perfectable humanity and perfect society. Its outworking ought to be evident, if not compelling for all to behold. Unfortunately, history does not seem to comply with Islamic expectations. Granted, that Muslims may point to Islam's early conquests as confirmation of the truth and power of Islamic revelation when Islam was the global superpower that reigned supreme from Spain to Iran. However, as with the way of all human flesh and empires, stagnation and decline eventually crept in. Indeed, the last two hundred years witnessed the fragmentation and demise of Islamic political power, epitomized by the dismemberment of the Ottoman Empire by Western powers.

Contemporary Muslims are beset by an embarrassing historical incongruity. The perfect revealed book ought to nurture a perfect society if not a dominant society. But the reality is that its adherents continue to suffer political setbacks under the hands of "godless" Westerners. It would seem that the more Muslims up their rhetoric of the supreme truth of the Quran based on its alleged efficacy, the more obvious the discordance between Islamic rhetoric and the realities of history.

How then is Christian love to engage with Islamic political power? One calls to mind the Song of Mary (Luke 2:46–55), the reversal of social values, power, and hierarchy epitomized by the Incarnation and the cross. In the end, only eschatology can settle the issue. But until then, the Christian peacemaker can only plead with Muslims and all who tend to use

---

30. Cragg, *Muhammad and the Christian*, 33.

power in destructive ways (including fellow Christians) to take a hard and honest look at history. The way to hell is indeed paved with self-righteous intentions. Is it not the case that history has become the slaughter bench arising from mindless exercise of power? Did not King Louis XIV described cannons as the "ultimate argument of kings"? Should we not be profoundly disturbed by the endless cycles of violence, revenge and counter-revenge in inter-ethnic conflicts between Serbs, Croatians, and Bosnians? The Christian's humble but persistent message is that only love can break this mindless cycle of violence.[31]

Ultimately, the difference between Islam and Christianity is that the former views the relationship between God and man within the field of power. The Divine-human encounter becomes a contest of strength where human submission is a matter of expediency in the face of sheer dominant power. In contrast, Christianity views the relationship as one that is moral: God, despite his sovereignty, treats human beings as persons with inherent dignity (since they are created in his image). God seeks allegiance from man based not on expediency but as a grateful response to a God who passionately cares for his welfare (cf., pathos in Abraham Heschel's work). Man may fail to perceive the depths of divine pathos. Without a personal revelation from God, man can only be dimly aware of divine pathos in pale and fragmented forms, described as divine sorrow, pity, wrath, and compassion, because of his psychological limitations, although divine pathos must be perfect and complete within the divine Trinity. However, these partial perceptions of divine pathos are fully revealed and experienced as divine love when manifested at the cross. Hence the glorious declaration in 2 Corinthians 5:19—in Christ God was reconciling the world to himself.

---

31. Volf, *Exclusion and Embrace*, 99–165.

3

The Self-Revealing God and the Human Predicament

Burchell Taylor (Jamaica)

As the ultimate and the all-embracing subject of Christian faith, God is the primary theme of theological reflection. German theologian Jürgen Moltmann puts it well when he states that "[t]heology has only one problem: God. We are theologians for God's sake. God is our dignity. God is our suffering. God is our hope."[1]

The affirmation of the centrality of God has direct and inescapable implications both for the world and human life. Taken seriously, the assertion presupposes that God is the Source, the Ground and Ultimate Goal of creation. This stance operates with the conviction that the created order—which is the arena of our existence, and which is subject to human exploration, investigation, and analysis—is not a crude material reality that finds its explanation in itself. Rather, it is the outcome of the purposive and creative will of God, on whom it depends, and by whom it is sustained in its ongoing existence, as it moves toward its ultimate goal. This God alone is God—a God of infinite power, enduring presence, and providential care. This is essentially what the ancient Christian creeds sought to teach when

---

1. Moltmann, *God for a Secular Society*, 5.

they affirm that there is "One God, the Father, the Almighty, Maker of Heaven and Earth, of all that is seen and unseen."[2]

Regardless of the form it takes (discourse, debate, meditation, contemplation, critical reflection, or systematic articulation), when theology is properly done, it makes *God* the focal point of reflection. This means that when we do theology, we must have before us, in one form or another, the reality, character, meaning, and the acts of God.

This may be an obvious point, but nonetheless it needs to be stressed. For, in recent times, belief in the existence and reality of God has been called into question. Under the persistent influence of the Enlightenment's secularist mindset, there has been an overweening human self-confidence that has created a climate in which even the idea of God is considered redundant. Humans have asserted their ability to explain reality separate and apart from God. Thus, in such a context, God is deemed unnecessary. What seemed to emerge in the contemporary milieu, is an ethos of agnosticism and atheism that appears unassailable.

In fact, for a while, the anti-God wave was so strong that there even emerged the strange phenomenon of the so-called Christian atheism. While there were variations in the way proponents of this perspective stated their views, they shared the common conclusion that God was dead! According to them, the death of God had taken place in history, in culture, and principally in human existence. Harvard theologian Harvey Cox even expressed the conviction that the time had come for religion to come to terms with the fact of the death of God. According to these thinkers, the time had come to turn attention away from the notion of a transcendent being to a focus on humanity. Humans were said to have come of age, and thus become the measure of all things. We were told that if such a move was not made Christianity would soon cease to exist.[3] In keeping with this, even in Christian circles, there was a capitulation to the atheistic mood—albeit in a way that hoped for some form of theological adaptation.

The challenge of Christian atheism came at a time when Christian thinking about God seemed to fall into a complacent slumber. It was a time when Christian thinking started with belief in the existence of God as a basic premise. But what was not taken into account was the fact that that premise itself was being seriously challenged. Critics of Christian theism were quick to argue that God's existence was not as self-evident as its proponents claimed. Arguing pragmatically, others pointed out that belief in

---

2. *Documents of the Christian Church*, Henry Bettenson ed., p.24.

3. See Harvey Cox, *The Secular City: Urbanization and Secularization in Theological Perspective*.

God did not seem to make any appreciable difference to the life of persons. To those who held to such pragmatic view, ways of presenting God that assumed that his reality could be proved by means of abstract philosophical arguments or objective logical analyses were not convincing. For many, the memories and lingering legacies of questionable ventures, projects, and enterprises that were undertaken in the name of God, but which ended up having deleterious effects on people in vast areas of the world, as well as in the very centers from which belief was promoted, made the prospect for belief in God look grim.

NEW ATHEISM

But for a time, it seemed that the atheistic challenge had lost its edge. However, there is now a new atheism that is making its presence felt with a great deal of abrasiveness and aggressiveness. Many of the old arguments have been rehashed, although they are stated differently and in some instances with greater confidence.

New charges have also been leveled at faith in God. Some even claim that religion is responsible for all the evils and problems of the world. Sam Harris, for example, represents a view shared by many critics of Christian faith. He put forth the claim that it is only when all faith is abolished in the world that problems like terrorism will be banished. For him, faith is represented as basically irrational or credulous—it is belief held without evidentiary basis.[4]

Harris's critique displays something that is typical of the attitude of critics like him. As Karen Armstrong points out "The new atheists all equate faith with mindless credulity."[5] What we have here is the equation of genuine Christian faith with its misrepresentations, distortions, and oddities. But such a broadside seems to display an ignorance and a lack of acquaintance with the best representation of, and witness to, faith in God particularly the portrayal of God presented in biblical witness. The balance of this essay will be devoted to a distillation of this biblically based portrayal and its implications for human life in general and the human experience of the problem of pain and suffering in particular.

---

4 Harris, *End of Theism*, 58–73.
5 Armstrong, *The Case for God*, 305.

A DIFFERENT PERSPECTIVE

It is significant to note that even in the face of this aggressive broadside, the portrayal of God imbedded in the biblical witness continues to retain its strength and relevance for Christian thinking, living, and practice in areas situated outside the North American and European centers of reflection. In these places, theological reflection is not only carried out with greater reliance on the biblical witness; it is also done in closer proximity to the life and experience of the people. In these contexts, the "God problem" is not construed in terms of unbelief, but idolatry. In other words, in these places, the question that is often asked is not whether there is a God, but what kind of God he is. What people grapple with is the meaning of God for the life and hope of humankind and the creation. Phillip Berryman states this concern with stark clarity when he observes that:

> In North America and Europe the God problem is essentially one of how one can believe in God at all. . . . The situation in Latin America is quite different. In the first place, unbelief is not a widespread pastoral problem, except among a small elite. . . . Hence in a pastoral and theological sense, "the God question" becomes not whether there exists some referent to the term "God" but which God is meant.[6]

Even with the considerable penetration of North American and European culture into the Majority World that we've witnessed of late, the situation that Berryman describes has not changed. In fact, what he has seen in these centers of the Majority world bears considerable resemblance to what is conveyed in the biblical witness itself. Paul's comment on the situation in Athens is relevant here. The problem that Paul encountered in this ancient Greek metropolis was not whether there was a God who was real and who was worthy of belief. It was instead a problem of idolatry that was evident in the preeminence attributed to other so called gods. Atheism was out of the question. Idolatry was the real issue! Paul reinforces this position to the Corinthians when he writes:

> indeed even though there may be so-called gods in heaven and on earth as in fact there are many gods and many lords . . . yet for us, there is one God, Father from whom are all things and for whom we exist, and One Lord Jesus Christ, through whom are all things and through whom we exist (1 Cor 8:5–6).

---

6 Berryman, *Liberation Theology*, 152–53.

These sentiments confirm the fact that in the Bible, the existence of God is taken as a given. Nowhere does Scripture make a case for the existence and reality of God. What the biblical witness vehemently objects to, and roundly condemns, is the usurping of the divine status and the sharing of the title and prerogatives of deity with created things. True, in Psalm 14:1, the psalmist speaks of the fool who contemplates that there is no God (14:1. Cf. 53:1). But, the folly that the Psalmist chastises here is what Walter Brueggemann calls "practical atheism." The rebuke is directed at an approach to life that assumes the existence of God while the actual ordering of life runs counter to the assumed reality. This is lip service theism. Commenting on the Psalm, Brueggemann writes:

> In its main theme the Psalm is a statement about "practical atheism." It reflects on one whose conduct is disordered and without focus because it is not referred to God. A picture is drawn here of a creature whose life is not referred to the Creator. Notice in verse 1, the "fool" does not visibly announce atheism. It is only "in his heart," i.e. he thinks and decides that way.[7]

There is no theoretical or abstract discussion about God in the Bible. God is the living, active, encountering, and encountered Presence of ultimately definitive significance for all life. This is the witness of the Bible. The questions that arise about him are therefore of a different nature and category. They are practical, concrete and reflective. How does God act in the outworking of his purpose? What is God like in his nature and character? How does God relate to the universe—God's own creation? How is God known? These are questions that are addressed not by means of philosophical speculation or scientific examination and analysis. The answers to these queries come by way of response to, and reflection on, the revealed truths, insights that God himself communicates to us in the biblical witness. This is the revelation that Scripture speaks of in a unique fashion. Fundamentally, in the Scriptures, God is represented as Ultimate Self-revealing Subject.

ULTIMATE SELF-REVEALING SUBJECT

The defining and central Presence that we encounter in the biblical story is the living, self-revealing, and active God. This makes revelation the indispensable key to belief in, and knowledge of, God. God is not an investigable object; he is rather the ultimate and self-revealing subject. Karl Barth, in characteristic fashion, states that the very fact of God's revelation signifies that:

---

7 Brueggemann, *The Message of the Psalms*, 44.

> Man cannot of himself really believe in God. It is because man cannot do that that God reveals Himself. What man of himself can believe in are gods who are not really God. When his confidence in his ability really to believe in God of Himself goes to pieces, then the gods fall, in whom he can really believe. In the collapse of this confidence they are unmarked as god's who are not really God. But God is God in that we can know Him only on the basis of His revelation ....[8]

This focus on the revelation of God brings into sharp focus the reality of God as the central witness of the biblical drama. God is represented as being able to be known, understood, and responded to, adequately in terms of God's own self. This self-revealing God is made known in the activity of creation, in a covenant made with Israel, and ultimately in the history of Jesus Christ. In the process certain leading themes emerged in the stories. For example, God is encountered and experienced as executing justice, righteousness, peace and the fulfillment of hope. He is seen as well in the restoration of the creation after it was threatened by sin and evil. This restoration which conforms perfectly to God's purpose finds expression in the inauguration of the kingdom which will be consummated in a New Age, in the form of a new creation when the sovereign God will be all in all (1 Cor. 15:28).

What is critically important here is that the essential and fundamental dynamics of this self-revelation of God is definitively and absolutely bound up with the history of Jesus Christ. God's self-revealing wisdom, love, power, and freedom came to full flower in the coming of Jesus Christ who gave full embodiment to the identity and purpose of God. The writer of the letter to the Hebrews speaks to the decisive, definitive, and normative nature of the self-revelation of God in Jesus Christ.

> Long ago God spoke to our ancestors in many and various ways by the prophets, but in these last days he has spoken by a Son whom he appointed heir of all things, through whom he also created the worlds. He is the reflection of God's story and the exact imprint of God's being, and he sustains all things by his powerful word ... (Heb 1:1–3, NRSV).

Scripture, of course, speaks of other forms and means of mediation of divine self-revelation. However, we have here a bold affirmation that the absolute, decisive, and normative mediation of God's self-revelation is Jesus Christ, the Son. Brian Hebblethwaite underscores this further by locating it also in the foundational tradition of the church. He writes:

---

8. Barth, *Creddo*, 14.

> It is the central conviction of the Christian Church that God's self-revelation reached a unique and unrepeatable climax in the Incarnation—the coming of human form of God Himself in one mode of his eternal being, in order to enact and manifest the divine love in person and to win God's wayward creatures into a fuller, deeper life and fellowship in God.[9]

This confirms the insight that the meaning and purpose of the universe and, indeed, of all life, are located and expressed in the self-revealing activity of God in Christ Jesus.

The centrality of God's self-revelation in the history of Jesus Christ has direct bearing on questions regarding the meaning and significance of God. We have already noted the difference that exists between the position adopted in the traditional theological centers of the West, where the issue is about the existence of God, and the perspective adopted in centers located in the Majority World where the question relates more to the meaning and purpose of God in the face of the lived experience of the people. Gustavo Gutierrez notes that the first question asked by people whose daily experience is that of poverty and oppression is not about God's existence. Rather, it is about God's justice and love. What preoccupies the mind of people in these places is the challenge posed to God's justice and love when they reflect on their experience of poverty and all the anomalies that seem to separate the rich minority from the poor and oppressed majority. It is in the historical reality of Jesus Christ as the self-revelation of God that they find an answer that provides hope and assurance. In the God who is revealed in Jesus Christ, they meet a God who shows concern for, and attentiveness to, their welfare by upholding the cause of justice and righteousness.

In Jesus these realities are faced in the purpose of God. They are not explained away or denied. They are seen as a distortion and denial of God's purpose rather than as the predetermined fate of those who suffer. The purpose of the mission of Jesus was to challenge the way of life and the system that perpetrated evils of this kind. His announcement of the kingdom and the accompanying signs of liberating action and their consequences displayed an alternative order of existence that God purposed for all life and the creation. The messianic mission gives the assurance that the greatest forces of opposition will not succeed, but will ultimately be defeated as God's kingdom of righteousness, justice and peace, inaugurated by Jesus Christ is established and ultimately consummated (Rev 11:15).

As made known in the history of Jesus Christ, God is real. He is not as a figment of the imagination or an object of theoretical speculation. Through

---

9. Hebblethwaite, *The Essence of Christianity*, 41.

the presence and activity of the Spirit, he becomes contemporary, as an active and ongoing reality of everyday life. In the self-disclosure of God, the Spirit proceeds from God through Jesus Christ, making present the reality of what God has accomplished in and through the history of Jesus Christ. It is not surprising, therefore, that in biblical witness the Spirit is actually referred to as the Spirit of God as well the Spirit of Christ (Rom 8:9).

TRIUNE GOD

This brings into sharper focus the fullness of the self-revelation of God witnessed to in Scripture. Daniel Migliore brings out the significance of this insight in this way:

> The God of the biblical witness is God, the gracious Source of all life [Father] whose eternal Word became human to mediate abundant life to a world in captivity to sin and death [Son], and whose spirit of freedom and new life in communion is moving the people of God and all creation, to the consummation when God will be all in all.[10]

It is impossible to miss the fact that as the biblical witness to the self-revelation of God is set forth, Trinitarian language comes into play. This is the foundation of the church's articulation of the doctrine of the Trinity. The one God is self-expressed and is, in turn, experienced as diversity in unity, that is as a three-foldness of Being. While the church found it necessary to do this, as Jose Comblin says, it must readily be admitted that "Here, of course, we are entering into the secret of God and all that we can say stops short of the reality of God, which is inaccessible to us."[11] This means that the doctrine of the Trinity is really an attempt to express the inexpressible with the intention to communicate meaning that is graspable only very inadequately.

It is beyond the scope of this presentation to deal with the intricacies and the vast implications of the doctrine of the Trinity that have occupied Christian thought over the centuries. Yet, there are things of a more concrete, practical, and experiential import that need to be said in a discussion on the self-manifestation of God. It is often pointed out that the doctrine of the Trinity is a theoretical construct that is designed to make God understandable to the intellectual and philosophical mind. This leads to the claim that the doctrine is not supported by what the Bible teaches about God and

10. Migliore, *Faith Seeking Understanding*, 58.
11. Comblin, *The Holy Spirit and Liberation*, 163.

his ways. The truth is that there is indeed no full blown expression or explication of a doctrine of the Trinity in the biblical witness. Yet, the presence in Scripture of Trinitarian language in reference to God with respect to his work in creation and redemption is undeniable.

The New Testament's references to the Trinity are *unselfconsciously* Trinitarian.[12] By this we mean that it is almost in a matter of fact way that it refers to the experience of the reality of the Trinity. There is no felt need to offer any intellectual explanation. This cannot be overlooked. As Ralph Del Colle concludes in his essay on *The Triune God*:

> [T]he Christian doctrine of God is constructed as one of the foundations and capstone of Christian existence enacted in praise and worship. It is in this doxological event and context as the source and summit of Christian vision and understanding that the One God who is Father, Son and Spirit in known, proclaimed and adored.[13]

The New Testament offers the Trinitarian perspective, without articulating or expounding a Trinitarian doctrine. It is a perspective that is grounded experientially and devotionally. Theologically, it is the experience, the encounter, and the engagement that emerges out of the history and gift of creation and salvation that forms the basis for reflection. Because our reflection about God is such, its limits must be humbly recognized. In our effort to apprehend God and his ways, we must always recognize that we are dealing with a mystery the depths of which we will never be able to plumb.

When we take this consideration into account, we can understand why errors have always attended the effort to give expression to the reality of God. For instance, in some expressions of the doctrine of the Trinity, Father, Son, and Holy Spirit have been described in ways that suggest that they are three different centers of divine existence, giving the impression that the Christian view of God is tri-theism rather than monotheism. There is also a view that sees the divine persons as three different modes of the one and same being manifesting itself at different times and in different capacities. On this construal, which often bears the name of modalism, there is no real distinction in the person and the existence of the members of the Godhead; they are merely differing appearances of the same reality. Furthermore, there are those who prefer to see the members of the Godhead from the perspective of the position they occupy in the hierarchical order

---

12. See for example, Matt 28:19; 1 Cor 12: 4–6; 2 Cor 13:14; Eph 4:4–6; 2 Thess 2:3–4; 1 Pet 1:2; 1 John 4.

13. See, the essay, "The Triune God," in the *Cambridge Comparison to Christian Doctrine*, 138.

of supremacy that ranges from the Father, to Son, and to the Spirit. Known as subordinationism, this view denies that the members of the Trinity enjoy ontological equality among themselves.

While the challenge to offer an intellectually satisfactory explanation of the Trinity remains, none of the above theories seems adequate. For none fully matches the actual experience of God as Father, Son, and Spirit as revealed and affirmed in the biblical witness. They all seem to miss some critically important biblical insights about the nature and character of God, and about his relationship with humanity.

God is a loving, active, and personal being. He is not an impersonal entity or lifeless material reality. His reality is experienced in the creation, in the history of salvation, and in his ongoing work of generating, sustaining, and empowering life. The way that God works in the historical domain provides some insights into his inner nature as personal being and into the nature of the relationship that characterizes the members of the Godhead. Based on what is revealed in Scripture, we can affirm that, in the Godhead, we have a community of divine persons which maintains a relationship of mutual indwelling and interdependent actions. In every instance, each is involved in the being and expression of the others, even when the identity of one is specifically experienced, and even when his work is propelled at the forefront of the divine action plan. The divine community, thus, displays a relationship of faultless interrelatedness that, nonetheless, maintains personal distinctions and characteristics.

According to the biblical witness, the Triune God enters into covenant relationship with humankind in creation and redemption. Among other things, the purpose of this initiative is to provide a basis and a pattern for life in community. This means that in terms of a social order of existence, human life is meant to reflect the sociality that characterizes the life of the Triune God. If such is the divine intention, it follows that all that is disruptive of community is a deviation from the divine blueprint. Evils such as injustice, oppression, war, poverty, and the systems and structures that prevent people from participating meaningfully in community, and from fulfilling their human potential, are contrary to the nature of God. This explains why God is particularly attentive to the plight of the oppressed and their cry for liberation. There are persons of faith in certain parts of the world where faith in a Triune God is not grounded on abstract, philosophical argumentation, but is a lived, a lived out, and shared reality. It is a liberating reality to be embraced and proclaimed. Leonardo Boff comments:

> The Trinity understood in human terms as a communion of persons, lays the foundations for a society of brothers and sisters, of

equals, in which dialogue and consensus are basic constituents of living together, in both the world and Church.[14]

He also states that "this strengthens the cause of the oppressed struggling to liberate themselves so there can be sharing of community."[15]

ATTRIBUTES OF GOD

In our reflection about God, it is essential that we always keep in view his Triune nature. For, when the other aspects of the divine nature such as his attributes are considered separate and apart from an understanding of God as Triune, they are inevitably spoken of, and represented in, a negative manner. In my view, this amounts to a *via negativa* that presents a limited and one-sided view of God. For example, in Western theology, God is often portrayed as being limitless, emotionless, passionless, and changeless, and without any restriction of power, knowledge, or presence. Expressed in more abstract language, God is said to be infinite, impassible, immutable, and omnipotent, omniscient, and omnipresent. Of course, some divine attributes—love, just, and the like—are also applied to humans, and are thus known as communicable attributes. But even here, God stands in incomparable perfection in all such areas. Not even the most impressive instantiations of these attributes in human life can approximate the way in which they are exemplified in the life of God.

But even with this concession, it seems evident that, in traditional theology, the overall presentation of the attributes seems so skewed toward the safeguarding of the otherness and transcendence of God that, often, the biblical affirmation of his nearness to human life is overlooked. Yet, the biblical witness has a lot to say about God's involvement with, and within, the life and history of the creation. It portrays him as a personal, active, living, and caring Presence (Job 7:8; 33:4; 34:14; 34:15; Matt 5:45; 6:25–30; 10:29–30) who is not revealed only in terms of contrast and exclusion, but also in terms of engagement and embrace. We can say that essential to the biblical expression of the attributes, is a dialectical connectedness which belongs to the mystery of the Divine Being as Triune. When viewed in this light, the attributes take on a different meaning from the purely negative connotation that's often associated with them.

By way of explanation, let's touch briefly on the attributes mentioned above. Consider the attribute of omnipresence as a starter. It is my conviction

14. Boff, *Trinity and Society*, 118, 236.
15. Ibid.

that, as British theologian John MacQuarrie insightfully suggests, this notion is better rendered by the idea of *immensity*. In contradistinction to omnipresence, immensity expresses the way in which God is actually experienced in his encounter with humans rather than the way he is conceived abstractly. Immensity communicates overwhelmingness. God is encountered and experienced as *"Overwhelming Being."* He is experienced as the One who confronts, inter-faces with, and impinges upon fragile, vulnerable, and contingent beings. In this experience, true self-understanding is gained, awe is evoked, and possibilities for enhanced existence are disclosed. Yet, this close encounter requires no compromise of the differentiation that exists between God and humans. Nor does it leave room for manipulating God, or exhausting our knowledge of him, or reducing him to manageable, measurable, and controllable proportions.

How about the concept of impassibility and the idea of immutability that often accompanies it? Is the Triune God immune to being affected by the plight of humans as the concept of impassability suggests? Certainly not! As revealed in Scripture and experienced in human life, the biblical God is the living and active God. Revealed as personal Being in Father, Son, and Holy Spirit, he always responds with concern and compassion to realities and conditions of human life and the creation. In sovereign freedom, the Triune God has chosen to become identified with the human predicament and suffering, working for redemption and hope. God grieves over human rebelliousness and becomes identified with the predicament and agony that it causes. In loving response, God acts to provided redemption and reconciliation (Isa 5:1ff; Hos 11:8–9; Mark 15:34; Rom 8:26). God hears the cry of the oppressed and responds effectively to their pleas for help (Exod 3:7–12). Doesn't this raise questions about the idea that God is utterly immutable—that he does not and cannot change? Certainly, total immutability could be justifiably affirmed of a Being who never displays passion. But a God who shows so much pathos as the biblical God seems to do, must be subject to change in some way.

God is a God of impeccable integrity who always acts consistently with his own self-revealed character. This means that God is absolutely trustworthy and dependable. God is revealed in varying ways, in varying situations and circumstances, making responses that are themselves always consistent with God's own justice, righteousness, love, power, and wisdom. In this way, change and differentiation are seen but they do not mean inconsistency in God's character. God will not be proven to be self-contradictory or falling short of his own ideals (Heb 13:8). It is precisely God's consistency and trustworthiness that become the ground for the hope the poor and oppressed of the world. A creative and responsive God is not marked by a static sameness, but by a consistent dependability and unimpeachable integrity.

God is eternal. Generally, eternity expresses God's endlessness in a manner that places him outside of time. God is this seen as beyond time, utterly and absolutely. Yet, there are serious questions surrounding the matter of whether a timeless God is able to act in a temporal creation, and Christianity requires a view of God in which God does act in created space and time. He did so in a profound and decisive way in the Incarnation of Jesus Christ (Gal 4:4). Since this is the case, it follows that an understanding of eternity that locates God beyond time does not provide a complete picture of the biblical portrayal of him, nor give an adequate representation of his activity in the world. That is why the term "everlasting" has been deemed more appropriate by some than the concept of timeless eternity. The point is that the notion of everlastingness allows space for God's participation in time and history without being imprisoned or limited by them as is the case with creaturely beings. Brian Hebblethwaite describes the "everlasting" nature of God as,

> free from decay and the kind of change that characterizes our space/time world, God not part of, or limited to the space/time structure of creation. God's time is deeper, primordial, unaffected by relativity and thermodynamics.[16]

A God who is not indifferent to time, though not imprisoned or limited by it, is a God who can be trusted to act in time and give hope to those who are oppressed and exploited here and now. They do not live on deferred hope and vindication beyond time.

In the exposition of the doctrine of God, it is the attributes of the divine omnipotence, omnipresence, and omniscience that are often cited, both in popular piety and in philosophical discourse, to emphasize the contrast and overwhelming difference that exists between limited human power, presence and knowledge and the power, presence and knowledge of God. But when these attributes are understood in the light of God's self-disclosure as Triune, the challenges and contradictions that they purport to pose are put into proper perspective. We have already offered a different perspective on omnipresence above, hence we will reflect only on the remaining two other "omnis" here.

In our perspective, omnipotence does not simply mean God's ability to exercise brute power at will. While it is true that God's power is incomparable, and that no external force can ultimately exert control over his power,

---

16. Hebblethwaite, *The Essence of Christianity*, 48.

Scripture teaches that divine power is not exercised irrationally or arbitrarily. God's power is subject to God's own restraint. Its exercise is always consistent with God's own character and nature. The biblical God is just, wise, true, loving, patient, and faithful. Hence, paradoxically, in the mystery of God's ways, Scripture says that God's power was manifested eminently in the cross of Jesus Christ (1 Cor 1:18). It is power that displays its powerfulness in its capacity for creative and redemptive expression of love and hope.

The concept of divine omniscience which holds that God has endless knowledge—vast, unspecific, and open-ended—also needs to be clarified along the lines taken with respect to the other attributes discussed above. The incomparable knowledge of God that is mentioned in the Scriptures speaks more to the depth, fullness and the inexhaustibility of divine knowledge. Hence, some think that such knowledge is best understood as wisdom, in its purposive and effective nature. This is what Paul seems to be saying in his doxological exclamation as he reflects on the plan that God has effected for the redemption of the world "O the depth of the riches and wisdom of God! How unsearchable are his judgments and inscrutable are his ways..." (Rom 11:33). This is wisdom that is beyond our ability to grasp in its totality. And yet it offers much that reveals God's active nearness and self-givenness. Kenneth Grayston shows great insight into this aspect of the nature of knowledge of God when he says that "God is not dependent on our information or intercession. We cannot put him under obligation by piety or charity. All that God is, has been, will be, is in his creation and care. Hence the service of God is not harsh, grim, bleak, but splendid."[17]

This notion of divine knowledge serves as a restraint on the human presumptuousness that often attempts to exercise wisdom independently of God, and in so doing, renders God's wisdom unnecessary. Instead of such arrogance, we should humbly embrace God's wisdom and in so doing receive the hope and the confidence that all areas of life are covered by his understanding and will, however challenging and perplexing they may be to the human mind.

PAIN AND SUFFERING

One may ask "What is the practical relevance of the foregoing reflection about God?" Throughout the essay we have hinted at the implications of our understanding of God for human life and existence—particularly the life of the poor and the oppressed. But as we conclude the essay we'd like to

---

17. Grayston, *The Epistle to the Romans*, 102.

focus on the significance of this theology for the human problem of pain and suffering.

It is our conviction that the challenge posed by this nagging human predicament is best approached from the perspective of the theology of the Trinity and the understanding of the divine attributes articulated above. Traditionally, the problem is expressed this way: "wouldn't an All-Powerful, All-Knowing or All-wise, and All-Loving God be able to prevent and/or banish pain and suffering that frequently devastate human life?" Inherent in the question is the idea that God's perfection and integrity seem compromised by the reality of pain and suffering that is so integral to the human condition.

Admittedly, human ingenuity is yet to come up with a totally satisfactory response to the problem of pain and suffering. Yet, we are not convinced that it is necessary to conclude from this inability that faith in the God portrayed in the Bible is unreasonable and unjustifiable. Indeed, we contend that meaningful faith in the Triune God is not only justifiable in the face of the problem that confronts human existence; it is an effective response to the human predicament. How so? However limited our knowledge of the God portrayed in the biblical witness may be, such knowledge empowers us to engage the reality of pain and suffering by means of reflection and struggle. In openness to the guidance of the Spirit, faith apprehends and responds to the redemptive work of God in Christ as the expression of God's power, wisdom and unbounded love.

Essential to this understanding is the cross of Christ. This perspective takes seriously the fact that in Christ's crucifixion, God plumbs the depths of human pain and suffering, and through the resurrection, overcame the forces and powers that distort human life and existence. Pain and suffering are by no means denied and underrated. Instead, they are seen as being taken in by God's costly love and overcoming power. Such understanding empowers the sufferer to view pain and suffering from the proper perspective and thus put them in their proper place. Seen in this light, although troubling and disturbing, such vicissitudes of life are never granted the right to speak the ultimate word. Hence they can be endured and resisted in the light of God's vindicating power and grace that were so clearly manifested in Christ. Such assurance lies in the power of the Spirit whose enduring presence, life shaping activity, and life enabling work introduces and guarantees the blessings of the fullness of life to come.

A point that is often overlooked in this discussion is that prior to the time of the Enlightenment, people were aware of the difficulty posed by human pain and suffering for the vindication of God. But such awareness never rendered faith in a God of absolute power, wisdom and love impossible. It is interesting to observe that, while the Enlightenment spirit (*zeitgeist*) continues to prevail in the centers of its birth, it is not thriving in areas of our global village where pain and suffering are being experienced in some of their starkest forms. These include natural disaster, physical and environmental devastation, human exploitation, to name just a few. Indeed, it is precisely in these centers of suffering where Christian faith is showing the strongest signs of growth and vitality at this time.

Thus, while the witness of the Bible does not offer a full explanation of the origin or the "whys" and "wherefores" of pain and suffering in all their varied dimensions, it nevertheless, confronts such baffling reality, and deals with it in a manner that does not leave any doubt that God is sufficient to the challenge it poses both to human life and the creation. There is mystery that surrounds the problem and exposes human finitude. There is still more to be known by humans who do not apprehend the total picture of created existence, but who know that it is never closed to the dynamic liberating and redemptive activity of God. The Apostle Paul speaks effectively when he says,

> [N]ow we see in a mirror dimly, but then we will see face to face.
> Now I know, only in part, then I will know fully, even as I am fully known
>
> (1 Cor 13:12) (NRSV)

While such partial knowledge prevails in the face of the mysteries of life in creation, the enduring virtues of faith, hope, and love are gifts of the lived experience by God's grace. These are themselves virtues that give purpose to life in the face of the challenges posed by experiences of pain and suffering. Such purpose involves resistance and Spirit-enabled, and liberating action. This continues to give cause and space for worship of the Triune God.

PART 2

Christ and Salvation

4

Redeemer and Transformer: The Relevance of Christ for China's Cultural Renewal and Liberation

Carver T. Yu (Hong Kong)

CHRIST AND SALVATION—CONTEXTUAL AND CATHOLIC

EVERY THEOLOGICAL REFLECTION AND articulation is contextual in nature. The prevailing concerns of a context, the socio-cultural-spiritual predicaments it faces, and the unique mode of human corruption or the yearning for life fulfillment, all affect our proclamation of the gospel. The gospel is certainly the same gospel, but the way it is being proclaimed, the relevant answers coming out from it in response to life questions being asked are bound to be context-specific. Reflecting on Christ and salvation, a Chinese theologian cannot avoid having a unique Christological and soteriological perspective. Yet we have to ask, just how unique can this theological perspective be? The answer is quite simple: it can be unique as much as it is catholic and evangelical at the same time. Thus, before we go into the Chinese context to articulate that unique perspective, let us state briefly the common conviction about Christ and salvation among Christians who adhere to the historic Christian faith based on biblical revelation.

The gospel delivered to the Greco-Roman world and articulated by the early church fathers in their context is the same gospel for the Chinese in their unique context. The gospel is whole for all aspects, all dimensions of human life. It can address all forms of human needs that arise from our human fallenness. While human persons in different historical contexts may find themselves in different conditions with different forms of human distortion, which may find different aspects of the gospel more immediately relevant, the gospel is an integrated whole. Only the whole gospel can address the human person in a holistic way. However, in different contexts, addressing their different human conditions, proclamation of the gospel and theological articulations of it may need to place emphasis on certain aspects or dimensions of the gospel in order to bring in the full impact of the whole gospel.

However, something foundational has to be affirmed in whatever context the gospel is proclaimed. What is foundational, that which transcends all contexts, is the fact that Jesus Christ, the Word Incarnate, is our salvation. His life is one continuous saving act culminating in his crucifixion and completed in his resurrection. The Incarnation reveals the fact that God did not act through agents, instruments or schemes, effecting control of historical events to achieve the salvation of humankind. God came in person and acted in person. He affirmed his covenantal love in person in the face of utter human rejection, bore in person the consequence of human sin in fulfillment of his covenantal righteousness, acted out divine forgiveness in person for the restoration of covenant, and invaded the power of darkness in person to bring about liberation. Jesus Christ is the divine person in his saving act, actuating divine love, justice, righteousness, and power. Divine covenantal personhood is the core of this continuous saving act. Salvation starts with it and is brought to completion in it. In being saved, the human person, humankind and the whole universe are unified in this divine person. In being unified in him, the covenantal personhood of all things, particularly the human person, is healed and made whole. In him, covenant, the internal basis of creation, is restored, and creation, the external basis of covenant, is renewed.[1]

On this foundational understanding, different themes have been used to articulate the truth of salvation—themes like redemption, justification, reconciliation, participation in divine life leading to union with God, and

---

1. Here I am indebted to Karl Barth's covenantal theology of creation. Cf. Barth, *Church Dogmatics*, III/1.

liberation. However, the whole picture of salvation cannot be fully articulated by a single theme. A holistic picture of salvation involves the weaving together of all these themes. In weaving them together, certain theme may stand out in a particular context more than the others, like a certain strand of threads may stand out on a tapestry among many other strands which are there to sustain this distinctive strand. Thus the theme that stands out cannot do without the others if a full picture is to be yielded. In certain context, the theme of justification may stand out as vital in response to a particular form of human distortion within a particular life-system that oppresses people in certain ways. Or in certain cultural contexts, people are most receptive to the idea of participating in divine life, and thus salvation by union with Christ may prove to be highly effective in communicating the gospel. Justification in such a context, though, may be susceptible to a total misunderstanding if the theme of participation precedes it. After the theme of participation has laid the foundation, justification will have its place, and properly understood. Likewise, liberation may particularly be relevant to a context where injustice and oppression is prevalent, yet other themes like reconciliation or justification have to be there to facilitate a holistic articulation of liberation, or else, liberation can fall into an ideological trap.

NARRATIVE OF A WOUNDED SOUL—THEOLOGY IN A CONTEXT IN CULTURAL DISINTEGRATION

When the gospel came to China in full strength in the middle of the nineteenth century, the whole country was gripped by a deep sense of national crisis. The opium trade forced onto her by Britain devastated both the body and soul of a people who became widely addicted to the drug. Rampant corruption at all levels of society exacerbated the spread of this social and spiritual ill. Just when signs of socio-cultural disintegration were becoming apparent, the impact of Western culture came in full force through its military prowess. Whether China could survive as a nation in the onslaught of Western imperialism and colonialism was the question. After humiliating defeats in the Opium Wars (1839–60), the threat of China being divided among Western powers was real. A deep sense of survival crisis intensified. Not only did the Chinese people begin to question their cultural tradition, they were thrown into frantic quest for a cultural model that could make China strong again. A complete cultural overhaul became urgent. To survive, China had to modernize, and to do so it had to absorb whatever necessary from Western civilization unreservedly. As survival crisis deepened, a self-questioning of China's cultural past culminated into an iconoclastic rejection. However, the problem of identity crisis immediately surfaced. Culture is not like clothe which can be taken off or put on at will. It is a way of life unique to a people. It is a system of meaning and values ingrained in the human person, social relations, and economic structures. Reaction to the iconoclastic orientation was therefore equally strong, and there was thus, a recoil to conservatism. Anything foreign was greeted with hostility. The struggle to maintain historical continuity with her cultural past while assimilating Western civilization was a real issue.

The Chinese people were deeply divided in this quest for cultural transformation. For some, complete Westernization was the only answer to national survival. Western science-technology and democracy was the answer, and had to be taken in wholesale, except of course Western religion, which was being rejected by the modern mind as unscientific. The Chinese cultural past was regarded as a failure, and had to be abandoned. For others, the achievement of the Chinese humanistic spirit could be brushed aside just because of temporary technological setback. On the other hand, the Western scientific/mechanistic worldview behind all the technological achievements could in the long run be a real menace to humanity. The whole orientation of Western technological advancement pointed to the intrinsic drive within Western culture to conquer others and to subdue nature for the satisfaction of material needs as life-fulfillment. Despite its material strength on the outside, Western civilization was perceived to have a much deeper crisis at the core.[2] Such warning of course fell on deaf ears, and the iconoclastic approach had the upper hand. Unreserved Westernization was set into motion, leading to rapid disintegration of the Chinese cultural tradition, resulting first in a deep sense of identity crisis, and then axiological crisis—the crisis of values.

The old ghost of the Chinese cultural tradition just refuses to go away, and continues to haunt the Chinese soul. How can they maintain the spiritual values that have through centuries been ingrained in the Chinese personality and the Chinese way of life? How can they integrate their historic past with Western elements so as to maintain a cultural historical continuity? How are they to evaluate the Chinese emphasis on "inner life" over against the emphasis on efficiency and functionality in the modern world? The problem

2. Liang Su-ming's lectures at Beijing University in 1921, "Dong Xi Wen Hua Ji Qi Zhe Xue," (Eastern and Western Cultures and Their Philosophies) was prophetic in pointing to the inner problems of Western culture. Liang affirmed unequivocally the value of the Chinese humanistic tradition. In similar vein, Carsun Chang wrote a book in collaboration with German philosopher Rudolf Eucken, *Das Lebensproblem in China und in Europa* (Leipzig, 1922), in defense of the Chinese tradition while pointing to the spiritual predicaments in the west. His essay—"The European Cultural Crisis and the Direction of China's New Culture"—is highly instructive.

of assessing the value of the Chinese tradition over against that of the West continued to occupy attention of many Chinese intellectuals long after the May Fourth New Culture Movement. The intensity of spiritual anguish over the disintegration of the Chinese humanistic tradition was clearly expressed in a manifesto pronounced in 1957 by a small group of highly influential Neo-confucian philosophers, Carsun Chang, Tang Chun-I, Mou Tsung-san and Hsu Fu-kuan, "A Manifesto for Reappraising the Understanding and Reconstruction of Chinese Culture."[3] The Chinese cultural tradition was pictured to be in a state of fragmentation and dissipation, with the Chinese humanistic spirit withering. The call for renewal sounded desperate as the Chinese people was taken by the Communist regime onto a course of socio-cultural revolution based on the ideal of historical materialism, with the Chinese cultural tradition totally negated.

It was in this extremely difficult period that waves of missionary endeavors came into China with increasing propensity from 1850 to 1949. Poorly equipped for understanding the Chinese tradition and insensitive to her struggle for survival as well as cultural integrity, missionaries proclaimed a gospel infused with Western mindset and tainted with spiritual and cultural triumphalism. It was, therefore, quite natural that their mission was perceived as the cultural side of the Western invasion of China. Worse still, it was perceived to be a gospel that condoned the opium trade and thrived on military invasion. Emotional resistance to the gospel was almost insurmountable and yet, the real problem lay in the gospel of salvation that missionaries preached. With the exception of a few missionaries who were mainly liberals, most missionaries preached pure personal salvation completely oblivious to redemption in the socio-cultural dimension. Some even saw Chinese culture, with all her "religious superstitions" and "inhumane" customs, as utterly depraved. So, anyone converted to Christianity had to sever with the old way of life, and that means the old Chinese cultural tradition. Not only were they not concerned about the cultural struggles, they rejected Chinese culture itself in the name of Christ. The result of this is that Chinese intellectuals thus saw the gospel as totally irrelevant to their struggle for national and cultural transformation.

Under Communist rule, the Chinese people went through utter spiritual and physical devastation. Starting from 1949 to the end of the Cultural Revolution in 1976, for almost three decades, traditional moral values were trampled on as feudalistic, human relations were subjected to scrutiny under the lens of class struggle, mutual trust evaporated, fear and suspicion

---

3. An abridged English version of this manifesto is printed in an appendix of Carsun Chang's *Development of Neo-Confucian Thought*, 455–84.

reigned, any form of personal or social aspiration became a costly liability, and the mind and heart were numbed by continual blare of ideological exhortations which propagated nothing but emptiness. Physical suffering was immense, but spiritual devastation was even worse as it cut deep into the soul of the people. Tens of million died of famine and class struggles in the Great Leap Movement and the Cultural Revolution. Those who survived were left to face the spiritual void in a society the moral foundation of which had collapsed, where basic human trust evaporated, where the abuse of power and corruption had spawned wide spread discontent and a spirit of despair, and where meaning and hope wore thin.

From 1980 onward, China was taken onto a new course. Market capitalism was mounted onto a totalitarian socio-political system rife with corruptions. With the traditional value system torn to pieces, with all forms of spiritual quest suppressed, with the communist ideology discredited, China, in spiritual vacuum facing the onslaught of market capitalism, which recognizes efficiency and functionality as the measure of all value, found itself in a most critical situation. The economic boom in recent years is merely a façade pasting over severe social cracks and spiritual emptiness. There is a strong sense among intellectuals that the moral foundation of social life has to be rebuilt. The cry for reviving the traditional spiritual values is growing stronger everyday. Popular religions are making a come back not only in rural areas, but also in big cities. There has been a trend among intellectuals for promoting Confucian values in society. There is a movement calling for the reestablishment of the long abandoned Confucian Religion, with Confucian temples and rites restored. Equally astounding is the revival and spread of Buddhism in China. It is quite clear that there is a deep spiritual hunger in China. However, this spiritual hunger is not merely "spiritual," it has a strong socio-cultural orientation. The quest for social and cultural regeneration remains a core concern. On the other hand, in no other time than this period of Chinese history have the Chinese people seen so clearly the depravity of human nature. In the Anti-capitalist Movement, the Great Leap Movement and the Cultural Revolution, the worst of human nature was let loose. Right after the Cultural Revolution, the so-called "Literature of Wound and Scar" became the main stream of literary creation in the 1980s. They not only narrated and lamented the immense suffering of a people who were so intoxicated with hope for the Communist Revolution, but went beyond socio-cultural phenomena to reflect on human nature.[4] In the face of this flood of narratives, some Neo-confucianists, who in the past would

---

4. Dai Hou-ying's *Man, Oh Man* (人啊，人) and *The Death of a Poet* (詩人之死) are good examples of such reflection.

only emphasize the bright side of human nature, are beginning to talk about the "awareness of the dark side of humanity" (幽黯意識). More and more Chinese intellectuals begin to see that any attempt to regenerate the Chinese culture has to take into account the regeneration of human person. Culture and the human person are dialectically intertwined. The gospel of Christ as the redeemer of the human person and the transformer of culture has had great appeal to the Chinese people. It is no wonder that in a matter of three decades, tens of million, particularly the intellectuals, have turned to Christ. Thus the proclamation of the good news of Christ and his salvation cannot ignore this dialectical intertwining between the human person and culture.

THE RELEVANCE OF CHRIST TO CULTURE

The Confucian tradition takes an integral view about humanity and culture. Humanity and culture are seen as one and the same thing. As I-Ching asserts in *The Book of Change*, "Observe astronomical phenomena so as to discern the change of seasons, observe the logic of humanity so that life under heaven may be cultivated according to it."[5] Culture comes as the concretization of humanity. So, "cultivating personal life, keeping one's family in order, governing one's country, maintaining peace in all realms under heaven,"[6] interlock with one another as different dimensions of a single whole, which is culture, the concrete manifestation of humanity. To be fully human is to be able to cultivate one's personal life according to Heaven's Way (Tien Dao), to be able to keep one's family in proper order, to participate in the proper governing of one's land, and to facilitate peace in all realms. The starting point is, of course, the cultivation of personal life. But it does not stop there. It has to emanate to the other dimensions of life. Thus personal life and culture interlock into a single whole. Transforming personal life cannot be separated from transforming culture.

Such an understanding of humanity and culture resonates with the Augustinian-Reformed perspective. In this Christian perspective, which I regard as highly biblical, Christ is the transformer of personal life as well as culture. For Augustine, as Richard H. Niebuhr puts it most succinctly, "Christ is the transformer of culture for Augustine in the sense that He redirects, reinvigorates, and regenerates that life of man, expressed in all human works, which in the present actuality is the perverted and corrupted

---

5. Quoted from I-Ching in *The Book of Change*, Commentary on the 22nd Hexagram.

6. Confucius, *The Great Learning*, Part 1, Verse 4.

exercise of a fundamentally good nature . . . ."[7] Calvin, very much like Augustine, is convinced that "what the gospel promises and makes possible, as divine (not human) possibility, is the transformation of mankind in all its nature and culture into a kingdom in which the laws of the kingdom have been written in the inward parts."[8]

Having understood the continual and intense quest for cultural regeneration in China for more than a hundred years, the proclamation of Christ has to bring out the implications of the gospel for the regeneration of Chinese culture. To do so, Christ cannot be presented merely as the personal savior. His being the foundation of all creation has to be spelt out at the same time. As the New Testament shows, all things are from him, created by him, through him, and for him (John 1:3, Rom 11:36, Col 1:16). Humanity is of Him and from Him, so is culture as the manifestation of humanity. Christ's incarnation reveals the fact that humanity belongs to Him. He is the Lord of humanity, and he can freely bring it into union with his divinity, despite the ontological distinction between the human and the divine. The humanity of Christ is truly authentic humanity—humanity as it should be. It is in this authentic humanity that all possibilities for a holistic culture are in store. It is in him that a culture, no matter how distorted and wounded, may find healing, transformation, and regeneration. That means a culture has to get all the way back to its true ontological source to reinvigorate itself and to redirect itself from the wrong path of fulfillment.

To acknowledge Christ as Lord, the source of all things created, is to affirm the kingdom perspective of salvation. Salvation does not stop at the individual personal realm. All forms of human creativity, all levels of human life, all structures of human relation, and all dimensions of human interaction, belong to Christ and have to be brought under his reign. Salvation thus touches all aspects of human life—personal and socio-cultural. These include the socio-structural, political, legal, economic, religious, educational and creative-communicative realms. The kingdom of Christ has to "invade" these realms and transform them in accordance with the Way, the Truth, and the Life manifested in Christ (John 14:6).

Now it should be quite clear that if we preach Christ without taking notice of the deep sense of cultural crisis in China, then the Chinese people would have no interest in a "Christ" that has nothing to do with their culture. Yet, we do not preach Christ as relevant to culture because it is expedient to do so—to gain Chinese acceptance. No, the context does not dictate the gospel. Rather, it is the whole gospel that demands us to address

---

7. Niebuhr, *Christ and Culture*, 209.
8. Ibid., 217–18.

the cultural crisis in China. Christ—the Way, the Truth and the Life—is totally relevant to the cultural crisis in China. A holistic preaching of Christ and his kingdom in China will bring personal salvation as well as cultural transformation and regeneration.

CHRIST THE FULFILLMENT AND JUDGMENT OF CULTURE

Before we go further to explore the relevance of Christ and his salvation to the Chinese culture, we need to clarify what culture really is from the theological perspective.

What is culture from the perspective of the Christian faith? In response to this question, we may begin with a simple statement that "Culture means humanity."[9] A human being does not live *in* culture, his/her very being is actualized and concretized as culture. In so far as humanity is a gift from God, culture is also a gift from God. Thus "seen from the point of view of creation, the kingdom of nature (*regnum naturae*), culture is the promise originally given to human being he/she is to become."[10] What human being is to become can only be found in the fulfillment of the image of God. "The image is not in the human person; it is the human person."[11] As image of God, human being shares the sanctity that belongs to God. A sanctity that even God himself would not violate. We can thus even say that human being shares the kind of absoluteness that belongs to God. In this sense, it is quite understandable why early church fathers such as Athanasius as well as Basil the Great, and subsequently the Eastern Orthodox tradition, have put so much emphasis on the idea of the "deification of human being." Athanasius, referring to the logic of Christ's Incarnation would say, "He was made man that we might be made god." Basil also put it thus, "man is nothing less than a creature that has received the order to become god."[12] Referring to the biblical tradition, Jewish philosopher Abraham Heschel points out that "It is an important fact, however, that in contrast with Babylonia and particularly Egypt, where the preoccupation with death was the central issue of religious thinking, the Bible hardly deals with death as a problem. Its central concern is not, as in the Gilgamesh Epic, how to escape death, but rather how to sanctify life. And the divine image and likeness does not serve

---

9. I have borrowed this simple statement from Barth, "Church and Culture," 338.
10. Ibid., 341.
11. Heschel, *The Insecurity of Freedom*, 152.
12. "Athanasius: Select Works and Letters" in *Nicene and Post-Nicene Fathers*, vol. 4, ed. Philip Schaff and Henry Wace, 65.

man to attain immortality but to attain sanctity."[13] Ensuring the sanctity of the human person as that which is holy to God is the most fundamental directive of culture as the manifestation of humanity. A culture, if it is to fulfill its task for the actualization of humanity, cultivates a sense of sacredness for his neighbor. "Thou shall love thy neighbor as thyself" (Lev 19:18) is an inevitable implication drawn from the fact that behind and above each human person, there is the Absolute God. At the same time, human being hears inside himself the call from God, "you shall be holy for I, the Lord, your God, am holy" (Lev 19:2). Culture should also give expression to the sense of the Sacred (or Holy) intrinsic to human being. Only when a culture cultivates commitment to the unconditional would it be true to its task. A culture that alienates itself from the transcendent would ground itself on itself and end up absolutizing itself. Self-absolutization is the root of human sinfulness. A society that closes its eyes to the transcendent light would start turning its own darkness into eternal light.

The reality of sin puts authentic culture on the defensive. What has been a promise now hangs over human being as a judgment of his/her unfaithfulness. In so far as the freedom of human being is a real gift from God, his/her will to distort the promise of God is allowed with its full effect, though contained within God's providence. And so, the distortion of humanity sets in and permeates every aspect of culture. The land still prospers, but prosperity can become destructive. There will be thorns and thistles which will block and disrupt human being's attempt for order and abundance (Gen 3:17). What should have been positive directives for fulfillment can now become guidance towards a blind alley. Culture thus contains implications of the curse from God as well as the working of human being's own sinful design. All cultures are to be judged by the Word of God, while at the same time, they are to be affirmed by the Word of God as his gift, even in their corrupted form.

In the Asian cultural traditions, we see the promise as well as judgment of God. In so far as human being is affirmed without losing sight of his utter dependence on the transcendent, this fundamental insight has to be taken as a sign of God's original gift. In Hinduism, Buddhism, and Taoism, the Nothingness of human existence is stressed. This understanding of the nature of human existence in itself agrees in a profound way with the Christian belief in *creatio ex nihilo*. It also depicts the condition of human being as sinner, whose attempt to ground her existence on herself leads her to Nothingness. So attachment to the self is a delusion leading only to suffering. Confucianism, on the other hand, seldom dwells on Nothingness.

---

13. Heschel, *The Insecurity of Freedom*, 152.

Yet it puts tremendous emphasis on human participation with heaven and earth to bring fulfillment to all things. In the Confucian outlook, the human being does not live in isolation but in a community of beings, which should exist and relate to one another in accordance with the mandate of heaven. Participation in the mandate, and participation with one another, is the key.

SOTERIOLOGICAL PERSPECTIVES IN RESPONSE TO THE CHINESE CULTURAL TRADITION

For the Confucian tradition, a very fundamental attitude in one's approach to reality and life is "Jing" (敬—reverence). "Jing" is the intuitive confidence of the infinite value of human being and the cosmos.[14] This attitude opens the human heart to the transcendent dimension, to that which is beyond the human realm. It is a positive directive that points the human person as well as society as a whole to the Lord Creator. There has been thus in the Chinese tradition a strong sense of the Mandate of Heaven, of Dao (the Word) that governs all things. "Jing" was originally a religious concept, referring to the feeling of *mysterium tremendum*, not to gods, but to that which is the ultimate.[15] This fundamental attitude originally holds promise for the Chinese people to recognize their utter dependence on the Creator. Unfortunately, it was later turned into a political concept, and became the virtue of a ruler seeking mandate from heaven to rule. A ruler who had been affirmed to have the mandate of heaven to rule would then have absolute power. But as Lord Acton has formally said, "Absolute power corrupts absolutely." This means that to avoid this deleterious effect, an important modification needs to be made in this feature of the Chinese culture and psyche. To redeem Chinese culture, the attitude of "Jing" has to be affirmed but re-directed to the personal God creator. The mandate from heaven is not a set of mandate to govern, but Dao (道—the Word, the Way) embodied in Jesus Christ, who came in person to make it concrete and real.

The Confucian tradition puts tremendous emphasis on human being as the locus for the manifestation of Dao, and Dao can shine through human existence if the human person allows it to do so. Thus, allowing Dao to shine forth is of paramount importance to one's being human. To achieve that, one has to go deep into one's self to grasp the heart and the nature of one's being, in order to focus on it, not allowing oneself to be distracted by desires stirred by sensations. Thus, the practice of inwardness is a core

---

14. Tang Chun-I, *Zhong Guó Wen Hua Zhî Jing Shén Jiá zhí* (The Spiritual Values of the Chinese Culture), 136.

15. Mou Tsung-san, Zhong Guó, *Zhe Xue De Te Zhi*, 16.

spiritual exercise. This line of thinking is particularly prominent in Neo-confucianism. Neo-confucianism goes further to affirm that Dao is immanent in the human person. Everyone can achieve sagehood (saintliness) by just allowing what is already in him/her to flow forth from one's life. But to do so one has to go through a process of "self-emptying"—emptying one's mind and heart of self-centeredness until one's mind and heart becomes an unobstructed mirror to the principles of heaven, which actually resides within oneself.[16] As a mirror can be tarnished by dirt and stain, one's heart and mind can be marred by desires. As one can clean a mirror, so too one can clear one's heart and mind of desires. A constant exercise of self-awareness and self-discipline can restore one's identity as being one with heaven. The sense of relying on oneself is strong. There is no sense of human depravity. Sin is nothing but aberration which can be rectified by one's effort of spiritual discipline. There is a strong optimism about human nature, and thus a strong orientation in relying on one's own effort to achieve full humanity in the Neo-confucian tradition.

Achieving or restoring full humanity is definitely a central concern for the Confucian and Neo-confucian tradition. Evangelical theology has to retrieve theological resources from church fathers to articulate a theology of salvation that takes the restoration of full humanity seriously. Thus the theological theme of the image of God, of Christ being the full manifestation of that image, of his personal life being the paradigm of true humanity in personal form, has to be presented in our articulation of the doctrine of salvation. Christ's self-emptying is particularly relevant here as the Neo-confucian tradition puts tremendous emphasis on self-emptying. Yet the full force of Christian salvation has to come out in two points of critique of the Neo-confucian tradition. First, due to human depravity, the original image of God, the mirror within human being for the reflection of God's glory and goodness, is not only tarnished but broken. Salvation means more than cleaning the mirror. It means "making whole again". This cannot be done by self-effort. The broken mirror has to be renewed by union with Christ, and through such union the human person takes on the true and full image of God in Christ. Secondly, Christ's self-emptying is not for self-fulfillment, for achieving full humanity for himself. His self-emptying is for others. It is an act of covenantal love. Full humanity lies precisely in the fulfillment of covenantal commitment.

This brings us back to Confucius and Mencius who put more emphasis on mutual commitment and mutual enrichment within a community of beings. "Ren" (仁—Commitment-communion) is state of life where full

---

16. Cf. Theodore de Bary, *The Unfolding of Neo-confucianism*, 164–87.

humanity is manifested. "Ren," according to Mou Tsung-san, means "life-communion with the aim of enriching one another"[17] It is a life attitude based on a particular perception of reality. To the Confucian, one's being is always being-with others and being-for others. This being-with and being-for is not limited to communion and commitment among human beings, but also includes heaven and earth. Human being, in order to accomplish full humanity, has to participate with heaven and earth (與天地參) to transform and nourish all things under heaven, thus coming into union with all.[18]

This concept of Ren resonates with the Christian conviction about full humanity. Full humanity is realized in covenantal fulfillment—the fulfillment of human being as being-with and being-for others, as it is revealed in Jesus Christ. Here the challenge to the evangelical soteriological perspective is quite obvious. The theme of alienation and covenantal restoration is particularly relevant here. Salvation through reconciliation, participation and mystical union can become very powerful. In the face of the Confucian tradition, evangelical theology may need to broaden its soteriological perspective by retrieving theological resources from early church fathers and the Eastern Orthodox tradition.

In soteriological articulation in response to the Confucian tradition, theological critique should not end in negation and judgment, it has to bring out at the same time the promise in this tradition for fulfillment in Christ. If, indeed, the articulation of salvation makes it possible to affirm certain aspects of the Chinese cultural tradition then salvation gives hope to the Chinese people who struggle so hard to maintain the historical continuity of their cultural identity.

From the Christian perspective, Daoism and Buddhism, likewise, hold promise as much as distortions.

Daoism seeks liberation, liberation from stifling oppressions of cultural constructions as well as unnatural desires of the human heart. Both cause distortion of the human person, which is the source of all forms of human suffering. Human culture which originally aims to cultivate full humanity becomes oppressive when it imposes on nature strictures that reflect nothing but human desires and fear, thus rendering nature unnatural. Human desires and fears which subvert nature are the cause behind these strictures.

---

17. Tsung-san, *History of Philosophy*, 178.

18. "It is only he who is most authentic in his existence that can cultivate his humanity to the full. Only then can he can he cultivate others to full humanity. Only then can he cultivate animals and things to their full nature . . . he then can participate with Heaven and Earth to transform and nourish all and come into union with Heaven and Earth." Confucius, *The Doctrine of the Mean*, chapter 22.

Even the pursuit of saintliness or the pursuit of wisdom can be obstructive and destructive. They are used as pretext to boost one's status or fame, in short, one's ego. They may also be desperate responses to chaotic human condition, but these futile actions can only make things worse. The path to liberation is to return to simplicity of life, to the natural way, to the approach of "effortlessness" (Wu-wei—無為), a state of freedom comparable to what Christians call "beatitude".[19] Again, the key lies in emptying and renouncing the fabricated self. There is a strong sense of judgment on culture. Culture means fabrication, the source of inauthentic human existence.

Buddhism dwells on the reality of human sufferings, the source of which is the illusion about the self. Self-attachment is the root of human predicament and suffering. The self is in reality empty, its "substance" is nothingness. All the human inventions and cultural constructions serve to hide this reality from us, and hold us captive in this castle of illusion. Salvation, therefore, means liberation from this castle of illusion. Self-negation is the key, and the discipline of self-denial is the path to salvation.

Liberation from captivity of self-deception through cultural fabrications or acts of consciousness is a very powerful soteriological theme that the Daoist and the Buddhist mind will be able to understand. Christian theology can affirm the Daoist and Buddhist perception of humankind's spiritual predicaments and draw spiritual resources from them to understand forms of human self-captivity. Theological articulation of salvation can then be greatly enriched.

SOTERIOLOGICAL PERSPECTIVES IN RESPONSE TO THE CHALLENGE OF MODERN CHINA

The failure of the communist social experiment has revealed to the Chinese people the emptiness of human visions for a just society. Having gone through tremendous sufferings in the Cultural Revolution, the reality of human sinfulness manifested in various forms, particularly corruptions of political systems, has become all too obvious. With the old tradition in tatter and the communist ideology bankrupt, the quest for a new spiritual orientation has never been as urgent as it is now. While movements to revive the old tradition are emerging and gathering momentum, the dominant force that is shaping the national consciousness now is market capitalism, bringing with it its collaborator, liberalism humanism.

Market-driven capitalism is taking off and accelerating phenomenally in China. The market-capitalistic logic in a context where traditional

---

19. Cf. Slingerland, *Effortless Action*, 78–88, 176–82.

spiritual values have been uprooted will go unopposed. Market capitalism, with functional rationality as its highest value, has been making far reaching cultural impact in Western society right before our eyes. All values other than functional and marketable values are being marginalized. Even the sacred, the sublime is to be commoditized. This in the Chinese context uprooted of traditional spiritual values will surely be devastating. As China is now in a spiritual vacuum, the moral foundation of values is drastically undermined. The family, for example, which has been for centuries the core value of Chinese culture, is now in fragmentation. Confucian nurture of moral character and inwardness in the Chinese soul has long evaporated. After a century of cultural disintegration, China is surely a spiritual wasteland. The Nobel Prize winning novel, *The Soul Mountain*, by Gao Xingjiang catalogues the chaotic fragments of past traditions being scattered into oblivion. It is a testimony to the death of the Chinese soul. In such a condition, China is to face the onslaught of market capitalism. Corollary to market capitalism is a culture of narcissism and consumer personality. Individualism is already a problem as the result of the one-child policy. The situation will be exacerbated by a form of liberalism that embraces a liberty of indifference and rejects any form of common social vision as a reaction against the Communist authoritarianism. The form of market capitalism and liberalism rising out of the ruin of communist social experiment will be much more blatant and aggressive than the form we are experiencing in the so-called postmodern West. It will boomerang back to the West almost like revenge as China becomes the world's most formidable economic power twenty years from now. A theology of covenantal economics for developing a new form of capitalism in which values are defined, created, and redistributed in such a way that functional rationality, self-interest, and competition are transformed in a new configuration of values.

In a context with deep awareness of human depravity, with yearning for a personal spiritual anchor in the midst of commoditization of the human person, with desire to restore the inwardness of the human person being dissipated by outward activities and overwhelmed by incessant flows of information, personal salvation is particularly relevant. Acknowledging the need to restore the personal realm of being, the personal presence of God in Christ is most powerful for this generation of Chinese caught in the maelstrom of socio-cultural forces, which converge to reduce them to things. Attention to human depravity is particularly important as corruption of all forms from the personal to economic and political levels reveals itself most blatantly. There is a deep yearning from the heart for moral regeneration in the individual human person. There is a pervasive awareness that the deep divide in human society stems from human selfishness. Right relation and the uprightness of the human character cannot be separated. The human person has to become upright before she can have right relation with others. The outcry against unrighteousness and apathy in human relation is so strong that Christ's crucifixion by the unrighteous and for the unrighteous can be easily understood.

The gospel of Jesus Christ, restoring the right relation between human being and God as well as among human beings, however, cannot be preached in abstraction from the gospel of liberation. The gospel has to be relevant to social and political reform, a reform that can free the Chinese from a political structure that has been perceived to be oppressive and corrupt. There is a deep yearning for socio-political liberation. However, what is being perceived by intellectuals as a more fearful menace is market capitalism in close alliance with liberal humanism. Liberation from the "totalitarian" market logic and radical individualism is even more desperately needed. The market logic and radical individualism feed on each other. The two have to be dealt with together.

The gospel of liberation calls for a new form of liberty beyond the liberty guaranteed by a democracy shaped by market capitalism. Liberty here means personal autonomy understood in terms of the freedom of choice. It is a liberty free from external constraints of all kind. Democracy catering for this kind of personal autonomy is basically "rule by the many in accordance with their wills". However, the will of the mass is "will-less" as it is being shaped by the media controlled by corporations with all but one objective of making the biggest profit in the most efficient way. Liberty has to be redefined in terms of freedom made real in covenantal commitment. God's freedom, absolute freedom, is not a boundless license for arbitrary actions. Rather, his freedom has its actuality in his love. The content of his freedom is freedom to love. This has been most clearly revealed in Jesus Christ and his cross. Freedom should be understood as the capability to transcend oneself in the very act of affirming it. Freedom in this mode can only be found in the act of covenantal love. And, Jesus Christ is the embodiment as well as the out-pouring of this covenantal love.

Thus socio-political liberation goes beyond radical political reform that aims at a democracy of universal suffrage. What is needed is a "democracy" founded on the vision of freedom in mutual commitment, as a concrete expression of covenant love where justice and compassion are intertwined as a single whole. For this form of covenantal democracy to realize, covenantal character has to be formed as the indispensable asset in society. Our society has to be envisioned as community (*Gemeinschaft*) and not contractual association (*Gesellschaft*). The church, despite all her failures, is gathered by Jesus Christ as the eschatological community manifesting the social relation in the *eschaton* where covenantal love binds people together. In her being the eschatological community, the church is gathered by Jesus to live a life of covenantal love together, through the exercise of kenosis exemplified by him.

Here salvation as participation in the life of Jesus Christ has its particular significance. Jesus Christ is not merely a life example. His mode of personhood, his moral character, his act of sacrificial love, cannot be acquired through learning. It can only be realized in mystical union with him by the act of the Holy Spirit.

CONCLUDING REMARKS

The Chinese theologian faces a three-fold challenge. He has to be firmly anchored on the catholic evangelical faith in proclaiming the salvation of Jesus. Firmly grounded she has to translate the gospel into the Chinese context where personal depravity is entangled with structural-systematic injustice, where erosion of personal identity goes hand in hand with cultural identity crisis, where fragmentation of the Chinese humanistic tradition coincides with the breakdown of moral foundation under the impact of market capitalism. In translating the gospel, she has to affirm certain core elements of the tradition from the Christian perspective in order to maintain the historical continuity of the tradition. In so doing she has, on the other hand, to critique the Chinese tradition where distortion of image of God is manifested. In this exercise of "redeeming" a cultural tradition, the Chinese theologian may be able to retrieve spiritual resources from the Chinese tradition to enhance the effectiveness in the proclamation of the gospel in modern China where market capitalism puts functionality and efficiency as the measure of all values, where human persons are reduced to commodities, where moral values are regarded as obstacles to the free marketing of any sort of commodities so long as there are demands, including pornography, for example, where systemic poverty is treated as the necessary evil of free competition. The attempt above is nothing but a small exercise to bring demands together. It serves merely as an illustration as the sort of challenges a Chinese theologian has to face in translating the gospel to her context.

5

Christ and Liberation: Toward a Messianic Christology for a Postcolonial Society

Delano Palmer (Jamaica)

Dieumeme Noelliste (Haiti)

INTRODUCTION

> Contextualization has both strengths and weaknesses. The strength [sic] lies in making ideas relevant to a particular cultural context. The weakness [sic] lies in precisely that fact: the more it speaks to a particular culture, the less it speaks to others—Colin Brown[1]

BY AND LARGE, THE history of the Caribbean is a history of the deprivation of freedom. It is a history marked by centuries of slavery, colonialism, and neocolonialism. As is true of the places where such experience has been the dominant feature of life, the Caribbean has always evidenced a

---

1. Brown, "Christology and the Quest of the Historical Jesus," 68.

strong impulse for freedom and liberation. This thirst for emancipation in a freedom-denying context is one of the factors that explain the pull that many dwellers of the Caribbean Basin have felt toward Jesus and his message of liberation that the New Testament writers, particularly the authors of the Gospels, have written about.

We believe that this penchant toward Christ and his liberating message is good and correct. Jesus is the bearer of freedom. As John expresses it in the Fourth Gospel: "If the Son sets you free, you shall be free indeed" (John 8:36). Further, his Spirit is the Spirit of freedom. As Paul declares, "the Lord is Spirit, and where the Spirit of the Lord is, there is freedom" (2 Cor 3:17). Having said this, however, we need to stress that in order to be truly beneficial to the Caribbean region, the idea of messianic liberation must be construed holistically, and not in a reductionistic fashion. In our construal of a perspective on freedom that purports to find its anchoring in Christ, we must avoid embracing a doctrine of purely spiritual liberation that is so totally oriented to the future and the world beyond that it mutes the note of social engagement that is sounded so clearly in the New Testament. Conversely, such a doctrine should not be so completely bound to, and enmeshed in, the present socio-political domain that it loses sight of the spiritual and eschatological vision of the salvation that Christ came to bring.

In keeping with this conviction, focusing on the theology of Luke and Paul, this essay will survey Jesus' work of a holistic salvation with a view to exploring its liberating significance for the Caribbean region.

The Jesus Tradition and Liberation

A perusal of any of the Gospels shows that the idea of liberation was a major theme of the Jesus tradition. For example, Mark, considered the first of the historical bio-narratives, declares, "For even the Son of Man did not come to be served, but to serve, and to give his life as a ransom for many" (Mark 10: 45, NIV; cf. Matt 20:28). With the mention of the theologically pregnant term "ransom," Mark's concern seems to emphasize the basis of the Messiah's liberating work. Beside Matthew who repeats Mark's saying almost verbatim, John also stresses the liberation theme. However, we note an important difference in the Johannine depiction. While Mark and Matthew focus on the basis of the liberation brought about by the Messiah, John draws attention to the finality of the process. "If the Son sets you free, you will be free indeed" (John 8:36), he declares. In the tradition relayed to us by the evangelists, we also find the resurrection accounts (Mark 16:1–8; Matt 28:1–20; Luke 24:1–12; John 20:1–10) which, in light of Philippians

3:20–21 and 1 John 3:1–3, are paradigmatic of the holistic liberation previously mentioned.

It is our contention that this tradition which portrayed Jesus as bearer of salvation considerably influenced Paul and the other New Testament writers. We see a hint of this, for example, in Acts 20 where Luke quotes Paul as saying:[2] "You yourselves know that these hands ministered to my own needs and to the men who were with me. In everything I showed you that by working hard in this manner you must help the weak and remember the words of the Lord Jesus, that he himself said, 'It is more blessed to give than to receive'"(Acts 20:34–35). Beside citations such as this, we should also take note of the fact that Luke was Paul's missionary companion and that both showed keen interest in Gentile conversions and congregations (2 Tim 4; Acts 9–28). If we take these clues seriously, it is inconceivable that the apostle to the Gentiles could have been ignorant of the Jesus tradition which stands behind our canonical Gospels. Indeed, it can be argued that if the Third Gospel is Lucan, there is a sense in which the book of Romans is the "Gospel" according to Paul. This suggestion should not be considered farfetched; for in Romans, one hears echoes of several of the Christological themes found in the bio-narratives produced by Mark, Luke, Matthew, and John. The following table provides a glimpse of this convergence:

Matthew	*Incarnate Royalty* (perfect King; cf. Rom 1:1–4)
Mark	*Incarnate Ministry* (perfect Servant; cf. Rom 15:8)
Luke	*Ideal Humanity* (perfect Man; Rom 5:12–19)
John	*Incarnate Deity* (perfect *Imago Dei*; Rom 10:13)[3]

---

2. Cf. also Luke's (chapters 1–3 and passim) comprehensive incarnation record with Paul's brevity in Gal 4:4–6.

3. The "Word" that became flesh (John 1:14) was a theological and redemptive necessity; the Son of God had to become human in order to die as the spotless Lamb of God (John 1:29). And he had to retain his divinity (John 1:1c), in order to give global and eternal value to his sacrifice. If Jesus were a sinner, he could only have died for his own sins (Rom 6:23a); if he were only a perfect human, he could only have died for one other person—most likely for someone in the Caribbean (conventional substitution)! But being the unique (*monogenēs*) member of the God-head, the only one to have taken on permanent human status, his death has value for all humanity, and his resurrection by the Spirit (Rom 1:1–4), the Father (Rom 6:4), and the Son of Man (John 2:19) makes available a right relationship with God (Rom 4:25).

THE LIBERATOR'S GOSPEL ACCORDING TO LUKE

If from the four canonical Gospels, we single out Luke's Gospel, along with its sequel in the book of Acts, for our exploration of the person and mission of Jesus, we come face to face with the picture of ideal person who came to bring a holistic salvation which is experienced as persons are transformed into his image and likeness by the power of the Spirit.

Jesus the Ideal Human

Among the evangelists, it is Matthew and Luke who record for us the circumstances under which Jesus came into the world. But Luke's narrative contains certain features that seem clearly intended to underscore the uniqueness of the person whose birth he was relating. Luke, for instance, traces the lineage of Jesus back to Adam, highlighting his universal significance for the fulfillment of the hopes and aspirations of the human race. There may also be here a hint at the unique relationship that obtains between Jesus and God, the Father. Luke ends his genealogical account with "the son of God" (3:38). While in context this speaks of the relationship of Adam to God, the designation is even truer of Jesus and God, as Luke mentions repeatedly (e.g., 3:22; 9:35). Furthermore, while both evangelists include David in their accounts of the human descent of Jesus, Luke takes pain to distance Jesus biologically from Joseph by stressing his virgin conception (3:23, 34–35). Moreover, to remove all possibility of a purely biological happening engineered by Mary alone, Luke stresses the supernatural agency of the act, and concludes that that which was formed in Mary's womb was "holy" and nothing less than the "son of God" (1:35). In keeping with his understanding of the lofty origin of the son to be born, Luke speaks of this greatness in a threefold fashion. In terms of his divine status, he is "the son of the Most High (1:35). In respect of his titles and mission, he is Savior, Christ, and Lord (2:11). And, in regard to his career he is the rightful heir to David's throne (1:32)

Beside all this, Luke shows particular interest in the human development of Jesus. He tells us that "Jesus increased in wisdom and stature, and in favor with God and man" (Luke 2:52). For him, there was nothing lacking in our Lord's intellectual, physical, spiritual or social maturation. He was the perfect human from birth and remains the perfect human forever. His perfection is not something he acquired along the way as a result of his performance. From Luke's portrayal of Jesus, it is clear that we are in the presence of a unique person. Indeed, we can say that what he wants us to contemplate in Jesus is the picture of an ideal person.

Jesus the Humble Human

And yet, alongside his lofty depiction of Jesus, Luke sounds another note: the humility of the Messiah—the anointed one. This is underscored in two themes that are noticeable characteristics of the Third Gospel: prayer and the ministry of the Holy Spirit. Prayer in general is a focus of Luke's. But what is striking is the focus that he places on the prayer life of Jesus. We always thought that only imperfect people like you and me need to pray regularly and earnestly. Surprisingly, however, we find the perfect man constantly praying: "One day Jesus was praying in a certain place. When he finished, one of his disciples said to him, 'Lord, teach us to pray, just as John taught his disciples'" (see further, 3:21; 5:16; 6:12; 22:32–40; 22:44–45; 23:44).

Jesus, the perfect human, not only prayed regularly, he always allowed the Spirit of God to guide and control him. This too is surprising. We can understand ordinary mortals with all their weaknesses seeking the supernatural help of the divine Spirit. But Jesus—the ideal human? Yes indeed! Throughout his Gospel, Luke belabors the point that Jesus' life was a Spirit-infused life. (3:22; 4:1). He not only lived by the power of the Spirit, but the redemptive mission that he came to fulfill could only be carried out in the power of the Spirit (Luke 4:16–18).

There is a lesson here that should not be missed. If Jesus is our exemplar in our quest for complete humanity, clearly, his dependency on the Spirit tells us that from God's perspective, real humans are those who lived in the power of the Spirit, who meet temptations head on with the Spirit's help, and who come out victorious with the Spirit's enabling (Luke 4:1, 14). In other words, like the Messiah, real humans are Spirit-anointed persons.

Jesus, the Bearer of Holistic Messianic Salvation

For Luke, this focus on the role of Spirit is not immaterial to the question of holistic salvation. For him, the Spirit that empowered the Messiah *is* the Spirit of liberation. At the very beginning of his ministry, Jesus himself brings out the connection of the Spirit's unction and the quest for liberation.

> The Lord's Spirit is on me,
> because he has appointed me Messiah
> To proclaim the gospel to poor.
> He has sent me on a mission to announce
> liberty to the incarcerated, heal the blind, take care

of the oppressed, and to proclaim the time of
the Lord's welcome intervention (Luke 4:18–19)

In a word, the Messiah came to ameliorate human suffering and oppression as well as promote human liberation from sin, oppressive structures, and satanic bondage, through the power of the Spirit. As Luke makes plain in Acts, no one today has an excuse not to come under the sway of the liberating and life transforming Spirit, since the last days have arrived (Acts 2:15–17; cf. Joel 2:). As a consequence of the redemptive work of the Messiah, the liberating Spirit has been poured, and is ready to be poured, on all flesh.

As we will see shortly, Luke notes specific instances of the work that the Spirit's outpouring has wrought in the lives of persons resulting in their genuine freedom. But for the moment it is important that we complete his depiction of the Messiah by mentioning Luke's interest in Christ's concern that the salvation he brought be made accessible to the weak, the vulnerable and the outcast. Here one thinks of passages like 8:1–3; 13:10–17 (women), 17:11–19 (men), 18:15–17 (children), and 23:39–43 (the dying). Not even the rich escaped his notice (18:18–30; 19:1–10).

Paul's Experience of Holistic Messianic Salvation

One of the ways Luke advances his plot in Acts is by the provision of series of progress reports as the trajectory of his narrative moves from Jerusalem, the religious capital, to Rome, the imperial capital. A central part of the narrative relates the conversion of three prominent individuals who experienced the transforming power of the Messiah and the Spirit he has just sent. After citing a few instances of "mass" conversions, Luke begins a triadic show-piece by telling the story of the Ethiopian Eunuch, the Gentile treasurer who was going to his homeland after attending the earthshaking Pentecostal event recorded in Acts 2. The conversion of this eunuch (Acts 8) may well be regarded as part of the first-fruits mentioned in Psalm 68:31 (Acts 8).

Acts 10 provides the story of the Cornelius. This Roman soldier is the third example of an individual who came under the influence of the Messiah and his life transforming Spirit. His conversion is clearly an adumbration of the final episode of Acts that is played out in Rome itself (Rom 28).

Between these two episodes, Luke locates the centerpiece of the triad, which seems to be his main interest. In chapter 9, Luke relates to us the conversion of Paul, the former Semitic zealot who became the chief agent in carrying the gospel beyond the borders of Palestine into the very center of the Roman Empire. Saul of Tarsus becomes, for Luke, the best example of a person who has come under the sway of the Messiah and his transforming Spirit. Paul, himself will give credence to this in his own reflection on his life before and after his Damascus Road experience (Acts 9, 22, 26).

Luke's interest in Paul is clearly evident in the amount of space dedicated to his story in the book of Acts. From his conversion to his incarceration in Rome, Luke makes him the main protagonist of his second volume. But for our purpose here, it is the three accounts of his experience of the Messianic salvation that are of particular significance. (Acts 9:1–19; 22:6–16; 26:12–18).

In Acts 9:1–9, Luke tells that Saul requested and received authorization from the Judean authorities to go to Damascus to carry out his mission against the early disciples of Jesus. While he was near his destination he was confronted by a light from heaven out of which came a voice saying, "Saul, Saul, why are you persecuting me?" (v. 4). Saul immediately responded: "Who are you, Lord?' (v. 5a); then came the surprising response: "I am Jesus whom you persecute" (v. 5b). Barrett sums up the significance of this verse for Paul's life and theology in this way:

> The question corresponds to the *egō eimi* that follows. Saul is aware that he is confronted by a superhuman being; . . . The question leads to identification: the superhuman stranger is Jesus. . . . The discovery that the crucified Jesus was in fact alive agrees with Paul's own account of the origin of his Christian life (Gal. 1:15, 16; 1 Cor 9:1; 15:8; cf. Phil 3:7–11), and was the root of the new understanding of the OT and the reinterpretation of Judaism that were the foundation of his theology.[4]

So in Acts, the writer seems eager to show that the early followers of the Messiah not only sought to understand their world, but they also wanted to engage it with theological values that were transcendent and life transforming. As Stephen Neil and Tom Wright aver, "All the ultimate questions about man and his life are theological. The moment I begin to think about my own existence, I am faced unfathomable mysteries."[5] What this means is that the Lucan plot is not just mere narrative, but a story which invites us to share its world, the commitment of its leading characters, and their enthusiasm for life.[6] The world that the writer invites his readers to join was permeated by the influence of the Messiah and the presence of his Spirit. In the first volume (and in the first chapter of Acts) the dominant figure is the

---

4. Barrett, *Acts of the Apostles I–XIV*, 450.
5. Neill and Wright, *The Interpretation of the New Testament: 1861–1986*, 146.
6. Ibid., 445.

Messiah himself, with others in the background. In the second, Peter takes center stage in chapters 2–11, while Paul makes his entrance in chapter 9, and maintains his prominence until the end. Of course, for Luke, although the Messianic presence is mainly in the background in Acts, the Messiah is still large and in charge of Empire, for "he must reign[7] until he has put all his enemies under his feet" (1 Cor 15:25). This means that Messiah is large and in charge of the Caribbean as well. The reign is along the lines of the already-not-yet construct (see below) and is only evident to people of faith. Caribbean theologians, though quite attuned to the need for this fulsome liberation, seldom mention this already/not yet perspective of divine deliverance that is perhaps best summarized in the words of Philippians 1:6 ("being confident of this, that he who began a good work in you will carry it on to completion until the day of Christ Jesus"/*So mi nuo dis fi shuor se a Gad imself staat op da gud wok ya iina unu, an im naa go tap nou. Im a-go gwaan du we im a du iina unu laif, til Jiizas Krais kom baka ort*).[8] We all need to bear in mind, then, that the liberated-in-Messiah "live a life of . . . [victorious freedom], but it is qualified victory. We are not yet what we shall be. We are not yet totally like the Messiah (1 John 3:2). We live in the tension between the 'already and the not yet.' We are genuinely new persons but not totally new."[9]

From whatever vantage point we view God's enterprise of liberation, then, the prospects of its present application are staggering in their reach and richness; and such potentials render any effort to reduce this liberation to a strictly personal matter or to an exclusively socio-political frame of reference meaningless. A close reading of Luke or Paul (and the other NT corpora for that matter) seems to confirm this.

After relating Paul's life transforming experience with the Risen Messiah, Luke presents him as witnessing before the Jewish authorities (Acts 22), and subsequently before the civil authorities (Acts 26). After receiving

---

7. Present tense.

8. NIV and *Di Jamiekan Nyuu Testament* (Kingston: Bible Society of the West Indies, 2012), respectively. We think the point is also made in Bob Marley's Redemption-Song lyrics: "Emancipate Yourself From Mental Slavery!"; the song in which in "four minutes Marley tells of a history that spans 400 years" (Dawes, *Bob Marley: Lyrical Genius*, 308).

9 Hoekema, "A Reformed View," 190. See also the Appendix below. The analogy between the already-not-yet perspective and Caribbean experience of postcolonialism may be extended to include what needs to take place in the interim; in both cases serious work must be carried out to ensure that lack of productivity (e.g., Gal 5:22–23; 2 Pet 1:3–10) does not jeopardize or call into question the initial stage of spiritual liberation/ or political independence. Perseverance to the end will therefore serve as evidence of the genuineness of commitment. On this, see especially Thomas, *A Case for Mixed-Audience with Reference to the Warning Passages in the Book of Hebrews*.

permission to speak (v. 1), Paul proceeds to share his revolutionary and life transforming experience. For the first time we are explicitly told that the resurrected Messiah spoke in the "Hebrew language" (v. 14; RSV). Again, we have a contrastive *egō . . . egō* (I . . . I) as in 22:8. The fact that *egō* is placed on the lips of Jesus in all three Lucan passages shows the writer's interest in the Messianic "I." It seems that this experience has made an indelible impression on Saul. But his own employment of "I" would never approach anything like that which he encountered on the Damascus Road. From now on, for Paul, there is only one supreme "I" clothed in humanity—the One who spoke from heaven and confronted him on the Damascus Road. As Paul says throughout his writings, this encounter profoundly transformed both his previous self-understanding and his previous theology. A. B. du Toit brings this out with great clarity:

> We have seen that Paul's previous self-concept portrayed the features of someone who was highly satisfied with his religious achievements. This self-appraisal was totally shattered by the Damascus event. . . . He realized that, because of human sin, man not only has no ground for any self-boasting before God (Rom 3:27, 4:2, 7:1–25; 2 Cor 12:5); he is totally and irrevocably dependent on grace. [Therefore] Paul's new self-understanding also becomes clear in the radical way in which he understands himself as transformed by God.[10]

THE LIBERATOR'S GOSPEL ACCORDING TO PAUL

What Luke has recorded in respect of Saul's initial transformation and liberation is corroborated by the apostle Paul himself in several of his letters particularly in the autobiographical statement he provides in Galatians 1:11–17:

> I want you to know brothers and sisters that the gospel I preach is not of human origin. I did not receive it from any man, nor was I taught it; rather, *I received it by revelation from Jesus Christ*. For you have heard of my previous way of life in Judaism, how intensely I persecuted the church of God and tried to destroy it. I was advancing in Judaism beyond many of my own age among my people and was extremely zealous for the traditions of my fathers. But when God, who set me apart from my mother's womb and called me by his grace, was pleased to reveal his Son in me so that I might preach him among the Gentiles, my immediate

---

10. Toit, "Encountering Grace," 71–87.

response was not to consult any human being. I did not go up to Jerusalem to see those who were apostles before I was, but I went into Arabia. Later I returned to Damascus.[11] (NIV)

This text acts as a window through which we see the radical new self-understanding and revolutionary orientation that Paul experienced as a result of his conversion. Along with passages such as 1 Tim 1:12ff.; 1 Cor 15:1ff., 10; Gal 2:20; Phi 3:1ff.; Eph 4:24, it speaks eloquently to the transformation that the Messiah wrought in Paul's life by the Spirit. His personal transformation became a part of the foundation for his argument that the new self is fully realized only as one becomes conformed to the image of Christ, the ideal person. For Paul, then, full liberation lies here: total transformation into Christlikeness—both personally and socially. Societies can only change for the better as they are populated by people who are transformed into the likeness of the ideal human; truly transformational societies are never self-generated. Societies, like cultures, are created by people. To the extent that such transformation remains incomplete, fulsome social liberation will also be incomplete. This is a key element of the Pauline good news: the more Messiah-like we become, the more human-like we will be, until we all attain perfection (Eph 4:13; 2 Cor 3:18). And, of course, the more Christ-like we are the godlier we become. This is part and parcel of the Pauline proclamation. While the Pauline gospel is more than Christlikeness, it cannot anything less.[12] In what follows we will turn our attention to this holistic messianic salvation that Paul has experienced and which he is committed to proclaiming as God appointed herald.

Liberation as Justification, Celebration, and Glorification

Paul's perspective of holistic salvation may be gleaned from the structure of Romans, his *magnum opus,* as the following sketch shows:

A   1–5 Gospel for Sinners: *Liberation in terms of Justification*[13] (International Dimension)

B   6–8 Gospel for Saints: *Liberation from Sin's Power and Presence* (Doctrinal Dimension)

---

11. Italics mine.

12. E.g., the cosmic character of the liberation is seen especially in Rom 8:18–23, and from a comparison between the old and the new creation: in the former, the Creator-turned-Liberator started with the material universe before the creation of humanity (Gen 1); in the latter, humanity takes precedence. The comparison reveals the following chiastic macro-structure: A-Material Universe (Gen 1:1–25), B-Image-bearers (Gen 1:26–31), B'- Image-bearers (2 Cor 5:17), A'- Material Universe (Rev 21–22; cf. 2 Pet 3).

13. On this, see Pearson, "Justification by Click," 55–57.

A′ 9–11 Gospel for Sinners: *Liberation from Sins' Penalty* (National Dimension)

B′ 12–16 Gospel for Saints: *Liberation in terms of Sanctification* (Practical Dimension)

Justification

In the first four chapters of the epistle, Paul demonstrates that human beings viewed both ethically and ethnically have no ground of boasting before God, because they are rebels. However, by God's grace, these rebels can be justified. They have been declared righteous on the basis of the atoning work that the Messiah accomplished on the cross. The case for justification (i.e., declaring repentant and believing sinners right in God's sight) is advanced and strengthened by invoking two prominent Old Testament witnesses—Abraham (an "Iraqi") and David (an "Israeli")—in chapter 4. The end of the A-section (chapter 5), then goes on to itemize some of the advantages and benefits of justification. The justification motif is again treated in chapters 9–11 (A′-section), with a special focus on unbelieving Israelites. But let us examine the first A-section that deals with the matter of justification for the Gentiles in Romans 4. Here we believe that Keener[14] has shed some light on this section by providing the following contrastive sketch, which we have adapted for our purpose.

Pagans (Rom 1:20–27)	Patriarch (Rom 4:17–21)
Pagans' failure (1:20, 25)	Patriarch's faith (4:17)
Pagans' culpability (1:20, using *dynamis*)	Patriarch's confidence (4:21, using *dynatos*)
Pagans' disregard of God's glory (1:21)	Patriarch's regard for God's glory (4:20)
Pagans' dishonored bodies (1:24)	Patriarch's newly honed body (4:19)
Pagans' negative sexuality (1:26–27)	Patriarch's positive sexuality (4:19)

14. Keener, *Romans*, 67.

The schema is useful in drawing attention to the necessity for liberation (Paganism) as well as the possibility of global salvation (patriarch), since Abraham himself was once an idolater (Josh 24:1–4; 14–15).

The opening verse of chapter 4 inquires into the discovery of Abraham with reference to the issue of righteousness. The question is to be understood against the background of Jewish opinion which believed that the merits of this forefather commended him entirely before God. The apostle follows up the argument in verse 2 by reasoning something like this: "Let us assume for argument's sake that Abraham was justified by works, wouldn't he have had ground on which to glory? Yes, but certainly not before God!" A keyword in this verse is the term "boast" (*kauchēma*). It is not only important in the development of Paul's argument, it also "exemplifies both literary and emotional 'color.'"[15] Paul already uses a cognate term (*kauchēsis*) to demonstrate that the principle of faith precludes human boasting (Rom 3:27). Here, he probably links the word to the greatest religious role model before the Christian era. "But," a Jew might ask, "can you prove that Abraham was not indeed justified by works?" "Well, let us turn to the Scriptures," says the apostle. To support his claim, Paul invokes Genesis 15:6, which declares that it was Abraham's faith that brought him a right standing before God. It would seem that the apostle not only attempts to substantiate his point from Genesis 15:6 but also to correct a misunderstanding of the verse based in part on the following: "Was not Abraham found faithful when tested, and it was reckoned to him as righteousness?" (1 Macc 2:52, NRSV).

Having turned to Old Testament revelation for support of his claims that faith, not works, is the basis on which a person is justified, Paul now draws on the experience of daily life (v. 4). The analogy states that which was common knowledge in the first century: remuneration is commensurate with output ("Now when a man works, his wages are not credited to him as a gift, but as an obligation"—NIV). There is nothing gratuitous here. Two word-pairs are set in stark contrast; each pair marking out a fundamental approach to God. Taking verses 3 and 4 together, the couplets are summed up as follows: "works" and "obligation" on one hand versus "faith" and "gift," on the other. "The contrast is instructive. 'Works' and ['obligation'] belong together as correlatives; 'faith' and 'grace' similarly correspond, and it is to this pair that ['credited'] belongs."[16]

In contrast, then, to the natural affairs of verse 4, verse 5 declares the heart of the gospel proclamation. In order to grasp fully the import of this declaration, we need to look at four key terms. The first key word to be

---

15. Liefeld, *New Testament Exposition*, 87.
16 Barrett, *A Commentary on the Epistle to the Romans*, 88.

examined is the verb "believe." In its active form, Paul used it twice before: in chapters 1:16 and 3:22. Like these occurrences, it is also employed in a soteriological sense and setting in chapter 4. Its meaning in 4:3, 5 is wholehearted trust and confidence. It is the only kind of faith that brings justification. This happens when the believer (*pisteuonti*) comes face to face with the Justifier (*ton dikaiounta*), most likely a New Testament metonym for God.

This brings us to another key term of verse 5: righteousness. "Justifier" and "righteousness" are cognate terms and both relate to the concept of justification ("*righteoustification*"?). It is the verb form ("was justified,") which occurs in verse 2 and elsewhere, that Bible students find problematic. The difficulty does not seem to be merely with the lexical idea which has to do with righteousness but with the theological import of the term. The question is: should we view justification as forensic (i.e., imputed righteousness) or intrinsic (imparted righteousness)?

While exegetes like Sandy and Headlam[17] have serious reservations about the concept of forensic righteousness in Romans, the idea seems to fit Paul's intention better than the other view. One reason for this is that the suffix of the verb (*dikaioō*) appears to carry the declarative/causative idea. Secondly, the Septuagint (LXX), which Paul had already quoted, seems to have influenced the Apostle along forensic lines. So to be justified is to be pronounced and treated as righteous.

The meaning of "counted" (KJV) or "credited" (NET) in verse 5 also bears out the forensic view of justification. Faith is credited or put to the "account" of the believing sinner.

This brings us to the other key-term in the verse: "ungodly." As an adjective, it is found one other time in Romans where we are informed that Christ died for the "ungodly" (5:6). The term is a strong one, denoting gross impiety; it is a deep-seated lack of reverence for God. Although God's wrath is unleashed against every form of impiety (1:18), in the *eschaton*, God is going to remove it altogether (11:26). It is by sheer grace that God justifies such a person, based on the loving release of his Son (5:6). The context demands that even the patriarch Abraham falls under the category of the "ungodly;" after all, how else could he have been an example of justification, *sola fide*?

Celebration

A new witness to the phenomenon of justification is now called to the stand. The apostle will now show that the testimony of David is in harmony with that of the patriarch Abraham, thus proving his case from the Law and the

---

17. Sanday and Headlam, *Romans*, 36.

Prophets (cf. 3:21). The phrase "Even as David" (KJV) shows the closest possible connection between verses 5 and 6, and is followed by the key referents discussed above. The correspondence between the two verses seems to underscore Paul's point of righteousness being credited to a person who believes in God. The stem for "trusts/faith" is used twice in verse 5 (*pistis, pisteuonti*) and the idea it conveys is further defined by the phrase "without works." A quotation now follows in which we have an exact reproduction of the Psalm 32:1–2 (LXX). Psalm 32 is traditionally understood to be one of seven penitential poems. However, it should be observed that there are strong elements of thanksgiving and celebratory expression in the song. Reflecting on the gladness that results from the experience of divine forgiveness, the psalmist exclaims in exultation:

> Oh, what joy for those
> whose disobedience is forgiven,
> whose sin is put out of sight!
> Yes, what joy for those
> whose record the Lord has cleared of guilt,
> whose lives are lived in complete honesty! (Ps 32:1–2, NLT)[18]

The stanza which pertains to our discussion describes the happy estate of the person who has experienced forgiveness. But what has forgiveness to do with justification, and how do these verses from Psalm 32 serve Paul's purpose at this point? In connection with the quotation from Genesis 15:6, it has already been pointed out that, in all likelihood, the Apostle is employing a Rabbinic form of exegesis to substantiate his claim (see verse 3 above). The catchword of the two passages is "reckoned"(*logizetai*). On the one hand, righteousness is credited (v. 3=Gen 15:6) and on the other sin is not taken into account (v. 8=Ps 31:2 LXX). Since Paul's use of the two Old Testament passages is not just formal but substantial, he is certainly highlighting two dimensions of justification: (1) the receiving of righteousness (positive side) and (2) the removal of retribution (negative side).[19] This twofold act of God on behalf of the sinner is for Paul good news that evokes elation.

---

18. Several Caribbean peoples are now learning to celebrate their salvation in their heart language; see for example, Richards, "Creole Songs and Scripture!" 326–29.

19. Verse 8 seems to summarize the concept of this removal (i.e., forgiveness), while gathering up the parallel lines of the previous couplets. The plural terms for evil within the couplets may serve to emphasize both the gravity of sin and the graciousness of the pardon that removes it.

Glorification

It is the B-section (6–8, Good News for Saints: *Liberation from Sin's Power and Presence*) that takes up the various strands of salvation and weaves them into the beautiful tapestry of glorification. It is this segment as well that emphasizes the already/not character of divine liberation, which, if not understood correctly can cause confusion and misapplication in the lived-experience of people of faith everywhere. If we invoke the theological construct of the already-but-not-yet character of divine liberation, the problem may not be solved completely but some light may be shed on the tension we observe in the B-section (6–8). There, it is said, on the one hand, that the believer is free from sin (6:7—the "already" dimension of liberation), and on the other hand, s/he is not fully free (7:14?) but anticipates with certainty (8:21) a final act of liberation which can be existentially and proleptically celebrated (7:25a; 8:31–39), even in the midst of agonizing struggle against the internal foe (8:12–14). The B´-section (12–16) hints at the same thought when it promises a bruising of Satan (16:20) that has effectively taken place (cf. Col 2:25; Gen 3:15) in anticipation of final vindication and glorification.

INAUGURATED ESCHATOLOGY AND CARIBBEAN REALITY

The theological construct referred to above (the already-not-yet nature of messianic liberation) goes by the official nomenclature of Realized Eschatology, a term first employed by Englishman Charles Harold Dodd. In his seminal work on the Synoptic Gospels, Dodd advanced the thesis that the eschaton (relative to the Messiah) "has moved from the future to the present, from the sphere of expectation into . . . realized experience. . . . It represents the ministry of Jesus . . . as the impact upon this world of the 'powers of the world to come' in a series of events, unprecedented and unrepeatable, now in actual progress."[20] Although Dodd used this concept to deny, for example, a future millennial reign on the part of the Messiah, his essential point of the "already/not yet" messianic hegemony can still stand up to scrutiny (cf. Luke 11:20; 17:20–21; 1 Cor 15:25). While initially Dodd saw far more "already" than "not yet" in the NT documents, he later conceded that the latter category (the "not yet") is just as much an integral part of NT eschatology as the former. This is seen, for example, in his comments on Romans 13:11–13, "The early Church lived in an atmosphere of crisis: a New Age was dawning; the Present Age was passing away; any day might

---

20 Dodd, *The Parables of the Kingdom*, 50–51.

turn out to be 'The Day of The Lord.'"[21] In light of this, a better expression for the construct is "inaugurated eschatology," which incorporates both a feature of a *fait accompli* and an element of future consummation.

There may an application here to the nations of the Caribbean which have already experienced emancipation/independence from colonial powers.[22] In some sense they are free, but in the words of Nelson Mandela, "The truth is that we are not yet free; we have merely achieved the freedom to be free."[23] This tension may be further elucidated by a contextual study of the final verb in Rom 8:30 ("glorified")—a proleptic aorist akin to the "prophetic perfect" in the OT.[24] Stanley Porter construes the "glorified" aorist in Rom 8:30b as timeless and translates the verse in question thus: "whom he sets apart, these indeed he calls; and whom he calls, these indeed he justifies; and whom he justifies, these indeed he glorifies."[25] The timelessness of the aorist, then, would underscore the nature and salvific purpose of the One who knows the end from the beginning (Isa 46:10), without doing violence to the realized eschatological point we have stressed above. In fact, Keener picks up the thought of Isaiah 46:10 in his comment on the verse in question and argues that: "Paul presents all the elements in 8:30 as a *fait accompli*, since from the standpoint of God's foreknowledge it is already done . . . ."[26] So from the perspective of the holistic messianic provision, the people of God in the Majority World (and wherever they are to be found) impoverish themselves if they fail to take seriously the biblical affirmations with respect to the present reality of messianic salvation in spite of the fact that not all the blessings promised will be experienced in this life (Heb 11:13). Here and now we have "every spiritual blessing in Christ" (Eph 1:3) and "everything we need for a godly life" (2 Pet 1:3). And since the messianic liberation is multi-dimensional, the pursuit of a purely socioeconomic solution or a privatized personal salvation to our world's ills is surely misguided.

21 Dodd, *The Epistle of Paul to the Romans*, 209. Dodd appears to grudgingly affirm the futuristic pole of the eschatological tension when he writes: "there remains a residue of eschatology which is not exhausted in the 'realized eschatology' . . . the element of sheer finality."

22. See especially, Davis, *Emancipation Still Comin'*.

23. Mandela, *Long Walk to Freedom*, 624.

24 Cf. Eph 2:6 ("*seated* in the heavenlies with Messiah . . . ." and Isa 9:6; 53:5; although passive participles are used in the latter, the thought is similar. On the prophetic perfect or "perfective of confidence," see Waltke and Connor, *An Introduction to Hebrew Syntax*, 490, and Fanning, *Verbal Aspect in New Testament Greek*, 269–74; for the proleptic aorist, Wallace, *Greek Grammar Beyond the Basics*, 330. For other perspectives, see Kruse, *Paul's Letter to the Romans*, 357–58.

25 Porter, *Verbal Aspect in the Greek of the New Testament*, 237.

26. Keener, *Roman*, 110; he also refers to Isa 53:5.

SUMMARY AND CONCLUSION

Using the twin testimony of the Jew-Gentile fraternity (that of Paul and Luke) which functioned powerfully under Empire, we have sought to forge a perspective of liberation that is suited particularly for peoples operating in a postcolonial milieu. For a liberative theology in the Majority World to approach anything like maximum beneficence, its practitioners can ill afford to ignore the total witness of the New Testament, particularly the Pauline and Lucan corpora. Here the fundamental frame of reference must always remain the Messianic Liberator, the One who exemplified the dictum, "All that is not eternal is eternally out of date."[27] The NT witnesses in one way or the other all point to a way of doing theology that manifests itself "only in concrete action."[28] This alone is authentic soteriology—a liberating messianic theology which interprets faith, like James, as philanthropic engagement with especially the poor "to whom the good news is addressed as a way of understanding the hoped-for horizon of God's new creation."[29] Only this way of theologizing transforms a person into a real *Mensch*—where, at the end of the day, s/he can say, "*bin ich mir ein wertes Ich*"[30]—I am myself a worthwhile "I." And only self-consciously worthwhile persons, filled with the messianic Spirit, can liberate a society from sinful and oppressive structures.

---

27. Heitzig, *When God Prays*, 187.

28. Gutierrez, *A Theology of Liberation*, 199.

29. Cited in Murrell *James Barr's Critique of Biblical Theology*, 343, as part of his critique of what he perceives to be Barr's truncated hermeneutical agenda and theology.

30. Moltmann, *Weiter Raum*, 363; English rendering mine.

APPENDIX

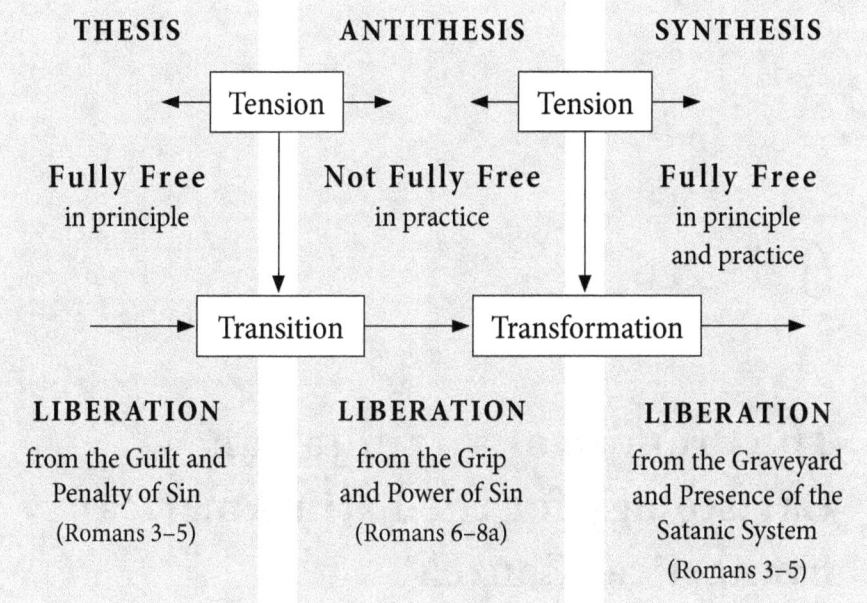

The Dialectic of Messianic Liberation

(Romans 6:7; 7:14; 8:21)

The second column is where the struggle for excellence is to be located; whereas the other two sections represent crisis (i.e., a momentary experience) events, the antithetical experience of "transition" and "transformation" demands constant vigilance along with "all kinds of prayers and requests" (Eph 6:18a), including the following Hebraic exemplar:

> From the conscience that shrinks from new truth,
> From the laziness that is content with half-truth,
> From the arrogance that thinks it knows all truth,
> Oh, God of truth, deliver us.[31]

---

31. Cited in Lim, "Beyond Success," 179.

6

The Promise of a Trinitarian Christology for the Latin American Evangelical Church

David del Salto (Equador[1])

A CLEAR CONSEQUENCE OF living in a globalized world is that now more than ever we are open to considering and consuming products from other parts of the world. That is true in every aspect of life, including theology. Although the conscious development of local theologies as expressions of particular contexts started in the second half of the last century in many parts of the world, only now is interaction among so-called global theologies taking place. That development began as it became evident that every theology is contextual.

A shift in perspective, concentrating on the role that circumstances play in shaping one's response to the gospel, first became evident in regions

---

1. David del Salto, from Ecuador, currently serves at Comunidad Nueva Creación, a church of immigrants in the Chicago area, and teaches theology in Chicago and in Latin America. This essay is an adaptation of a chapter from his PhD dissertation: "The Promise of a Trinitarian Christology for the Latin American Evangelical Church." A version of this chapter was published with the title, "Latin American Evangelical Christology" in *The Journal of Latin American Theology* 5, no. 2 (Feb. 2010), 51–106.

where Christianity was relatively new. It started coming to the world's attention in the 1950s in parts of Africa and Asia. There was a growing sense that the theologies being inherited from the older churches of the North Atlantic community did not fit well into these quite different cultural circumstances.[2]

The urge to think in that direction in the centers of traditional theological production comes, however, mainly due to the changing geography of Christianity in the world. As Kevin J. Vanhoozer states, "The single most significant methodological development that stems from the changing demographics of Christianity is the new appreciation for context."[3]

He then affirms, "Context is simply shorthand for seeing theology as ineluctably tied to and rooted in particular social, cultural, and geographical networks. It is context that gives theologies their specific *texture*."[4] Regardless of the reasons for that new awareness, what is important to notice is that it represents a significant step toward maturity for the church of Jesus Christ in the world.

When considering the Latin American contribution to the evangelical faith, especially during the last three decades of the twentieth century, two thinkers deserve particular consideration, C. René Padilla and Orlando E. Costas, due to the significance of their work for the evangelical family around the world. Although neither has produced a Christology per se, both thinkers have used Christological motives to advance their main theological work, that is, their theologies of mission and evangelization.

Padilla and Costas represent a generation of Latin American evangelicals that dared to think for themselves, in a context where theology was always an imported and translated commodity. As part of the theological movement that saw the inextricable unity between theology and theological community, they arrived at the conclusion that just as some theological and missiological conclusions had to be revised, the very nature of theology was in question. If theology is contextual, it cannot be simply translated into another language as if theology were sacred. As long as theology is a human production, it always responds to the concerns and interests of a particular group of people. Each church not only has the possibility but also the responsibility to do its own theology if the gospel will speak anew to them.

Although Padilla's and Costas' theological production incorporate elements that transcend their ecclesial and geographical location, it is quite clear that their main interlocutor has been the evangelical family, especially

2. Schreiter, *Constructing Local Theologies*, 1 . See also Kraft, "The Development of Contextualization Theory in Euroamerican Missiology," in *Appropriate Christianity*.

3. Vanhoozer, "One Rule to Rule Them All? Theological Method in an Era of World Christianity," 93.

4. Ibid.

in Latin America, and that they have produced their work mainly in conversation with other members of the *Fraternidad Teológica Latinoamericana* (FTL, Latin American Theological Fellowship[5]). Their main concern has always been the church and the role it plays within Latin American society. For that reason, when thinking of Latin American evangelical work in Christology, it is appropriate to call it "missiological christology."[6]

On the occasion of the fortieth anniversary of the Latin American Theological Fellowship, In this article we propose to give an account of the contributions made by Padilla and Costas to the field of Christology. In the process, we will stress some of the issues that most concerned them, especially in reference to their missiological work. At the same time, we will explore what appears to be a clear theological and methodological evolution in their thought. This exploration will be done in reference to José Míguez Bonino's proposal to the Protestant family in Latin America for a more comprehensive approach to theology. Míguez Bonino made his proposal at the close of his insightful historical and theological interpretation of what he calls "faces" of Latin American Protestantism.[7] When considering the evangelical church, he affirms that instead of churches "without theology," as René Padilla pointed out in the 1970s in reference to evangelical churches in the Majority World,[8] evangelical churches in Latin America hold to a reduced theology. The weakness of Latin American Protestantism "is not so much the absence of theology, nor its deviations—which, as we have seen, exist—but rather its 'reductionism.'"[9] This theological reductionism, explains Míguez Bonino, is the reason for what could be called an ecclesiological, and for that reason, a missiological and ethical reduction. Míguez Bonino explains that the evangelical heritage of the Anglo-American "awakenings" has resulted in a double reduction: Christological and soteriological.[10] Moreover, soteriology arrived wearing the individualistic, subjectivistic, and ahistorical clothes of modernity, resulting in grave theological

---

5. For many years the official name in English of the *Fraternidad Teológica Latinoamericana* was the *Latin American Theological Fraternity*. Given that the word "Fraternity" in North American English usually refers to male-only organizations, the title "Latin American Theological Fellowship" was adopted in 2006 as the official title in English to better express the composition and spirit of the organization.

6. Escobar, "Evangelical Theology in Latin America," 322.

7. Bonino, *Faces of Latin American Protestantism*.

8. Padilla, *Misión Integral*, 91.

9. Bonino, *Faces*, 111.

10. Míguez Bonino's thesis is also applied to other "faces" of Latin American Protestantism: Pentecostalism and liberalism. The manifestation of the reduction, in those cases, is different.

and practical deformations. "Thus, theology is practically swallowed up in Christology, and this in soteriology, and, even more, in a salvation which is characterized as an individual and subjective experience."[11]

Míguez Bonino recognizes that several attempts have been made within the evangelical church in Latin America to go beyond these narrow views. However, he finds that another separate but related problem has prevented them from succeeding. Their theologies have been worked out basically in what he calls "Christological key," which has made it difficult to place theology within the total framework of revelation. Míguez Bonino would say that it is not sufficient to add a few themes to round out the theological discussion. A proper framework is necessary to avoid repeating some of the problems we are trying to overcome. A new key is necessary, one that could provide a more comprehensive account of the totality of God's revelation, which brings us back to the discussion about criteria in a theological system.

To properly fulfill this task and to overcome the above-mentioned limitation of the Protestant church in Latin America, Míguez Bonino proposes the Trinity to be the criterion for theology.[12] The doctrine of the Trinity, he argues, should be the framework for theology. It can function as a hermeneutical criterion for theology because it is a formulation of the church which attempts to integrate the totality of the experience of revelation. "The doctrine of the Trinity is the expression of what the Scriptures reveal to us about the history of God with his people."[13] In that history, God reveals himself as the beginning of all things, whose Word originates all that is and all that will be. It is the history of that very God who decides to "pitch his tent" and live among us. It is the history of the presence of God manifested as the outpouring of life to the assembly at Pentecost. Thus, a Trinitarian framework will not only broaden but also enrich and deepen the understanding of the gospel and its witnesses.[14] It will play a crucial role as a principle which allows the church to distinguish, to discern, and to correct.

---

11. Bonino, *Faces*, 112.

12. Míguez Bonino observes that generally speaking, the Latin American Protestant church embraces a Trinitarian theology. In most cases, however, the doctrine of the Trinity has remained merely as a generic doctrine that has not informed the theology, the piety and the life of the church. For that reason he also affirms that although some Latin American Catholic theologians, particularly theologians like Juan Luis Segundo, José Comblin, Leonardo Boff, and Ronaldo Muñoz, have recently drawn attention to its significance and have made important contributions in that matter, much needs to be done among Protestants (*Faces*, 113).

13. Bonino, *Faces*, 114.

14. Ibid., 112.

With that hermeneutical tool in mind we now consider the contributions made by Padilla and Costas.

C. RENÉ PADILLA (1932–)

In an essay entitled "Toward a Contextual Christology from Latin America," Padilla explains a basic theological and missiological concern that defines his work. His concern is the difficulty of Christians to relate their faith with social, economical, and political matters. That situation, he believes, corresponds to the lack of an adequate Christological foundation for action and thought.[15]

He engages in Christological reflection, moved by specific pastoral, ethical, and missiological concerns. Therefore, Christology, and theology in general, become an expression of a pastoral and a missionary concern, which are contextual in nature. This is a key feature of Latin American theology. But, for a theology to be evangelical, it has to be nurtured and defined by the Scriptures. "The role of theology is to interpret and clarify God's Word for the sake of obedience to Christ in the concrete historical situation. . . . And for it to fulfill its purpose it must be based on biblical revelation, in the context of real life and for obedience of Christ today."[16]

The task of theology is also to analyze our commonly accepted theologies and theological traditions, following the guidelines previously described, to determine whether or not they do justice both to the historical situation and to the Word of God. In that sense, it is valid to test traditional images of Christ prevalent in evangelical circles in Latin America, because they do not always do justice to the image that comes out of the Gospels. "The search for ways to articulate faith in Jesus Christ is an unfinished task. This is not to deny the absolute character of God's revelation in his Son, but to recognize that all our Christological formulations are imperfect and therefore have to be examined in light of the Scriptures."[17]

Traditional Christology, explains Padilla, was fixed in philosophical categories, to the point that the historical dimension of revelation became secondary in relation to dogma. Nicaea and Chalcedon were able to characterize the identity of Jesus Christ as a divine and human being but were unable to give an account of his concrete historical actions. The Jesus of Nazareth who identified with the poor and oppressed became lost.[18]

---

15. Padilla, "Toward a Contextual Christology from Latin America," 81.
16. Padilla, *Mission Between the Times*, 104.
17. Padilla, "¿Quién es Cristo Hoy?" 24.
18. Padilla, "Toward a Contextual Christology," 81.

Padilla's problem is not with philosophy itself but fundamentally with the consequences of it for Christology and for the development of the church in general. The type of Christology that was produced opened the door to different forms of misrepresentations of the Christ of the Gospels. On the one hand, because of its link to the empire, it was used as a tool to justify the imperial power.[19] The Lord was conceived as a heavenly king invested with power on earth, giving support to the Christian emperor ruling in his name. Due to this false political image of the glorified Christ, the political relevance of the historical Jesus became lost. On the other hand, popular religiosity conceived of Christ as a dead, defeated, and helpless man. In this conception he was also unable to answer the cry of the poor, and Christ became a symbol of their passivity.[20] Padilla concludes:

> The Christ of traditional Western Christianity failed to provide an adequate basis for Christian social and political responsibility. The traditional images of Christ have made it very clear that a Christianity that disregards the historical Jesus may be useful for personal piety or civil religion, but it is neither faithful to the witness of Scripture concerning Jesus Christ nor historically relevant.[21]

This image of Christ, Padilla believes, has been especially problematic in the Majority World. "The images of Jesus Christ imported from the West have on the whole been found . . . too conditioned by Constantinian Christianity with all its ideological distortions and cultural accretions, and terribly inadequate as a basis for the life and mission of the church in situations of dire poverty and injustice."[22]

Consequently, it has not been uncommon to be confronted not only by distorted images of Christ but also by images that absolutely contradict the ideals and example of Jesus Christ. "For some reason it has been possible

---

19. About this whole discussion see González, *Mañana: Christian Theology from a Hispanic Perspective*, 139. González describes the problem this way: "By showing the 'rationality' of this notion [the Greek notion of God]—on the basis that only the fixed and given is strictly rational—and the anthropomorphism of the images with which Scripture and early Christian theology described the living God, the exponents of the theology of the status quo were able to do away with a great deal of the biblical picture of an active, just, loving, and avenging God. At the same time, allegorical interpretation dehistoricized the Bible, and thus God's activity in history was transmuted into perennial and supposedly 'higher" meanings." See also Kasper, *The God of Jesus Christ*, 182–84. Wolfhart Pannenberg discusses the issue in his *Systematic Theology*, 278 ff., when dealing with "The Method of Christology."

20. Padilla, "Toward a Contextual Christology," 81–82.

21. Ibid., 82.

22. Padilla, "Christology and Mission in the Two Thirds World," 18.

for Christians, in the name of Christ, to ignore or even contradict fundamental principles and values that were preached and acted upon by Jesus of Nazareth."[23] In this regard, Padilla quotes Roman Catholic African theologian Albert Nolan, who affirms that:

> Jesus has been more frequently honoured and worshipped for what he did not mean than for what he did mean. The supreme irony is that some of the things he opposed most strongly in the world of his time were resurrected, preached and spread more widely throughout the world in his name.[24]

Although professing strong allegiance to the Bible, Padilla finds that the prevalent images of Christ among evangelicals in Latin America do not do justice to the New Testament teachings about Christ. Without denying the humanity of Christ, evangelical Christianity in Latin America, as in the rest of the world, is deeply affected by docetism.[25] This type of faith helps the individual but is unable to relate to public life. With this type of Christology, the believer contemplates the transformative power of the gospel basically at a personal level; however, it does not touch, at least not directly, the serious problems that affect human life at the social level.[26] What is needed in Latin America is a clear understanding of Christ which relates the historical Jesus with the Latin American situation, for the sake of obedience to the gospel in our context.

Although these images of Christ have dominated the theological landscape for centuries, a new awareness has been taking place all over the globe, especially among the poor nations of the world. In this regard, Padilla praises what he calls the "discovery" of the historical Jesus that has taken place in Roman Catholic circles in Latin America since the early 1970s.[27] "One need not agree with this Christology in every detail to recognize that this return to the historical Jesus is beyond doubt the most significant

---

23. Ibid., 17, quoting Sobrino, *Christology at the Crossroads*.

24. Ibid., quoting Nolan, *Jesus Before Christianity*.

25. Padilla, "Toward a Contextual Christology," 83. Justo González makes a similar point in *Revolución y encarnación*.

26. Padilla, "¿Quién es Cristo Hoy?" 25.

27. It is important to notice the effort made by Jon Sobrino to distance himself and what he calls Latin American Christologies from European Christologies in their modern search for the historical Jesus: "Christological reflections done in Latin American in the last twenty years introduce themselves in the process to return to the historical Jesus but with different reasons and a different understanding about what is historic in Jesus" (*Jesucristo liberador*, 88).

theological development that has taken place within the Roman Catholic Church since it was established in Latin America."[28]

In the 1940s, however, elements of the emergence of a new image of Christ were seen in Latin America through the work of the influential Protestant missionary John A. Mackay. In line with the Gospel of Luke, this new image of Christ understood Jesus as the one who brings good news to the poor, proclaims liberty to the captives and recovery of sight to the blind, sets free the oppressed, and announces the year of the favor of the Lord.[29]

In 1965 Justo L. González published a short book that became influential in Latin America.[30] It was an effort to develop a Christian social ethics for Latin America using a Christological paradigm as a foundation. González wrote out of the belief that the doctrine of the incarnation has serious implications for living the Christian faith. In 1974 González published another study on the subject. He affirmed the centrality of the doctrine of the incarnation for the Christian faith, using it as the basis for reflection on the life of the church. He insisted that the doctrine of the incarnation was an explicit statement of a particular understanding of God's relation to the world. It affirmed that God acts in history. If either the incarnation or God's action in history is denied, the other is also denied. The doctrine of the incarnation, then, is a key piece to defining not only the church's beliefs but also its relation to the world and its role in society. For González, then, every Christian social action includes an implicit Christology. In the last analysis, our answer to the question of social action depends on our view of who Jesus Christ is.[31]

Christology and the Identity of Jesus of Nazareth

Fundamental to Padilla's Christology is the question of the historical existence of Jesus of Nazareth. Its historical foundation gives Christianity the basis to be a historical faith. Jesus of Nazareth is a historical reality, and his existence is established through several documents coming out of the first century of our era, especially by the witness of the New Testament.[32]

Because the New Testament is the fundamental source of Christological research, Christological reflection has to include the task of establishing the historical reliability of the Gospels. A confidence in the New Testament

28. Padilla "Toward a Contextual Christology," 83.
29. Ibid. See Mackay, *The Other Spanish Christ*.
30. González, *Revolución y encarnación*.
31. González, "Encarnación e historia," 152–54.
32. Padilla, "Jesús: ¿Mito o Historia?" 34

writings, affirms Padilla, is a basic characteristic of Latin American theology. "A fundamental premise of contemporary Latin American Christology is that the Gospels are essentially reliable historical records and that the portrait of Jesus that emerges from them provides an adequate basis for the life and mission of the church today."[33]

The implication of such understanding is clear; there is no disjunction between the Jesus of history and the Christ of faith. Thus, Christology and the Jesus of Nazareth are inseparable. Christology is possible only in reference to the history of Jesus of Nazareth as portrayed in the New Testament. Although Padilla believes that the historicity of the Gospel records as the basis for theology and Christian ethics can be safely assumed, he also recognizes that the Gospels are not "biographies" of Jesus in the modern sense of the word. Though reliable historically, they are also theological constructions.

The affirmation of the historical reality of Jesus Christ, in any case, is the way to promote a faith that is historically relevant and not just a pious feeling. Padilla believes that only a faith rooted in history can be historically relevant. This is the only way to establish a real connection between Jesus' mission and that of his disciples. "Unless the humanity of Jesus is given full weight, no real link can be established between his mission and that of his followers."[34]

The emphasis on the humanity of Jesus is in complete harmony with the notion that he is also truly God. Jesus of Nazareth is the Christ, the Son of the living God. Thus, a Christology that claims biblical support cannot ignore the New Testament teaching about Christ's preexistence and cosmic significance, just as it cannot dismiss what is said about his life and ministry.[35]

So who was this man from Nazareth? According to the New Testament testimony, Jesus of Nazareth is the promised Messiah for Israel.[36] Jesus introduces himself to his contemporaries as God's Messiah, as the bearer of the kingdom of God. "Jesus Christ not only proclaimed the coming of the kingdom of God, but interpreted his own mission as the inauguration of the

---

33. Padilla, "Toward a Contextual Christology," 83.
34. Ibid., 84.
35. Ibid.

36. A key question in our investigation is the manner in which Padilla understands the identity and mission of Jesus Christ, with regard to the Word-Spirit relation. In dealing with the Messiahship of Jesus, and the kingdom that he proclaims and bears, there is no reference to the action and role of the Spirit. Without denying the Trinity, Padilla does not work here in real Trinitarian terms.

christ and liberation 111

kingdom in the midst of history, and as the fulfillment of the prophesies of the Old Testament."[37]

To the New Testament writers, Jesus not only proclaims the kingdom; he is the kingdom in person. He is the one who inaugurates a new order in which God's rule of love and justice is established in anticipation of the end. This new order is marked by love for God and for one's neighbor, and it demands renunciation of privilege, material wealth, and earthly power. Jesus' messianic role leads him to suffering and to death, as the suffering Servant of the Lord. In this way, he takes the sins of his people and restores their relationship to the Father as well as their relationships with each other. By the power of the Holy Spirit, his followers are called to continue his mission on earth.[38] Padilla paints a word picture of this man from Nazareth called the Messiah:

> He affirmed that the kingdom of God was present in history and being manifest in the healing of the sick, the raising of the dead, and the preaching of the gospel to the poor. . . . He saw himself as a prophet who had been anointed to preach good news to the poor, to bring freedom to the prisoners, sight to the blind, and liberation to the oppressed—to proclaim "the year of the Lord's favor." . . . He was "a friend of publicans and sinners." . . . As a result, he surrounded himself with people who, according to the common convictions of the time, were rejected by God and had no hope of salvation. . . . He concentrated his ministry on the uneducated, the ignorant, and the disreputable. He spent much of his time going through all the towns and villages of the underdeveloped province of Galilee, preaching, teaching and healing. . . . He attacked religious oppression and rejected empty religious ceremonies, self-assured piety, and the idea that one's relationship with God is dependent on merit. . . . He vividly expressed God's judgment on the religious establishment of his day by the cleansing of the Temple. He claimed that justice and mercy are the great objectives of the law. . . . He condemned wealth and regarded greed as idolatry. He himself was poor and lived simply. . . . He defined power in terms of sacrificial service. . . . He summoned his disciples to social nonconformity patterned on his own and to a community of love and justice, forgiveness and sharing.[39]

37. Padilla, "El Reino de Dios y la Iglesia," 48.
38. Padilla, "Toward a Contextual Christology," 86.
39. Ibid., 87–89.

Padilla believes that this picture of Jesus represents the view of Christ preferred by the emergent Majority World Christologies. It stresses the humanity of Jesus and challenges us to discover the social dimensions of the gospel. It understands that Jesus' death is the historical and political outcome of his life. Padilla welcomes this new awareness and promotes it, but he also warns us. If we place too much emphasis on the humanity of Christ, at the expense of his divinity, we run the risk of reducing Christian activity to pure human effort. If the death of Christ is seen basically as the outcome of Jesus' confrontation with the leaders of Israel but not as God's provision for our sins, we have no basis for the forgiveness of our sins and for our justification.[40]

From the other side, however, although it is true that the New Testament assigns salvific meaning to his death, it is also true that the Gospels portray his death as that of a political figure whose messianic claims and public activity were considered subversive.

From a Trinitarian perspective, Padilla's relative silence about the Holy Spirit's role in Jesus' life and ministry is noteworthy. The New Testament gives testimony of a rich outpouring of life and power called the Spirit, acting in creation; in and by the power of that Spirit, Jesus is not only conceived but also anointed to accomplish his mission, dies, and is resurrected. Jesus' identity and his mission as the bearer of the kingdom of God cannot be explained apart from the action of the Spirit of God. Padilla develops the role of the Spirit later.

Christology and Social Ethics

Foundational for Christian ethics, Padilla believes, is the fact that the risen and the exalted Lord is the same as the Jesus of Nazareth; that the Christ of faith is the Jesus of history. "The starting point for *Christian* social ethics is the fact that God has revealed his purpose for humanity in a unique man: Jesus of Nazareth."[41] The incarnation of the Word affirms history as the context of God's redemptive work. Because the Word became flesh, there is no room for a dualistic separation of body and soul or for a mission, or ethics, or a church not committed to the social realities. Interestingly, and contrary to what Padilla sees as a trend in traditional theology, the doctrine of the incarnation serves him to affirm history. It is clear then, that the Christological definition of Chalcedon itself is not a problem for Padilla.

---

40. Padilla, "Cristología y misión en los dos-terceros mundos," 58–59.
41. Padilla, "Toward a Contextual Christology," 90.

The problem is the use of it to deny history, and consequently, the church's proper understanding of its own role in the world.

The church's calling is to assume a prophetic role in society, following the example of Christ. Those who confess Jesus Christ as Lord are supposed to make his options theirs, that is, to turn their attention to the impoverished in their societies. There is no other option for the followers of Christ. Just as the cross was the expression of Jesus' solidarity with us, just as through suffering God accomplished his redemptive purpose in Jesus Christ, so we are called to give our lives to serve others.[42] For those who follow Christ, there is no other ethic than the ethic of love and sacrificial service. "Jesus' death was not only God's atonement for sin but also his act of liberation from selfishness and his norm for a lifestyle that asserts love and justice."[43]

The cross, however, is nothing without the resurrection. The resurrection is the culmination of a life rooted in history. Through the resurrection, God brings into history the powers of the new era and makes its resources available to men and women through the Holy Spirit. Through those resources, sinners are transformed to live lives of sacrificial love and service, following the new lifestyle patterned by Jesus.[44]

Christology and the Christian Message

Padilla deals with the question of the Christian message in the context of the discussion of the mission of the church. When he deals with the question of the mission of the church, he does not deal precisely with methods, as is common among many evangelicals who are concerned with the spread of the gospel. Padilla emphasizes the nature of the gospel that is proclaimed and lived out by the church. This emphasis has been key for evangelical theologians like Padilla in Latin America. Their theological support has been Christology.

The gospel makes reference not only to the life and mission of the church but also, and fundamentally, to the founder of that church, Jesus Christ. "In the final analysis, he himself (including his person and his work) *is* the gospel."[45] The subject matter of the apostolic preaching in the New Testament is the gospel of Christ, which must be understood in light of the dynamic message of the kingdom. For that reason, the question about the gospel and the question about the church are Christological questions.

42. Ibid.
43. Ibid.
44. Ibid., 91.
45. Padilla, *Mission Between the Times*, 70.

The gospel is the good news that God has placed himself within our reach. "To accomplish this, he has broken into human history through the breach made by Jesus Christ in the time-space reality."[46] God made himself known to us in the person of his own Son, at a particular time and in a definite place. The Word of God became like one of us, and that is God's way of communicating with his creation. God's approach to revelation is incarnation. "The climax of God's revelation is Emmanuel. And Emmanuel is Jesus, a first-century Jew! The incarnation unmistakably demonstrates God's intention to make himself known from within the human situation."[47] The conclusion for theology, spirituality, and ethics, is significant:

> *The knowledge of God . . . takes place in the context of our bodily existence in the world.* The God whom the gospel proclaims is a God who has entered into human history in order to put himself within man's reach and to participate in all the contingencies of everyday life. The incarnation is a negation of every attempt to reach God by means of mysticism, asceticism, or rationalistic speculation; we know God through the Word who takes on concrete form in our own culture.[48]

To the New Testament authors, God has definitely acted in Christ's life and work, to fulfill his redemptive purpose. "The incarnation establishes the insertion of a new world inside of history . . . however . . . the consummation of the new age belongs to the future."[49] The New Testament pictures Jesus Christ not only as proclaiming the coming of the kingdom of God but also as interpreting his own mission as the inauguration of the kingdom in the midst of history, as the fulfillment of Old Testament prophecies.

> The kingdom that Jesus proclaims is the power of God active among men in his own person and ministry. Before the end of the age God has irrupted into history to accomplish his redemptive purpose, and he has done so in Jesus Christ. In announcing that "the kingdom of God is at hand," Jesus does not mean that the end of the world is within sight but that through his own mission God is visiting his people, thus fulfilling the prophetic hope.[50]

---

46. Ibid., 83.
47. Ibid.
48. Ibid., 90.
49. Padilla, "El Reino de Dios y la Iglesia," 45.
50. Padilla, *Mission Between the Times*, 71.

Once he has established as a basic premise that God has revealed himself in the history of the people of Israel which was brought to fulfillment in the person and work of Jesus Christ, Padilla moves to the next step. "According to the New Testament, the Word that God has spoken in Jesus Christ is inseparable from the preaching of the apostles."[51]

The emphasis now is on the written aspect of the Word of God. A basic premise of Christian preaching is that "the Word of God includes both the historical facts of Christ and their apostolic interpretation, the cross and the Word of the cross."[52] That means that without the mission of the apostles the mission of Jesus Christ would have been left incomplete. "Redemption is the substance of revelation but there is no revelation apart from the apostolic interpretation of God's redemptive work."[53]

The last premise of Christian proclamation is that God's final Word, spoken in Jesus Christ, is still active in history through the proclamation of the gospel in the power of the Holy Spirit. Note that the proclamation of the gospel is far more than a mere repetition of biblical concepts.[54] "If the message is to have a ring of truth, the Christ of apostolic tradition has to take shape in God's people by the power of the Spirit."[55]

It is important to notice the connection Padilla establishes at this point between Word and Spirit. He even says that Word and Spirit are inseparable. The connection, however, makes reference fundamentally to the work of the Spirit in relation to the nature and role of the written Word. "The Scripture does not fulfill its function apart from the work that the very Spirit that inspires them achieves in the heart of the human being. . . . The Word and the Spirit are inseparable; bibliology and pneumatology complement each other."[56] The Spirit's action in the person is vital to appreciate and to receive this message because the action of the Word and the action of the Spirit are perfectly united.

This connection between Word and Spirit was already expressed during the first theological gathering of the Latin American Theological Fellowship in 1970 in Padilla's presentation on the authority of the Bible. Yet that connection appears mainly in relation to the nature of the Bible or the reading and appropriation of its message. The joint action of the Word and the Spirit appears mainly related to the appropriation of the written Word of

---

51. Padilla, "God's Word and Man's Words," 219.
52. Ibid.
53. Ibid., 222.
54. Ibid., 223.
55. Ibid., 226.
56. Padilla, "La autoridad de la Biblia en la teología latino Americana," 149.

God. Of course, in this and other similar essays Padilla deals fundamentally with the Scriptures. However, more could have been done. Something similar occurs in his work on "The Contextualization of the Gospel." This work deals not only with the reading and interpretation of the biblical message but also with the church's appropriation and "translation" of that message to its situation and context.[57] Although Padilla explains that the purpose of theology is the obedience of faith, he fails to emphasize the fundamental action of the Spirit. Why not talk about the Spirit as the power of God that makes the contextualization of the gospel possible?

Christology, the Church, and the Kingdom of God

The identity of the church comes from its relation to the kingdom of God made present in history in Jesus Christ. It is by the action of the Spirit that the church becomes the community of the kingdom.[58] "The Holy Spirit is the agent of the 'eschatology in process of actualization.' It is through the Spirit that the kingdom of God, made present among men in Jesus Christ, continues implementing its action."[59] The particularity of the church, according to this explanation, is the action of the Spirit upon the church. In other words, the church exists by virtue of its relation to the Holy Spirit, through whom the church receives the benefits of the new age, the age of the kingdom of God. "If the church is the body of Christ, and as such the sphere in which operates the life of the new age unleashed by Jesus Christ, the Spirit is the agent through whom that life is imparted to the believer."[60]

The kingdom of God which came in the person of Jesus Christ and which will come at the end of "this age" is in process of actualization here and now in the midst of the people of God by the action of the Spirit. The power of the proclamation of the gospel, and the spiritual fruits that characterize the Christian life, are manifestations of the action of the Spirit. Note, however, as Padilla states, that "the kingdom of God is not an abstract principle . . . but a dynamic power active in the creation of a new humanity. It is a present reality among humanity and it takes shape in a community that lives and proclaims it;"[61] but the kingdom is also hope. The kingdom has come in the person of

---

57. Padilla, *Mission Between the Times*, 83–90.

58. This section comes mainly from a work presented at the second gathering of the Latin American Theological Fellowship held in 1972. The subject to be discussed was "The Kingdom of God and Latin America."

59. Padilla, "El Reino de Dios y la Iglesia," 51.

60. Ibid.

61. Ibid., 57.

Jesus Christ; however, it has not arrived in its fullness yet. According to this reality, then, there is no place for any absolutization of a church or a social structure. Both the church and society are called to a continuous reformation according to the principles of justice and peace of the kingdom of God.[62] "Beyond the structures created by the human powers, the church's hope is in a new heaven and a new earth, where 'justice resides.'"[63]

If there is a correlation between the church itself, the kingdom, and the Spirit, there is also a correlation between the mission of the church, the kingdom of God, and the Holy Spirit. "The mission of the church is defined by the 'already' of the kingdom of God. The same Holy Spirit that brought about in the church the life of the kingdom empowers the church for the proclamation of the 'gospel of the kingdom.'"[64] The conclusion is clear: the life and mission of the church are the concrete expression of the kingdom of God that has irrupted in history in Jesus Christ and continues to become manifest among humanity through the action of the Holy Spirit.

The emphasis on the present reality of the kingdom of God makes sense in reference to what Padilla calls the devastating effects of the futurist eschatology in the life of the church in Latin America. "The unilateral emphasis on the 'not yet' has eliminated the possibility that the 'already' of the kingdom would serve as a firm base for a responsible action of evangelicals in the social arena."[65]

This treatment reveals an important progression in Padilla's thought. The Spirit is shown as the agent of eschatology and as the agent of the church. The Spirit is the one who brings the benefits of the new age to the church. The church shares with Jesus Christ the same Spirit who made present the kingdom. There are, however, at least two issues that still need to be developed: the role of the Spirit in defining the identity of Jesus Christ and the role of the Spirit in the world outside the church.[66]

Christology, Christ, and the Spirit

In a more recent essay entitled "El Espíritu Santo y la mission integral de la iglesia,"[67] Padilla makes a significant development in his reflection on Chris-

62. Ibid., 60.
63. Ibid., 61.
64. Ibid., 53.
65. Ibid., 55.
66. We understand that Padilla is dealing in this essay with the kingdom and the church.
67. Padilla, "El Espíritu Santo y la misión integral de la iglesia."

tology, which is crucial for our investigation. This development expands his Christology and explicitly includes his reflection within a Trinitarian framework. Even though this is a reflection on the doctrine of the Spirit, it is valuable for Christology because of its Trinitarian approach.

Padilla begins by affirming that the work of the Spirit is inseparable from the work of the Father and the work of the Son, a reality that in fact corresponds to the very identity of God himself. "In the God revealed in Jesus Christ, unity and diversity are combined in such a way that in everything he does there is a perfect correlation and interpenetration proper of the perichoretic communion that characterizes the Trinitarian union of Father, Son, and Holy Spirit."[68] The type of communion is such that each person contains the other and resides in the other. Thus, the action of the Spirit can be understood only in relation to the action of the Father and that of the Son. This affirmation, however, does not deny the distinctive actions of each person of the Trinity. After establishing these fundamental Trinitarian principles, Padilla discusses the action of the Spirit in creation and history, in Jesus' mission, and in the church.

The image portrayed by Genesis 1:2 and Deuteronomy 32:10, where the *ruach* (Spirit) of God extends its wings and touches the surface of the waters, suggests that the Spirit of God accompanies the whole process of creation to produce cosmos out of chaos. Clearly, the action of the Spirit does not limit itself to the sphere of "the spiritual." It extends to the material world, the arena of human history.[69] The conclusion is that "the totality of creation both material and immaterial is the product of God's action through his Word . . . , by the power of the Spirit."[70]

The purpose of the entire creation is to reflect the glory of God. The action of the Spirit leans toward the fulfillment of that goal. From the original creation through the new creation, everything proceeds from the Father through the Son by the power of the Spirit, and everything returns to the Father in glory through the Son by the power of the Spirit. Meanwhile, the Hebrew Scripture explains that the *ruach* of God is the power through which God manifests his presence in creation and among his created beings. The creative work of the Spirit takes place in every sphere of life: social, political, economical, cultural, ecological, biological, or religious—producing life, solidarity, justice, and peace.[71]

---

68. Ibid., 117–18.
69. Ibid., 121.
70. Ibid.
71. Ibid., 122.

An important element for the New Testament doctrine of the Spirit is the relation of God's *ruach* to two Old Testament figures: the Messiah and the suffering Servant of Isaiah. To the prophets, the *ruach* of the Lord will dwell in a descendent of David. The promised king's sphere of the action is the whole creation, and in his kingdom, justice for the oppressed will play a major role. The prophets Ezekiel and Jeremiah share the notion that the new era for Israel will come through the action of the *ruach* of God. The prophet Joel emphasized the universality of that promise.[72]

In the Synoptic Gospels, Jesus is preeminently a man anointed by the Holy Spirit to fulfill the ministry which God entrusted to him. Since God's presence is active in the world through the action of the Spirit, God's action in Jesus is precisely the action of the Spirit of God in him. Padilla finds, in this regard, that the New Testament explicitly establishes a link between the leading role of the Spirit and the events by which Jesus fulfills the work of redemption: his incarnation (Matt 1:18; Luke 1:35), his ministry (Luke 4:18), his crucifixion (Heb 9:14), and his resurrection (Rom 1:4).[73]

The fact that the New Testament relates the action of the Spirit of God to Jesus' ministry must be explained in reference to his mission. The purpose of Jesus' anointing by the Holy Spirit is the fulfillment of the Messiah's mission as the one anointed by God. The mission of the Messiah anointed by the power of the Spirit focuses on the most vulnerable people in society: the poor, the captives, the blind, and the oppressed. Thus, it is a mission of *shalom*. It leads to the restoration of life in all of its dimensions, according to the purpose of God, and it includes the restoration of every relationship: between human beings, with God, and with creation.

In Padilla's interpretation, Jesus' mission has a clear eschatological dimension, according to the Gospels. Jesus believed that the Old Testament prophecies about the Messiah, particularly Isaiah 61:1–2, were accomplished in his person and ministry. What was really taking place in Jesus' announcement was the arrival of a new era in the history of humanity. "Anointed by God's Spirit, the Messiah is the agent of the eschatology in process of realization. . . . Therefore, Jesus' announcement must be understood as the proclamation of the beginning of a new era of justice by the power of the Spirit manifested in his own person and work."[74]

The conclusion is that the Spirit of God is the eschatological gift that makes possible the presence of the kingdom of God in the person and ministry of Jesus Christ.

72. Ibid., 124–27.
73. Ibid., 127.
74. Ibid., 130.

Jesus' project was the creation of a new humanity where God's purpose for humanity and for creation could be fulfilled. Jesus' followers participate in his project as witnesses, by the power of the Spirit. Just as Jesus was baptized at the beginning of his ministry as a fulfillment of it, Jesus' disciples are also baptized at Pentecost. By this baptism, God empowers the church to continue the mission of Christ, oriented to the transformation of human life in its entire dimension.[75]

Clearly, Padilla establishes a correlation between Word and Spirit, but this relation is understood basically as functional. The action of the Spirit in Jesus happens and makes sense mainly in reference to his redemptive mission in the world. Although Padilla begins by affirming that the work of the Spirit is inseparable from the work of the Father and the work of the Son, he does not explore that inseparability in reference to the identity of Jesus Christ as a person, much less as the God-man of incarnation.

Final Remarks

Padilla believes that Latin American evangelical theology, just as traditional theology, has overemphasized the divinity of Christ. That problem originates in Chalcedon where Christ is conceived in philosophical categories. From that moment on, the daily aspects and historical realities of his life were slowly relegated to the point that his life and work became foreign to the image of Christ promoted by the church. The outcome of this trend is a theology and a Christology that has nothing to do with the historical realities of the believers. It is good for personal piety but paraplegic in regard to history, justice, and poverty. It promotes a private spirituality with little or no help for life. Padilla proposes to give true attention to the historical Jesus, who for him is the Jesus of the Gospels. Jesus Christ is the man from Galilee who, by the power of the Spirit, announces and brings the kingdom of justice, peace, sacrifice, and love from God. Empowered by the same Spirit, as agents of the new age, his followers take up the same path and fulfill their mission in service and solidarity as an expression of their faith and commitment to the Messiah. Jesus Christ is the Son of God made human, the Messiah of God who introduces a new reality in history. The kingdom of God inaugurated by Jesus, by the power of the Spirit, is in the process of being realized, but no human institution can be equated with the kingdom, because the kingdom is also a reality that waits for fulfillment.

A significant evolution has clearly taken place in Padilla's Christology. The inclusion of the Spirit in the conversation makes the difference. For that

75. Ibid.

reason, we would like to conclude that although he is a Trinitarian, Padilla does not always articulate his missiological Christology in a Trinitarian framework. The notion of the kingdom seems to be the key to articulating his theology. Only more recently does he explicitly bring all the significant components together, including the kingdom, under the larger umbrella of the action of the Triune God in creation and redemption. This conclusion does imply that originally Padilla's theology was not Trinitarian. On the contrary, the seeds of a Trinitarian approach are there from the very beginning of his career, but the adoption of the Trinity as the framework for his theology is something relatively new in Padilla's work.

ORLANDO E. COSTAS (1942-87)

Orlando Costas' primary theological interest is the theology of mission and evangelization. The object of his inquiry is focused mainly on the mission of the church. He finds that the church has problems in its interaction with the social realities that surround it, has isolated itself from the world, and has promoted a spirituality that does not do justice to its very nature. In the process, the church has preached to the world as if the gospel were another product of consumer society. Therefore, the gospel has become unable to respond to people's real needs, especially to those in the lower strata of society. The church has not understood the world and has not appreciated the world, becoming incapable of seeing its own proper role in the world. On the basis of this diagnosis Costas develops his theology of evangelization. His overall project includes the construction of a theological framework to support the church's action in the world.

Although the theology of mission is the subject matter of Costas' investigation, the figure of Christ occupies a central place in his work. Instead of a direct treatment on Christology, Costas develops a theology of the mission of the church, profoundly influenced by Christology. It is also important to note that Christology for Costas is not simply another theological topic on the theological menu. Christology, and theology in general, is part of a more comprehensive project that includes not only the "theory" but also the "praxis" of the church. Theology is the work of the church, and it is produced for the sake of the church's mission in the world.

In 1983, during a conference on Mission in the Third World, Costas made an important observation. He declared that "Christology represents in the Two Thirds World an exciting and dynamic awakening."[76] He added that two Christological themes are prominent in that part of the world: the

76. Costas, "Proclaiming Christ in the Two Thirds World," 11.

rediscovery of the Jesus of history, especially in Latin America, and the emphasis on a proper understanding of the cosmic Christ of the Pauline Epistles, especially in Asia. In regard to the first theme, he noted the emphasis being placed on the historical Jesus as a starting point for Christology and also on the active presence of Jesus in the struggles of the poor, the powerless, and the oppressed. This new emphasis on the historical Jesus produces not only a new image of Christ but also a fresh understanding of the mission of the church in situations similar to those with which Jesus Christ identified during his ministry. In regard to the emphasis on the cosmic Christ, he noticed that the subject is particularly important in the context of other religious traditions of the Majority World. In a provocative manner he asked his evangelical colleagues: Is there a total discontinuity between the cosmic Christ and the religious traditions as was suggested by some missiologists from the West several decades ago? Or is there a continuity, and if so, of what kind? Costas finds that a deep and profound reflection on Christological themes is needed if the church wants to be faithful to its call.[77]

If the rediscovery of the historical Jesus has been a prominent theological subject in Latin America, it expresses itself in a particular way in that part of the world, especially among evangelicals. It is not a project motivated by the modern mentality that denies any supernatural reality and promotes a notion of a "closed world." The problem is not the disjunction between natural and supernatural but between the spiritual world and the historical world. The problem in Latin America is not the denial of the supernatural but the denial of history. As a result, God's relation to the world is just tangential, which then leads to an understanding of the Christian place in the world as accidental and peripheral. The importance of the emphasis on the history of Jesus lies in the presupposition that history has been neglected and that the church has adopted a spirituality detached from history. The goal, then, is to affirm history and "the world" as realities in which God himself is immersed, making it also the church's responsibility.

In light of this reality, Costas begins his reflections on mission in *Christ Outside the Gate*, discussing precisely the biblical notion of the incarnation, and based on it, the notion of contextualization.[78] "Biblical contextualization is rooted in the fact that the God of revelation can only be known in history. . . . In the New Testament . . . this revelation reaches its peak: God is known in human flesh."[79] The New Testament witnesses to the fact that the Word which was from the beginning with God and is God has become flesh in

---

77. Ibid.
78. Costas, *Christ outside the Gate: Mission Beyond Christendom*.
79. Ibid., 5.

Jesus of Nazareth (John 1:3, 14). Through the life of Jesus of Nazareth, God has come within the reach of every human being because God has become one with us: Emmanuel (Matt 1:22–23).[80] The implication is enormous. Because of the incarnation, we cannot think of God as an abstract being, removed from human history and experience, faceless and unidentifiable.

> God has a historical identity: that of Jesus, the carpenter from Nazareth and the prophet from Galilee who suffered death on a cross and was raised from the dead by the Spirit. God is not absent from human history, but continues to be present in the Spirit of the risen Christ (2 Cor. 3:17) who indwells the life and witness of the church.[81]

Of course, Costas recognizes that, chronologically speaking, the confessions which led to the doctrine of the incarnation do not belong to the beginning of the Gospel accounts.

> This act, which in the structure of at least three of the Gospels (Matthew, Luke, and John) appears as the starting point of New Testament faith, is nevertheless Christologically the point of arrival.... Indeed, it was not until the resurrection that the disciples were able to understand the cross as a revelation of God rather than a tragic accident, as Luke tells us they originally thought (Luke 24:18–26; Acts 2:32–36). The Easter event made theological sense of the cross and confirmed the understanding that the disciples had developed of Jesus through the years they had spent with him. Only through the experience of the resurrection did the early church discover the meaning of the cross. Only by the resurrection of the crucified Jesus was it able to interpret the theological significance of his life and ministry. And faith in him led it to the conclusion that God had become human in the man Jesus while remaining true to himself.[82]

The affirmation that "God is known in human flesh" testifies also to the fact that in the New Testament, Jesus Christ is a true human being. He was the son of a modest Jewish family who grew up in an insignificant town in the province of Galilee. He spoke with a Galilean accent, had a limited formal education, and was a carpenter by trade. He became an itinerant preacher and lived a poor life with no permanent residence. "He so identified himself with the poor and the oppressed that he dedicated himself to

---

80. God's special revelation according to the Old Testament occurs fundamentally in the history of Israel.

81. Costas, *Christ Outside*, 12.

82. Ibid., 6.

a suffering service in their behalf. It is this poor, humble, enigmatic, lonely Jewish preacher who fearlessly defended the cause of the hurt of his society whom the Christian faith confesses as the Son of God."[83]

In examining Costas' early work from a Trinitarian perspective, we do not yet see a clear role assigned to the Spirit in reference to Jesus' life and identity. That will become an important issue later in his work.

The Message of the Kingdom and Jesus' Life and Ministry

Jesus' ministry can be summarized as the ministry of the proclamation of "the gospel of God," as the announcement of good news from God. It is important to notice, however, that "the proclamation of God's name in Jesus' ministry was qualified by the announcement of God's kingdom."[84] At the same time, however, the kingdom that is proclaimed cannot be seen apart from his life and ministry. Since God became flesh in the person of Jesus Christ, he embodies the presence of God's kingdom. In Jesus, the kingdom of God has drawn near, and has come within everyone's reach. Thus,

> In Jesus' life and ministry God discloses the content of his kingdom far more clearly, comprehensively and deeply than in the life and history of Israel.[85]

The message of the kingdom reveals two fundamental notions: God's presence and work in history and God's final work of redemption.

> The kingdom is an indication of God's transforming presence in history.... It is a symbol of God's transforming power, of his determination to make "all things new" (Rev 21:5). This kingdom of God stands for a new order of life: the new humanity and the new creation which have become possible through the death and resurrection of Jesus. This new order includes reconciliation with God, neighbor and nature, and, therefore, participation in a new world.... This transforming power is also disclosed as an eschatological reality. It is the beginning of the end. As such, it awaits the final consummation of history. It is a force that anticipates the final redemption, which is made possible by the work of the Holy Spirit and which is borne witness to by what the Gospels call "the signs of the kingdom."[86]

83. Ibid.
84. Costas, *The Integrity of Mission*, 5.
85. Ibid., 6.
86. Ibid.

As important as it is, the message of the kingdom, as a present reality, has not received proper attention in the Christian church, producing not only a weak message but also a weak church. Since the kingdom, as a present reality, speaks of God's transforming presence in history, its message has a unique importance for a church that wants to understand its role in society.[87] The future aspect, or the "otherness" of the kingdom, has been stressed so much that we have forgotten its nearness and its implications. Costas identifies very closely with this problem.

> I come from a spiritual tradition (Protestant evangelicalism) which has stressed the proclamation of the gospel, but has, by and large, deemphasized the concept of the kingdom. Michael Green, speaking at the Lausanne International Congress on World Evangelization (1974), underscored this tremendous flaw in evangelical theology. He said that as evangelicals, "We tend to isolate what we call the Gospel from what Jesus called the kingdom of God."[88]

The notion of the kingdom of God is so central to the New Testament and to the person of Jesus that he himself was considered the kingdom. Anyone who believed in him experienced the kingdom. As such, the kingdom was understood not only as a transcendent and future reality but also as immanent and present: "the kingdom of God is among you" (Luke 17:21). The message of the kingdom was a central theme also to the preaching of the early church.[89]

The kingdom of God is a reality that cannot be explained except in reference to the Spirit of God. Costas, however, fails to give the Spirit sufficient attention when he deals with the kingdom. It is true that Jesus is the bearer of the kingdom of God, but it is also true that by the power of the Spirit the kingdom becomes a reality in the person of Jesus. In fact, Jesus becomes and acts as the Messiah, and fulfills his mission in the world, by the power of the Spirit. Over all, Costas agrees with our observation and, even more, he would affirm that the Spirit is the agent of God's action in the world, including in Jesus. However, he chooses to deal with this subject, in a sense, distantly from the Trinitarian emphasis that he will utilize later.

---

87. Wolfhart Pannenberg's theology of revelation became an important referent in regard to God's self-manifestation in history. Pannenberg, *Systematic Theology*, 230ff.

88. Costas, *The Integrity of Mission*, 7.

89. Ibid., 7–8.

The Cross and the Revelation of God and Humanity

The New Testament traditions concur in the description of Jesus' suffering and death as that of a poor and oppressed man, a blasphemer, and a political rebel. To the writers of the New Testament, however, these events were no mere accidents. They saw God's hand in the cross of Jesus Christ. The cross is God's plan for the salvation of the world. Thus, the cross of Christ becomes the place where the mystery of Jesus as the Son of God is most keenly revealed.[90]

The cross situates Jesus on the side of the poor and the afflicted, the sick and the oppressed. It is carried even further in Paul's linkage of the cross with the incarnation (Phil 2:8) and in Hebrews' location of Jesus' death "outside" the Holy City—the place where the leftovers of the cultic sacrifices were thrown (Heb 13:13). On the cross, Jesus takes the form of a slave, becoming totally identified with humanity in its lowest form. The cross is the ultimate test of this identification.[91] It cannot be forgotten, however, that "just as the crucified Son of man is the sign of authentic humanity, so his eschatological identity is a sign of the final redemption (and therefore of the absolute humanization) of humankind."[92] In the cross God identifies with us in our sin and in our sufferings. "The cross is not only the outcome of Jesus' life but also the consequence of our sin. It is the place where Jesus was made sin in order to take upon himself the death that belonged to every human being."[93]

In the cross and through the cross God identifies himself with us in every situation. The cross is the means God uses to reconcile the world to him. The cross assumes a situation of sin and death from which the work of Jesus Christ brings liberation and hope. That hope is depicted in the New Testament in terms of the hope of the Old Testament, that is, in terms of a new order, in terms of the messianic hope. In Jesus Christ, however, such messianic hope extends to all of creation, including nature and the whole of human society. "For Jesus, that new order was the goal of God's mission. God was in the process of inaugurating the kingdom."[94] The miracles and wonders attributed to Jesus Christ in the New Testament are signs of the new creation. They proclaim that creation will be made new. But the most outstanding sign of the coming into being of the new world is Jesus' death

---

90. Costas, *Christ Outside*, 7.
91. Ibid., 7–8.
92. Ibid., 12.
93. Ibid., 10.
94. Costas, *Liberating News*, 55.

and resurrection. The kingdom was made present in history, and through the resurrection, the messianic future was open for a final consummation.[95] Thus, the resurrection is the authentication of the cross and the central sign of the Christian faith.[96]

If the cross of this man from Nazareth caused scandal, his resurrection caused a revolution.

> [The Easter faith] . . . affirms that the so-called blasphemous and rebellious preacher who was forsaken and abandoned by his God and Father had indeed risen from the grave by the power of God's Spirit, and that he had been enthroned as the Lord of heaven and earth. This identity between the risen Lord and the crucified Jesus led early Christians to formulate the doctrine of the incarnation: the affirmation that the poor and oppressed preacher who died on Calvary was none other than the Son of God.[97]

Since in the cross Christ overcomes the power of sin and death, the cross becomes a sign of life and hope. In the cross we find life, we become new creation; we are made free to live for God in the service of the world. On one hand, the cross forces us to take suffering and death seriously, but on the other hand, the cross of the risen Christ reminds us that suffering and death are no longer ultimate, because there God dealt decisively with them, taking them upon himself. Thus, the message of the cross is a message of life through suffering and death but also a message of hope beyond it.[98] For that reason, the cross becomes vital to defining the church's role in the world. In the cross, Christ establishes a new pattern of existence, characterized by a hopeful service. "For the Christian community, hope is transformed into a call to obedience, and obedience is manifested in the labor of love, in Christian praxis, which means participation in the liberating transformation of the world."[99]

There is also strong testimony throughout the New Testament in reference to the fact that in the suffering of Jesus the Son, God himself is affected.[100] Paul's assertion is eloquent: "in Christ God was reconciling the world to himself" (2 Cor 5:19). In Jesus' death as the forsaken Son, God is revealed

---

95. Ibid.
96. Costas, *Christ Outside*, 12.
97. Ibid., 8.
98. Costas, *Liberating News*, 108–11.
99. Ibid., 29.
100. This is a clear Trinitarian statement, at least in regard to the Father-Son relationship. Cf. Moltmann, *The Crucified God*, 149–53; Sobrino, *Cristología desde América Latina*, 168–71.

as affected by suffering. The connection between the cross and the incarnation becomes apparent. The cross and the incarnation are expressions of the same act; they reveal God's total identification with us, especially with those who are suffering. From now on, any complete knowledge of God has to include the cross and the incarnation, since therein God has made himself accessible to us.[101]

> The Pauline expression "God was in Christ" refers not just to the fact that God delivered the Son and became thereby personally accessible to humankind, but also to the fact that God participated in the passion and suffering of the Son for the world. God refused to be identified at the cross by his power and glory. Rather, God was revealed in the helplessness and weakness of Jesus. The cross was both the culmination and the test of the incarnation. It was the point where the self-emptiness of the Son was revealed in its crudest form.[102]

What is surprising about the cross of Christ is that it reveals not only the true God but also the true meaning of humanity. The cross of Christ is the most authentic expression of self-denial and sacrifice for the sake of others. "The cross reveals Jesus as the man for others and in so doing locates authentic humanity in being at the service of others."[103] From this point on, humanization becomes possible through self-denial, obedience, and sacrifice. One must deny oneself, take up the cross, and follow Jesus through the wilderness of life (Matt 16:24; Heb 13:13). Thus, the incarnation bears witness not only to the fact that God has become part of history in the man Jesus but also to the fact that after the cross and the resurrection, this man reveals authentic humanity. The mediation of the God-man Jesus of Nazareth becomes necessary for the understanding of God and humankind. This is so because in the history of Jesus we discover the fullness of God and the fullness of humankind.[104]

Once more, Costas chooses to explore this crucial event in Jesus' life, but the role of the Spirit is still not yet prominent. The Father is mentioned as suffering the death of the Son, and pneumatology could be the resource to articulate that point. Gary D. Badcock develops this issue: "The basic question posed in the contemporary trinitarian theology of the cross is how it is possible to conceive of Jesus' death, the death of God's Son, as belonging

---

101. This reminds us of Luther's theology of the cross. See McGrath, *Luther's Theology of the Cross*; Hansen, "El uso político de la cruz."

102. Costas, *Christ Outside*, 10.

103. Ibid., 12.

104. Ibid.

within the being of God."¹⁰⁵ At this point, he argues, the Holy Spirit is frequently a key theme.¹⁰⁶ "Building on the traditional Western view, which understands the Holy Spirit's personal character in terms of the relation of love bonding the Father and the Son together, the theology of the cross is thus able to assume a pneumatological form."¹⁰⁷ Costas will later explore the Spirit in relation to the resurrection of Christ.

The Trinitarian Mission of God and the Mission of the Church

The mission of God is not only the model but also the foundation of the mission of the church. Costas' conviction is that the mission of the church is the mission of the Triune God in the world and for the world. Such Trinitarian foundation defines, motivates, empowers, and corrects the church's evangelization. "The evangelistic task is always carried out under the assumption that the God who has spoken in Jesus Christ addresses each and every human being in his or her time and space."¹⁰⁸ God did not only speak to us in Jesus Christ, however. In him "God became part of history."¹⁰⁹ In him and through him God assumes a human identity, and more concretely, the identity of the poor. This identification of God with the world finds its highest expression on the cross. Thus, "to understand the mission of Christians in any situation we need first and foremost to understand God's mission as it is revealed in his Trinitarian history."¹¹⁰

According to the Scriptures, God is not a static being, removed from creation. Nor does God exist as a solitary being, but as a being in communion. The biblical God has a communal identity and as such relates to the world. God's action in the world is always the action of the Triune God.¹¹¹ The persons of the Trinity always work in unity and cooperation: the Father sends his Son to save the world through the power of the Holy Spirit. He reconciles the world by the power of the Holy Spirit through the death and resurrection of the Son. The implication is clear: God can be known only as

---

105. Badcock, *Light of Truth and Fire of Love*, 185.

106. Eberhard Jüngel provides us with a great example of this kind of theology. He conceives of the Holy Spirit as the unity in love of the Father with the crucified Son. Jüngel, *God as the Mystery of the World*, 386–76.

107. Badcock, *Light of Truth*, 185.

108. Costas, *Liberating*, 24.

109. Ibid., 27.

110. Costas, *Christ Outside*, 88.

111. This statement shows Costas' acceptance of Augustine's principle according to which the Trinitarian works of God in the world are undivided.

a Triune God. In a similar fashion, the identity of Jesus Christ, evangelization and the gospel itself, have to be understood in light of the work of the Triune God in the world.[112]

The gospel, then, is the story of the sending of the only begotten Son of the Father to redeem the world. This is the foundation of God's very existence: the Father's holy love and the Son's loving obedience. The climax of such expressions of love is the cross of Christ. "The cross discloses God's identity as the holy loving Father and as the loving and obedient Son. . . . The cross can make sense only in light of the Father's holy love delivering the Son for the world and the Son's loving obedience in offering himself to the Father through the eternal Spirit."[113] But the gospel is not only the story of the sending of the Son by the Father to redeem the world. It is also the story of the Holy Spirit bringing the world to God through the Son for the glory of the Father. Through the Spirit, who is known as God in action, are the sending of the Son and, in fact, his whole work accomplished.

> Indeed, Jesus' identification with the world on behalf of the Father in his birth, baptism, and ministry; his suffering death as the Father's atoning offering for sin and the Father's true representative of the world who took upon himself the sins of the world; and his victorious resurrection, which confirmed the reconciliation of the world and set in motion a new creation—all of these aspects of the mission of Christ were accomplished by the power of the Spirit.[114]

This parabolic or chiastic model, as Catherine Mowry LaCugna calls it, is a great picture to illustrate the one ecstatic movement of God, from whom all things originate, through Christ in the power of the Spirit, and to whom all things return into union with God; from the Father to the Father.[115] This model provides the ground for a truly communitarian type of Trinitarian theology. "Christology is no more prominent than pneumatology. Nor is the immanent Trinity thought to be separate from the economy of salvation. United here are *theologia*, the mystery of God, and *oikonomia*, the mystery of redemption."[116]

Only within this historical framework can we begin to understand God. The Triune God must be conceived not fundamentally in terms of metaphysical categories, apart from history, but rather in terms of God's

---

112. Costas, *Liberating*, 24.
113. Ibid, 75.
114. Ibid., 75–76.
115. La Cugna, *God for Us*, 222–23.
116. Peters, *God as Trinity*, 72–73.

manifestation in history. Since God's mission is not grounded on metaphysical speculation and theoretical abstractions in the style of Greek philosophies, but rather on historical deeds, the outcome of any theological reflection also has to be practical in nature. "This is . . . the reason why I am motivated not by a theoretical but by a practical and pastoral concern."[117] Costas' final goal in his theological work is to understand the implications of God's Trinitarian activity in history for the church's task today.

Turning our reflection more toward the history of God's relation to his people, Costas finds that there is a basic theme in the Scriptures that encapsulates God's identity and mission. "The Bible states that 'God is love' (1 John. 4:8). God's relationships with the world are based on this affirmation."[118] The Old Testament presents Yahweh in a special relationship with Israel. At the root of that relationship, however, is God's interest in the well-being of all nations. It is true that Yahweh is the shepherd, the progenitor, the provider, and the protector of Israel (Ps 23; Isa 40:11; Ezek 34:12; Isa 43:1ff.; 44:2ff.; 66:1); however, the background of this parenthood is creation, in which Yahweh is revealed as the creator and sustainer of all humanity. God's plan includes the whole of humanity, and Israel is a prototype of the new humanity that God wants to create.

There is, according to the New Testament, a type of correspondence between Israel and Jesus of Nazareth. Jesus is the authentic Israelite (Matt 2:15) and the only one who fulfills the mission entrusted to Israel (Mark 1:8–11; John 1:49ff.; Luke 1:31–33, 76–77; Heb 1:1–4) because he is the man in whom God's eternal Word became flesh (John 1:14). As such, he is not only the model for the people of God but also the way to God. Those who follow him are born to a new life (John 1:12), are incorporated into the people of God, and are made to be his body.[119]

At the heart of God's relation to the world is the Father's love manifested by the Spirit. This is the same Spirit that

> "moved over the face of the waters" at creation (Gen 1:2); the breath that gave life to Adam's body (Gen 2:7); the power that rested on Israel and its leaders in times of national crisis and that fertilized the womb of the humble virgin (Luke 1:35) so that she could be the bearer of the Son of God; that enabled Jesus to offer himself to the Father as a perfect sacrifice for the sins of the

---

117. Costas, *Christ Outside*, 88.
118. Ibid., 88–89.
119. Ibid., 89.

world (Heb. 9:14) and by whose power Jesus was raised from the dead (Rom 1:4).[120]

The Spirit is the agent of God in creation and also the agent of love that the Father has revealed in the Son. The Spirit is the agent of God's love to men and women everywhere in the world. "The focus of the Spirit's work in the world finds its goal precisely in the reconciliation of all created things under the lordship of the Son and for the glory of the Father (Eph 1:14)."[121]

Yet, the Spirit's special function within the mission of God is eschatological. Jesus fulfills his ministry in the power of the Spirit (Luke 4:14ff.; Mark 1:8, 12, 14–15; Matt 3:16–17), and the content of that ministry is the proclamation of the kingdom of God. "This proclamation is not a mere reminder of God's sovereignty over all creation. On the contrary, something totally new is happening here: the eruption of a new era, a new order of life, the new creation. This messianic 'newness' is made possible by the death and resurrection of Jesus;"[122] by the power of the Spirit.[123]

This line of thinking is the basis for the affirmation that the mission of God, which is also the mission of the church, is both historical and eschatological. "The fact that it has as its goal the final consummation of the kingdom and that it is transcendentalized in the hope of new heavens and a new earth does not mean that this mission is either atemporal or beyond history. On the contrary, it is a mission whose stage is history."[124] It is a mission that has historical foundation and therefore promotes a historical hope: a redeemed creation without hate, chaos, or corruption; a redeemed creation in a world full of love, justice, freedom, and peace. This brings us back to the subject of the kingdom of God. In connection with the notion of the mission of the Triune God, the kingdom also acquires a Trinitarian dimension.

> The kingdom serves as the frame of reference for the mission of God. His working in history, as we have noted, is made known by the conclusive revelation of his liberating purpose and by the consistent denial of all tendencies that counter his will. The

---

120. Ibid.

121. Ibid., 89–90.

122. Ibid., 90.

123. Perhaps, more than from Augustine, Costas' influence comes from Pannenberg, who conceives of the Spirit as the dynamic field which unites the three persons of the Trinity and also as the uniting force between God and creation. See Kärkkäinen, "The Working of the Spirit of God in Creation and in the People of God," 94.

124. Costas, *Christ Outside*, 90.

participation of the People of God in his mission will have to be directed, therefore, by the message of the kingdom.[125]

The previous discussion provides a Trinitarian foundation for Costas' theology of mission. Costas establishes the identity of God as a being in communion and, in connection to that, the indivisibility of the Trinitarian actions in creation. He also affirms that the immanent Trinity is the economic Trinity and that the Father is the origin and the culmination of a process of sending and receiving through the Son and the Spirit to and from the world. Thus, God relates to the world through the Son and by the Spirit. The conditions have been established for an adequate Trinitarian Christology; let us see if it becomes a reality.

The Spirit and the Word in Creation and in Redemption

The Spirit is the uniting member of the Trinity,[126] the connecting link between the Father and the Son. The Spirit unites the community of faith with the Son and makes the unity of the world with God possible. The Holy Spirit's reconciling activity is the hidden force that unites the world with Father and Son in the all-embracing love of their eternal community.[127] But if the Spirit's reconciling action is the power of evangelization, the cross of the Son is its mediating sign.

The reconciling action of the Spirit does not take place isolated from creation.[128] Nor is it limited to the inner life of believers. "The sphere of action of the Spirit in evangelization is history, the concrete history of women and men."[129] The Spirit's work in individuals or a community expresses itself in their practical life, in society, in the transformation of their reality.

To speak of hope for a new world without engaging in concrete attempts to make this world a better place to live in is to deny that very hope; indeed, it is to escape into a vague and otherworldly abstraction that paralyzes the transforming force of the eschatological mission of the gospel and

---

125. Ibid., 91.

126. Here also Costas identifies with the Augustinian Trinitarian model.

127. Once again, this is a clear reference to Pannenberg's understanding of the Spirit as the uniting force within the Trinitarian life and between God and the world.

128. This clarification is important for the purpose of a more holistic understanding of the mission of the church. Much of the traditional theology has been individualistic in nature, limiting the action of God to the individual and to the sphere of the church, which in turn isolates the church from the world.

129. Costas, *Liberating*, 79.

ends up sacralizing the status quo. Hope for the transformation of the world without liberating action in the world is blasphemy.[130]

In our effort to give an account of Costas' theology of mission, we are looking for signs to help us understand his notion of God and, therefore, his notion of Christ. The relevance which the Spirit has taken in his work is clear up to this point. Although the framework adopted is valid—the Spirit as the uniting member of the Trinity—in the Augustinian tradition, not much is said about the Son. What is the role of the Son in creation and in redemption? Could it be that this "uniting member of the Trinity," acting in the name of and for the sake of the entire Trinity, obscures the other members of the Trinity, especially the Son, leaving the Son with a reduced role to play? Let us see if such is really the case for Costas.

The Triune God works through the action of the Spirit both in creation and redemption. Every aspect of God's work, from creation to consummation, is related to the action of the Spirit.[131] The Spirit is the wellspring, the energy, and the ground of life.[132] "This assertion proceeds from the conviction of biblical faith that the Divine Spirit is the Breath (*ruach*) that gives life, generates energy, and fills the needs of the world."[133] As the giver of new life, the Holy Spirit is the power of God in creation and redemption.[134]

The Spirit is the creator in action. While it is true that the heavens were made by the Word of the Lord (Ps 33:6), it is also true that the Word of God acts by the creative power of God's breath. "The Spirit is the energy of the Word; the Word acts by the Spirit."[135] The activity of the Spirit, as the giver of life, in creation is not limited to the very act of creation. The Spirit's work includes an ongoing creative process that renews the created order. This picture discloses the Spirit as the unceasing and dynamic communica-

---

130. Ibid., 79–80.

131. Could we say the same thing about the action of the Son and of the Father?

132. See Moltmann, *God in Creation*, 11 ff.; also Pannenberg's field theory of the Spirit by which the Spirit is the principle of the immanence of God in creation.

133. Costas, *Liberating*, 121.

134. The association of creation and redemption in Costas' theology is an emphasis that has a long history. In one of his initial writings, Costas wanted to make that point. "In the Bible, God introduces himself to us as Creator and as Redeemer. . . . Creation is an event that reveals the loving grace of God and finds its fulfillment in redemption. In other words, God's purpose in creation is redemptive." Costas, *La iglesia y su misión evangelizadora*, 27–28. This association has profound theological implications, especially important for evangelical theology and mission. If creation relates to redemption, then our missionary activity must also include the whole world. If creation relates to redemption, then this world becomes significant and has to do with our understanding of both the nature and the mission of the church.

135. Costas, *Liberating*, 122.

christ and liberation

tor upon every element and process of the material universe, the imminent and anonymous presence of God in the world.[136]

The Bible also gives witness to the Spirit as the restorer of the world. The Spirit is the restorer of the world in action. The Spirit is mentioned in connection with the salvation of Israel in very concrete circumstances. The Spirit of God is the liberating power of God revealed in the exodus event and the restoration from the exile.[137] The Spirit is also the power of the future, revealing the shalom of the messianic kingdom and the transformation of the earth. With this background the New Testament refers to the role of the Spirit in redemption. Here the Spirit's work appears intimately related to the person and work of the Messiah. Jesus himself appears as claiming the messianic Spirit upon his life and ministry. His death, resurrection, and continuing presence in history occur in connection with the Spirit.[138]

Costas makes a crucial point here when he says that the redemptive work of the Spirit and the person and work of the Messiah are intimately related. In reference to the role of the Word and the Spirit in creation he says that the Spirit is the energy of the Word and that the Word acts by the Spirit. These are key declarations that affirm the relational nature of God and his work in the world.

This takes us to the question of the identity of Jesus Christ. According to Costas, Jesus' identity is defined both in reference to his history as a Jew from Galilee and also in reference to his relationship to his Father, through the Spirit of God. Just as the identity of Jesus Christ can be understood only in reference to his particular history, so also his identity must be understood in reference to the history of the Triune God revealed to us in historical space and time. Both a historical and a Trinitarian framework are necessary to understand Christ's life, work, cross, resurrection, current work in the world, and future *parousia*.

The question of the unity of Jesus with God must be explained with a Trinitarian framework and eschatological key. In the New Testament "the deity of Jesus is expressed in the context of his particular relation with the Father and the Spirit. Jesus was possessed by the Spirit in his ministry and lived a life of total dependence on the Father."[139]

According to this view, the divine identity of Jesus depends on his relation with the Father and the Spirit. Therefore, it is as the Son of the Father that Jesus is called God. He is called God only in the context of the

---

136. Ibid., 122.
137. What about the action of the Son in the history of Israel?
138. Costas, *Liberating*, 123.
139. Costas, *Christ Outside*, 19.

Trinitarian fellowship. Such unity and, then, the divine identity of Jesus, are affirmed in the resurrection, "according to the Spirit."[140]

The New Testament distinguishes between the Spirit *in* Jesus and the Spirit *of* the risen Christ. When the New Testament talks about the Spirit *in* Jesus, it implies that he was a person full of God, which is a witness to the presence of God in human history. Such a statement also suggests that Jesus was obedient to the Spirit, demonstrating his faithfulness to God. As a result, he became the partner through whom a new humanity could be created; he became the true mediator of salvation. When the New Testament talks about the Spirit *of* Jesus, the implication is that he became not only the exalted Messiah but especially the life-giving Spirit, the Pneumatic Christ. In a word, he was made one with the Spirit. Christ and the Spirit, however, do not lose their proper identities. In evangelistic work, for example, the Spirit uses the prophetic and apostolic Word to impart new life to the world, and the Spirit calls people to Christ and empowers them for a new life.[141]

A person participates in this messianic reality by faith in Christ and in so doing is freed from the power of sin, experiences a new life, becomes part of the messianic community, commits to the cause of freedom, justice, and peace, and shares in the hope of new heavens and a new earth. Faith in Christ is verified in the development of a messianic lifestyle, active involvement in the messianic community, and participation in the struggle for a just and peaceful world in anticipation of the promised new heavens and new earth. Therefore, the messianic community, the church, is the result of the action of the Spirit.[142] "The church is thus that portion of humanity who experiences God's grace in Christ made present by the Spirit. And because of this, the church is called to witness to the world about her marvelous experience in Jesus Christ."[143] The church is the "first fruits" of the new creation. The church is the instrument of God's mission to the world. The church is the community sent by Christ to the world, in the power of the Spirit, to operate the miracle of the new creation.[144]

The new order of life can be seen in any transformation that takes place within history, as long as it points in the direction of the kingdom, that is, as long as it shows the signs of the new order of life: love, justice, freedom, and messianic peace. The new order of life, however, is not easy to discern. "Just as wheat and chaff grow together, so signs of the new order appear in the

---

140. Ibid.
141. Costas, *Liberating*, 124.
142. Costas, *Christ Outside*, 90.
143. Costas, *The Church and Its Mission*, 8.
144. Ibid., 57.

middle of contradictory situations and thus make it very difficult at times to distinguish clearly between a real signal and a short circuit."[145] In other words, social and political justice and the structural and cosmic liberation, implicit in salvation, are not clearly perceptible in history. "Justice and liberation, as aspects of the Gospel, can only be verified eschatologically."[146] But we know that in the present, by the action of Christ through the Spirit, there are historical anticipations of the eschatological future. For that reason we do not have to wait until the second coming of Christ to discern the justice of the kingdom and the liberating power of the gospel active in the social and political structures of society. As long as an action dignifies human life and promotes justice, peace, and fraternity, that action becomes a manifestation (though partial) of the salvific power of the gospel.[147] Therefore, in our evangelistic and missionary activities we have to discern the "signs of the times" through the Holy Spirit's guidance and by the orientation of the Word of God.[148]

Only when we understand God's activity as the creator and sustainer of life, as the ground and starting point of Christian mission, are we being faithful to the gospel. The implications are immense. First of all, we need to recognize all aspects of life as the sphere of evangelization. No space of life should be left out of the province of evangelization.[149]

The Triune God is present everywhere making evangelization possible. By this approach, a clear connection between creation and redemption can be appreciated. Second, suffering is incorporated within the divinity, in the cross of Jesus Christ. In this manner, suffering becomes a key missiological referent. Third, the Spirit's action in the world produces reconciliation: the world with itself and the world with God. Such reconciliation takes place in history and expresses itself in the transformation of lives and communities, in hope of a final transformation of creation.[150]

Based on such theological foundation, Costas proposes a definition of evangelization. To evangelize is

> to reproduce, by the power of the Holy Spirit, the salvation that has been revealed in Jesus Christ. This reproductive activity is carried out by means of testimonies and signs that point to the transforming action of the kingdom of God proclaimed and

145. Costas, *Christ Outside*, 91.
146. Costas, "Pecado y salvación en América Latina," 279.
147. Ibid.
148. Costas, *Christ Outside*, 91.
149. Costas, *Liberating*, 123.
150. Ibid., 83–87.

> embodied by Jesus, anticipated in the experience of the Spirit, and consummated "eschatologically" in the new creation that has begun with the resurrection of Christ.... The fundamental elements in evangelization are love, faith, and hope incarnated in a ministry dedicated to the transformation of the world.[151]

Costas' theology of evangelization has been developed based on a profound Trinitarian theology. Such a foundation provides the basis for a Trinitarian understanding of Christ and also of the Spirit. Our question is, does he do justice to both the Word and the Spirit in his effort? Does Costas portray the action of God in the world as the action of both Word and Spirit in correlation? Our impression is that, in his effort to recover the role of the Spirit, Costas not only pays more attention to the Spirit but also gives a larger role to the Spirit to the point that the Son appears almost subordinated to the Spirit. We have highlighted some passages where Costas emphasizes the relationship of Word and Spirit, but the overall impression is that the Spirit is the main character in this drama.

Final Remarks

Reflecting on Costas' theological work, Plutarco Bonilla concludes that Jesus Christ was the center of Costas' thought.

> The Gospel is the Gospel of Jesus Christ. The church is the church of Jesus Christ. The mission is the mission of Jesus Christ. If I am allowed to put it this way I would say that the unique character of Jesus Christ is a nonnegotiable of his theology. That means that Jesus' life, his death, resurrection and glorification also have a unique and unrepeatable meaning, especially in relation to evangelization as the announcement of salvation.[152]

Bonilla recognizes, however, that the central focus of his theological reflection was the mission of the church. Yet Costas' understanding of the mission of the church, suggests Bonilla, goes through an evolution as the theme of the kingdom of God becomes more prominent in his thought.[153] Bonilla ends his essay mentioning that mission, as the mission of the Triune God, is another important motif in Costas' thought. Bonilla does not elaborate on the issue. However, after our analysis, Bonilla's suggestion seems to be confirmed. We also find that Costas' thought suffers a subtle but signifi-

---

151. Ibid., 133.
152. Bonilla, "Viaje de ida y vuelta," 57.
153. Ibid., 69.

cant shift. It moves from being a theology centered on Christ to a theology where the Spirit acquires prominence. The notion of the kingdom appears in the midst of that evolution and plays well to both sides. If in his early writing the Word incarnated in Jesus Christ is the center of attention, in his later writings, especially in *Liberating News,* the Spirit receives considerably more attention and prominence. The Spirit appears as the commander in God's missionary activity in the world. Everything God does in the world, from creation to consummation, is related to the action of the Spirit. The Spirit of God is the power of God, in creation and redemption. The Spirit is the energy of the Word; the Word acts by the Spirit. The Spirit is the one who commands Jesus' life and destiny. The Spirit, not the Word, seems to give Jesus his identity.

We conclude that in his earlier writings Costas establishes a more balanced relationship between the Word and the Spirit. Later, although he has the elements to develop a rich Trinitarian Christology, and for that matter, a rich Trinitarian pneumatology, he loses the necessary balance.

CONCLUSION

If there is a constant in the analysis of these two theologians, it is a tendency toward movement. There are several movements, horizontal and vertical, in Padilla's and Costas's writings that express the nature of their work and contribution. Let us consider those movements.

The first movement goes from mission to Christology to mission. They begin their theological work from the mission reality of the church. Mission motivates Christology, and Christology is produced for the sake of the obedience of faith in the world, that is, for mission. The movement becomes ascendant as long as a new image of Christ moves the church toward new forms of missionary activity in the world, which also motivates new questionings and new understandings of Christ.

The second movement operates in a similar fashion: from Scriptures to faith to mission/ethics. This movement has to do with theological method, and it complements the previous one. The hermeneutics and theological method proposed and followed by these authors include in a circular way the following elements: the context of mission, the worldview of the theological community (including traditions, notions, values, etc.), the Scriptures, and finally, theology. Although the Scriptures are the norm for the church, we always start from our particular situations and realities. That is why our theologies are always contextual.

The next movement goes from above to below to above. The question of the identity of Jesus Christ does not fit necessarily within just one of the two options. Although both authors value and emphasize the historical Jesus, both also do theology from above. To them, God is in Christ, and both consider that the incarnation of the Son of God is crucial to recovering a balanced understanding of the world and the mission of the church in the world. However, both authors want to give due attention to the history of Jesus Christ in his particular context: social, political, and economical. Such context defines Jesus' life and ministry, and as such, our own.

The next movement goes from the Logos, to the Spirit, to the Trinity. Padilla and Costas transition from a theology fundamentally Christological, without denying the Trinity, toward a theology more articulated in a Trinitarian fashion. Costas and Padilla are different in this regard. Padilla rarely mentions the Spirit in his first works, and when he does, it is mainly in reference to the reading and appropriation of the Scriptures. Later he makes the case for a theology of mission from a Trinitarian perspective. Costas gives more attention to the Spirit in his first works, and the Spirit becomes a preeminent figure in his system, to the point that the Spirit seems to opaque the Word.

The final movement goes from God to the world to God. This is the missionary movement, especially as developed by Costas. The mission belongs to God, and God takes the initiative and moves to the world and creation. He then brings the world back to himself in redemption by the action of the Word and the Spirit.

PART 3
The Holy Spirit and The Church

7

The Church as Pneumatic Community: Toward an Ecclesiology for the African Context

Isaac Zokoué (Central African Republic)

"THE HOLY SPIRIT AND the Church" is a subject which, seen from the angle of systematic theology, combines two themes that are commonly treated separately, namely, pneumatology (doctrine of the Holy Spirit), and ecclesiology (doctrine of the church). Just as it is not allowed to confuse the person of Jesus Christ with his work, so it is right to study separately the doctrines of the Holy Spirit and that of the church which he gave birth to. But the message of salvation and its proclamation around the world constitute an indissoluble whole that reflects the image of the Trinitarian God who is One. From this line of reasoning, it is pertinent to maintain a dynamic bond between the Holy Spirit, third person of the Trinity, and the church, the body of Christ, that started at Pentecost.

But the combination of pneumatology and ecclesiology in the same study is not supported only theologically. It is also dictated by the nature of the two events that occurred at Pentecost, namely, the coming of the Holy Spirit, and the birth of the church which immediately ensued. We have here, two intrinsically interlocking events, but the second can only be understood through the first. In the same divine breath, the Holy Spirit, who proceeds from the Father and the Son, appeared in the world and inaugurated the church era. From that point on, it is not advisable to separate the church from its Trinitarian source, and to treat it as a simple institutional and sociological entity. It exists and is built by the work of the Holy Spirit.

Another fundamental element justifies the joint treatment of the Holy Spirit and the church: it is the choice by God of the Day of Pentecost to carry out this double event. Pentecost was a Jewish holiday commemorating the gift of the Ten Commandments by God to Moses. It is precisely at the time when God's people assembled to celebrate the divine commands that God chose to give birth to the new Israel on the foundation of his word, namely, the Christ that Peter proclaimed on that day. It is the acknowledgement of Jesus as Christ, the Son of the living God, that day which became the foundation of the church, and all this happened by the work of the Holy Spirit through the preaching of Peter. The symbolism is striking. For, in order to create this unique event in the history of salvation, God took hold of the Jewish Pentecost, transformed it into a Christian Pentecost and gave birth to the church. Before that, it was the Jewish Passover that Christ, during the Pascal meal, transformed into Christian Easter. In both cases, we see at the same time, rupture, continuity, and progress. We see rupture in reference to Passover, because by offering himself as a sacrifice, Jesus put an end to the sacrifices of the old covenant whose victims were only animals. We also see continuity because it was indeed a sacrifice. And there is progress because the victim is Christ himself, who lay down his life *once and for all*. The same process is repeated with respect to the coming of the Holy Spirit and the birth of the church. Indeed, the coming of the Holy Spirit puts an end to the preeminence of the two Tables of the Law, because from now on, God wrote his law in the hearts and not on a material matter. However, there are also continuity and progress, because the law is not abolished but fulfilled by Christ. Thus, the Holy Spirit uses the word of God, this word that he had himself inspired, to give birth to and sustain the church.

THE HOLY SPIRIT AND THE PEOPLE OF GOD BEFORE THE PENTECOST

The Holy Spirit and the People of the Old Covenant

God's people under the Old Covenant constantly profited from the work of the Holy Spirit throughout all their history. But they were also recipients of

God's promises concerning the future works of the Holy Spirit. Because the Old Covenant was only the shadow of things to come, the Holy Spirit could not exhibit his works entirely during that dispensation. It was necessary to wait for the Messianic era. Hence, as far as the Holy Spirit is concerned, the Old Testament contains promises made to God's people—not only his ancient people who were still under the law, but also and more especially his new people, i.e. the church.

The Old Testament announced what the Holy Spirit was going to do in the New Testament. In Israel, the Holy Spirit made use of men and women, individually or in group, to carry out particular missions. But this dimension of the work of the Holy Spirit within the people of Israel will not be evoked here. We want to limit ourselves to some promises, to show how they went beyond Israel as God's people, to aim at future actions of the Holy Spirit in the church. My purpose in this survey is to stress the unity of God's plan for his people. Indeed, there is only one Spirit and only one God's people, if one recognizes Abraham as the father of all the believers (Rom 4:16–25). Furthermore, the image of the branch of the wild olive tree grafted into the good olive tree (Rom 11:24) clearly shows that for Paul, there are not two kinds of God's people—an old that is different from a new—but only one kind of people in a spiritual continuity.

Here are some examples of prophecies that link the Holy Spirit with the church:

Moses Asked God to Give his Spirit to all the People of Israel

In Numbers 11:25, an event similar to that of Pentecost occurred. In this passage we see the Spirit of God resting on the group of seventy elders of Israel who gathered around the tent of meeting. They began to prophesy, including two who were absent, Eldad and Midad, because they were in the camp but who received this blessing simply because their names were on the list drawn up by Moses. But according to Joshua, Moses' assistant since his adolescence, only Moses had the quality of prophet; the others were to remain silent. Yet Moses' reaction to Joshua's remarks reveals God's plan for his people: "Are you jealous for my sake?" Said Moses, "I wish that all God's people were prophets and that the Lord would put his Spirit on them!" (Num 11:29). Here clearly Moses expresses the wish that the gift of the Holy Spirit be not limited to some privileged few, but that it be granted to all God's people. This statement, springing from within Moses' heart, before the settlement of Israel in Canaan, is itself a prophecy which concerns not the natural descendants of Israel but, prospectively, "the children of the promise" (Rom 9:6–8).

Isaiah Prophesies on the Coming of the Holy Spirit

In the midst of Israel's desolation, prophet Isaiah announces future restoration of the nation. Misfortune will last, he proclaims, "till the Spirit is poured upon us from on high . . ." (Isa 32:15). The expression "poured from on high" brings to mind the effusion of the Holy Spirit at Pentecost; and "upon us" evokes God's people which will be the recipients of this grace. "His Spirit will gather them together," so that "none of these will be missing" (Isa 34:16). God shows mercy toward his people and, in tender and reassuring terms, promises them his Spirit: "Do not afraid, O Jacob my servant, Jeshurun, whom I have chosen. For I will pour water on the thirsty land, and streams on the dry grounds. I will pour out my spirit on your offspring and my blessing on your descendants" (Isa 44:2–3). It is a promise without discrimination; it is for the entire people of God. The colorful language, which compares the Spirit of God with water and brooks, will be used again by Jesus in John 7:38–39 on the subject of "the Spirit, whom those who believed in him were later to receive." The church is in the background of this promise which crisscrosses the two Testaments.

The Prophecy of Joel, a Projection of Pentecost

The wish of Moses for God's people becomes a firm and explicit promise in the prophecy of Joel: "I will pour out my Spirit on all people." (Joel 2:28–29). It is about God's people in all their dimensions: generational and social, males and females, old and young, male and female servants. This list is undoubtedly given as an indication that no social category, no generation, no gender will be kept away from the gift of the Holy Spirit. The prophecy gives a configuration which brings to mind the makeup of the church itself. Peter's preaching on the Day of Pentecost will be based on this prophecy and will establish the link between Israel and the church. Thus, the Holy Spirit and the church is a topic that is already present in the Old Testament. It is by his Spirit that God is present among his people, whether he works in them or through them. That was the case at the time of Israel, and has continued to be so during the age of the church.

Jesus' teaching on the Holy Spirit

After his death and the resurrection, and his return to the Father, Jesus' work continued by the Holy Spirit. And since Jesus Christ himself is the plenitude of the divine revelation, he has, during his earthly ministry, revealed what was going to be the mission of the Holy Spirit in the world: he will do the work of regeneration, illumination, and sanctification.

In his teaching, Jesus closely binds the Holy Spirit to the church. Admittedly, he did not explicitly mention the church as such; but the content of his teaching makes sense and can be implemented only in the context of a church community—a teaching which takes account of the great declaration of Caesarea Philippi: "I will build my church" (Matt 16:18). In fact, as Jesus mad his way the cross, he was preparing at the same time the disciples to become, not only the first recipients of the salvation, but also witnesses in the world of the redeeming work that he accomplished. This preparation proceeded on two axes: the announcement of the creation of the church, the community which he will call out of the world to constitute his people, and the announcement of the Comforter that he will send to keep this community alive. And as his physical separation from the disciples became imminent, he made an ultimate revelation to them: "And surely I am with you always, to the very end of the age" (Matt 28:20). Jesus Christ, builder of the church is present among his people by the Holy Spirit. This, in essence, is what the Master had planned as the continuation of the plan of salvation after his death and his resurrection.

The Sending of the Holy Spirit by the Father and the Son

In the Gospel according to John, it is during the last discussions with his disciples that Jesus spoke abundantly about the Holy Spirit. On several occasions, it was a question of the sending of the Holy Spirit; but in each occasion, he insisted on the fact that the Father and the Son are both at the origin of this decision. It is sometimes the Father who sends, but on the request of the Son (John 14:16) or in the name of the Son (John 14:26). Sometimes, it is the Son who sends, but on behalf of the Father (John 15:26). However, when he presented his departure as a prerequisite to the coming of the Holy Spirit, Jesus spoke only on his behalf. This double language has theological significance. Indeed, Jesus reveals initially that the Holy Spirit proceeds at the same time from the Father and the Son; thus he has a divine personality, distinct from the personality of the Father and the Son. In second place, he indicates that the Holy Spirit is in a more immediate relation to the Son, since he comes to continue the work of the Son. In other words, Jesus introduces in his speech the person and the work of the Holy Spirit.

The Sending of the Counselor to the Disciples

In his discourse to the disciples, Jesus mentions the Holy Spirit παράκλητος (paraklêtos). This Greek word comes from the verb παρακαλέω, whose first meaning is *to call near to oneself, to call for help*. *Paraklêtos* means: lawyer, defender, intercessor, helper, supporter, adviser. Some French versions of the Bible translate it by Comforter—he who provides relief. The various meanings of this word convey the idea of assistance to a person in difficulty or in need. The Holy Spirit is sent to *the disciples* in his capacity as *Paraclete* to bring them assistance.

Several passages show that the Holy Spirit is promised to the disciples, and by extension to all those who share their faith. They are, in a broad sense, Jesus' disciples, and they, exclusively, will welcome the *Paraclete* upon his coming.

- Luke 24:49. "I am going to send *you* . . . . But [*you*] remain in the city until *you* have been clothed with power from on high."
- John 14:16. "And I will ask the Father, and he will give *you* another Counselor to be *with you* forever . . ."
- John 14:17a. ". . . the Spirit of truth. The world cannot accept him because it neither sees him nor knows him . . . ." In other words, the world will have no part in the coming of the Holy Spirit. But on the other hand,
- John 14:17b. "But *you* know him, for he lives with you, and will be *in you*."
- John 14:26. "But the Counselor . . . *will teach you* all things. And *he will remind you of everything I have said to you.*"
- John 15:26. "When the Counselor comes, whom I will send to you from the Father . . ."
- John 16:7. "It is for your good that I am going away. Unless I go away, the Counselor will not come to you, but if I go, I will send him to you."
- John 16:13. "But when he, the Spirit of truth, comes, he will guide you into all truth; . . . he will tell you what is yet to come."
- John 16:14. ". . . taking from what is mine and making it known to you."

- Acts 1:8. *"you will receive power when the Holy Spirit comes on you; and you will be witnesses..."*

Reading again these passages, one might conclude several things: the Holy Spirit comes to live among the believers. He comes to stay with them, to stay eternally with them, to dwell in them, and to communicate to them the life of Christ, to clothe them with power, to teach them all things, to remind them of the Master's teaching, to lead them in all the truth, to announce them the things that are to come. This is his mission of regeneration, illumination, and sanctification. And the framework of this mission is the totality of the disciples confessing the same Lord, and sharing the same community of life, i.e. the church.

Another dimension of the work of the Holy Spirit is revealed by Christ in John 16: 8–11. There is in this passage a remarkable symbiosis between the work of the Holy Spirit and that of Christ. It is on the basis of the work of Christ that the Holy Spirit will act to convince the world. "When he comes, he will convict the world of guilt in regard to sin and righteousness and judgment." It is worth elaborating on this text:

- "... in regard to sin, because men do not believe in me." First of all, the world does not believe in the Son of God; this is the sin. By not believing in Jesus, people pass a false judgment about the work of salvation achieved by him. To be saved, they must be convinced that only Jesus is the Savior of the world.

- "... in regard to righteousness, because I am going to Father where you can no longer see me ...." In its unbelief, the world rejects Christ and his plan of salvation, whereas it is he who has fulfilled the righteousness of God, and went back to the Father in heaven, thus removed from people's sight. The warm welcome that is awaiting him in heaven proves that his sacrifice is approved by the Father, and that he is from now on our righteousness. People must be convinced about the truth.

- "... in regard to judgment, because the prince of this world now stands condemned." The triumphal return of Jesus to the Father shows that the judgment of the prince of this world has taken effect. The world must know that its prince is definitively condemned, and that there is nothing any more to be expected of him.

It is important to discern in the words of Jesus the final purpose of the work of the Holy Spirit: to take action for the salvation of those who would thus believe. Because the reasoning is such, the sinner should have no other choices but to believe in Jesus. This is why to resist the Holy Spirit is an unforgivable sin; because the refusal to convince oneself of this comes down to locking oneself in one's sin and to suffer all the consequences of that choice.

But what are the means the Holy Spirit will use to convince the world? It is here that we find the disciples. Their role in this undertaking will be paramount. "You will receive power, the Holy Spirit comes on you. . . . And you will be witnesses . . . to the ends of the earth" (Acts 1:8). It is thus through the disciples that the Holy Spirit will convince the world to believe in Jesus. The same truth is expressed when Christ declares that he will build his church, and that he will entrust to Peter, a man and one of the disciples, the keys of the kingdom. The church that Christ will build will be a living church, conquering and victorious, because "the gates of hades will not overcome it" (Matt 16:18). It is the church that is the context within which the Holy Spirit will act, because it is intended to welcome believers, to support them, and to build them up. Indeed, God did not plan on leaving men and women who would be convicted by the Holy Spirit, he gathers them together within a new life setting, in his "house" (1 Tim 3:15), in order to better care for them. This is why the church is at the center of the mission of the Holy Spirit in the world.

Jesus is Present in the Church Through the Holy Spirit

In his discourse to the disciples, as he reassures them of the permanent presence of the Comforter that the Father will give them, Jesus made an unexpected statement: "I will not leave you as orphans, I will come to you" (John 14:18). The coming of the Holy Spirit to the disciples will coincide with Jesus' own coming to the disciples. In his remarks, it is about an invisible presence, because the world will no longer see him. However, he will be seen by the disciples, "On that day you will realize I am in my Father, and you are in me, and I am in you" (14:20). More precisely still: "If anyone loves me . . . my Father will love him, and we will come to him and make our home with him" (14:23). He repeated the same message to the disciples just before ascension: "And surely, I am with you always, to the very end of the age" (Matt 28:20).

What one needs to understand, after all, is that the Holy Spirit does not come alone to the disciples; he does not come alone to remain in them. His coming paves the way for the Father and the Son also to dwell in the believer. Therefore, the Holy Spirit gives birth to the church, which becomes at the same time the body of Christ. The debate between charismatic believers and non-charismatic on the baptism of the Holy Spirit, should take into account the fact that it is not possible for somebody to become a Christian, i.e., to be in Christ and for Christ to be in him (John 14:18) without the regenerative action of the Holy Spirit. It is the Holy Spirit who convicts the sinners, prepares their hearts to receive the Lord Jesus, and finally the whole Trinity. The baptismal formula "in the name of the Father, of the Son and of the Holy Ghost" is the expression which attests to an authentic conversion. To say that the Holy Spirit intervenes in the life of the believer afterwards, after conversion, by a special experience called "baptism of the Holy Spirit," is not in conformity with the teaching of Jesus-Christ on the Holy Spirit.

THE HOLY SPIRIT AND THE CHURCH AT THE PENTECOST

At Pentecost, the Holy Spirit Fulfills the Promises Made about Him

The Holy Spirit appeared into the world at Pentecost; and he fulfilled what Christ had said about him. In his demonstration, the Holy Spirit simultaneously provided the foundations of his actions in the church. The events of Pentecost are so rich that they should be treated point by point.

The Holy Spirit Came "From on High"

Isaiah had prophesied that the Spirit would be poured "from on high". This is what happened on the day of the Pentecost when, "suddenly a sound like the blowing of a violent wind *came from heaven*" (Acts 2:2). In this movement from top to bottom, there is obviously the intent to pinpoint the heavenly and divine origin of the Holy Spirit. Indeed, the event seems to be produced so that the witnesses could follow very well the trajectory of the noise in question, from heaven to the house, where the disciples were assembled. The Holy Spirit does not emerge from the bosom of humanity; he is not of earthly origin, and he cannot, therefore, be comparable to the spirits which haunt this world. He comes from heaven, "God's throne," and not from the earth, "his footstool" (Matt 5:34). Although we must be careful not to overstate the theological significance of this aspect of the event, the manner in which it is described deserves attention, because it is not devoid of a message. It confirms a prophecy which states clearly that it is God who pours his Spirit from on high upon his people.

The Holy Spirit Is Given to All the Disciples Without Exception

After the ascension, those who associated themselves with Jesus, and who were in Jerusalem, were estimated at one hundred twenty people (Acts 1:15). At Pentecost, a common Jewish feast, "they were all together in one place" (Acts 2:1). They saw what seemed to be tongues of fire that separated and came to rest on each of them. All of them were filled with the Holy Spirit" (Acts 2:3). As it is noted, the Holy Spirit was poured upon all hundred and twenty disciples, not only upon the twelve. Not only the prophecy of Joel concerning the pouring of the Spirit upon *all flesh* was fulfilled, but also the wish of Moses to see "all the people of the Lord being made up prophets" (Num. 11:25) was materialized. Peter declares in front of the believers of the Old Covenant, that what occurs before their eyes was the fulfillment of the Scriptures. All collectively were filled with Spirit. But before that, "they saw what seemed to be tongues of fire that separated and came to rest on each of them" (Acts 2:3). The Holy Spirit is given to all and to each one in particular. This means that the life that he brings is to be lived at the same time in a community and individually. At this stage of the event, the preparation for the birth of the church was on the way.

The Disciples Began to Speak Other Languages, as the Spirit Gave Them the Ability to Express Themselves

This account is about an experience of speaking other languages, and one should certainly not equate it with the spiritual gifts of tongue-speaking reported, for example, in 1 Corinthians 14. For according to Paul, "He who speaks in tongues edifies himself . . ." (v. 4). This was certainly not the case in the event of Pentecost. All the disciples belonged to the same language group. However, "a crowd came together in bewilderment, because each one heard them speaking in his own language. Utterly amazed, they asked 'Are not all these men who are speaking Galileans? Then how is it that each of us hears them in his own native language?'"(Acts 2:6–8). Beside the bestowal of the gift of tongues, the manifestation of the Spirit may have been intended to underscore the fact that salvation was opened to all the nations. The disciples were not to address this crowd only in Aramean or Hebrew, but to transmit to them the wonders of God in a language that each could understand—a language which penetrates their hearts and the fiber of their beings. And since, humanly speaking, that was impossible for them, the Holy Spirit enabled them to accomplish it. Thus, the Holy Spirit started to prepare the Jews and the proselytes present at the event to become, in turn, disciples. He started to mold them by putting in them a seed of the gospel.

At Pentecost, the Holy Spirit Reveals the Purposes of His Mission

Actually, in his sudden coming, the Holy Spirit did not dissociate his presence in the world with the purposes of his mission. In this event of extraordinary intensity which occurs in such a short period of time, there is a concentration of all that the Spirit comes to do in the world through the disciples.

Spiritual Gifts

By making the disciples able to speak in languages which, thus far, were foreign for them, the Holy Spirit shows that his mission consists in distributing gifts to believers. It is necessary to add to the gift of tongues that of preaching given to Peter on that day, when one remembers the disquieting past of this apostle. In his message, Peter evokes the prophecy of Joel to authenticate the divine character of the event which occurred; then he moves on quickly to the heart of the subject: Jesus of Nazareth. The fear of the Jews which Peter felt previously, was replaced by boldness with no common boundary. This situation fulfills the promise of the Lord that the disciples were going to receive a power, the Holy Spirit coming upon them.

Evangelization

The Holy Spirit creates the conditions for *evangelization*. The noise coming from heaven was used to give the alarm to the inhabitants of Jerusalem and to gather them, as reported in the Scriptures: "When they heard this sound, a crowd came together" (Acts 2:6). Without this noise, how were the disciples going to convene the people scattered in the city to come to listen to them? Once the crowd came together, Peter, filled with the Holy Spirit, could then speak to them in these terms: "Fellow Jews and all of you who live in Jerusalem . . ." (Acts 2:14). And what follows is well known. It should be noted that the Holy Spirit did not come in the form of a strong wind; but the noise which accompanied this coming was like that of a violent breath. It was the concrete demonstration of an invisible power.

Church

The birth of the church is the result of Peter's sermon. The substance of this sermon was none other than the death and the resurrection of Jesus, the confirmation of his Messiahship, repentance, baptism, remission of sins, and the gift of the Holy Spirit. It is written: "When the people heard this, they were cut to the heart . . . " (Acts 2:37). In other words, the Holy Spirit *convinced them of sin, righteousness, and judgment.* In other circumstances, the conclusion of Peter's intervention would cause a violent reaction; because he affirms that Jesus is the Messiah that they were waiting for, and he accuses them of being responsible for his death. But the Holy Spirit convicted them of their unbelief and their culpability, and he prompted them to repent.

Mission

Mission is one of the actions of the Holy Spirit at Pentecost. When Jesus gave to the apostles the missionary mandate to go to the world make disciples of all nations, promised them the power of the Holy Spirit , he also said this to them: ". . . you will be my witnesses in Jerusalem, and in all Judea and Samaria, and to the ends of the earth" (Acts 1:8). The mission of the apostles actually started in Jerusalem on the day of the Pentecost. Spiritual gifts, evangelization, establishment of the church, and mission are works that the Holy Spirit has done through the disciples immediately on his coming, on the day of Pentecost. And he continues to do it until now in the church.

THE HOLY SPIRIT AND THE CHURCH AFTER PENTECOST

The Church belongs to Jesus Christ, since in his declaration about the church, the Lord uses the possessive pronoun "my" church. In fact, the Holy Spirit brings the church into existence by creating the first community. "And the Lord added to their number daily those who were being saved" (Acts 2:47). Here, one notes a perfect symbiosis between the action of the Lord Jesus and the Holy Spirit for the church. This is the reality that God's people continue to experience as they embark on the Christian journey. Jesus is the Lord of the church which he regards as his body. It is he who calls men and women, and entrusts with various ministries to them in the church, "for building up the body of Christ" (Eph 4:12). And the Holy Spirit sanctifies this body, nourishes it, maintains it, and ensures its growth. It is he who trains and qualifies for the ministry those that Christ empowers in the church. Christ being at the right hand of the Father, intercedes on behalf of the church on the basis of his atoning sacrifice. He seeks to obtain God's favor for his people. For his part, the Holy Spirit, himself the Paraclete, comes to the help of believers and compensates for their weakness. Besides, he intercedes for them to ensure that their prayers are answered by the Father (Rom 8:26–27).

The Paraclete in the Church

Jesus promised to send to his disciples the Paraclete, to dwell with them, and to be in them. They need to be supported in times of weakness, defended when Satan, the accuser, harasses them in various manners; reassured in times of doubt; comforted when they go through life's trials, and to have an effective intercessor who champions their causes and is permanently at their side. The Christian life begins with the Holy Spirit and continues with him for eternity. Without the help of the Paraclete, the Christian life is impossible. However, the Christian life is lived in the context of the church, the living community of God's chosen people. Peter urges Christians to get closer to Jesus, "the living stone . . . chosen and precious in God's eyes" (1 Pet 2:6). Thinking of the church as a building he exhorts believers: "you also as living stones are being built up into a spiritual house" (1 Pet 2:5). This idea is not disconnected from what Jesus said himself in his statement, "I will build my church" (Matt 16:18). The church is thus a spiritual house, built by the Holy Spirit; because "the Most High does not live in man made buildings" (Acts 7:48).

In addition, the Holy Spirit being invisible, his presence is manifest in the life of the believers by the fruit they produce: "love, joy, peace, long-suffering, kindness, goodness, benevolence, faithfulness, meekness, self-control" (Gal 5:22–23). In concluding "against such things there is no law," Paul is suggesting that this list is not exhaustive. The Holy Spirit is perceptible only through those in whom he operates. His action occurs in each believer; but the end result is to join them together in one body (Eph 4:3–4). In the same way, "to each one the manifestation of the Spirit is given for the common good" (1 Cor 12:7). Both the individual and community aspects of the Christian life are a divine mystery. Through the Holy Spirit, the Trinity lives in the heart of the believer, so that he/she is constantly being watered by the divine life; and is in personal communion with each member of the Trinity. At the same time, the three persons of the Trinity are at work within the church community to mobilize its members and to use them collectively. Thus by the Holy Spirit, the church is empowered to positively influence society and the political life of the nation, where she is situated and in so doing fulfill her prophetic role.

The Spirit of Truth

Throughout his teaching on the Holy Spirit, Jesus presents him as "The Spirit of truth" (John 14:17; 15:26; 16:13). This attribute of the Holy Spirit appears in a spectacular way from the beginning of the birth of the church. Ananias and Sapphira are "miraculously" struck to death for having *lied to the Holy Spirit*. Peter's reaction exposes the gravity of this couple's action. "[H]ow is it that Satan has so filled your heart that you have lied to the Holy Spirit? . . . You have not lied to men but to God" (Acts 5:3–4). Ananias and Sapphira tried to make a dangerous mixture, by associating a work inspired by the Holy Spirit, namely the sharing of the goods within the newly born church, with the duplicity concerning the proceeds of the sale of their property. However, the Spirit of truth cannot be associated with such duplicity. For this would be tantamount to an association with "the father of lies" (John 8:44). The reaction of the Holy Spirit was terrifying, an intervention which was necessary if the holiness of the body of Christ were to be preserved.

The apostle Paul wrote of "God's household, which is the church of the living God, the pillar and foundation of the truth" (1 Tim 3:15). In this world where the prince is Satan, the father of the lies, God builds his church, to be the pillar and the defender of the truth. The church is able to play this role because it is the work of the Spirit of truth. It is in his role of witness to the truth that the church denounces untruth in all its forms in society. The church, like a Trajan's column, proclaims the Truth to the world. Verses 15 and 16 of this text are remarkable for their theological density. In these two verses, Paul mentions all three persons of the Trinity in connection with the church. Indeed, the apostle speaks about the church of the living God, evoking by that, the Father; and without naming Jesus the Son of God, he presents him in his incarnation as "the one who was appeared in flesh"; and the third person of the Trinity is mentioned in reference to his role in the resurrection of Christ, who "was justified in Spirit." The place of this joint action of the Trinity is the church, column and support of the truth. It is not astonishing that the church is thus put forward as the carrier of the truth, because Jesus defined himself as the Truth, and that the church is his body, i.e., the visible expression of this truth in the world.

The Holy Spirit and the Missionary Action of the Church

In the New Testament, it is in Antioch that the missionary action of the church begins, under the impulse of the Holy Spirit. The missionary activity was already going on since the dispersion of the disciples propelled by the persecution of the early believers (Acts 11:19ff). But only individual initiatives were reported. The express intervention of the Holy Spirit was needed so that the first missionaries, emerging from a church community, became engaged in mission (Acts 13:1–4). Verses 2, 3 and 4 give a precision of utmost importance on this mission. "[T]he Holy Spirit said: 'Set apart for me Barnabas and Saul for the work to which I have called them'" (v. 2). Yet, while the initiative comes from the Holy Spirit, the church is deeply involved. She fasts, prays, lays the hands upon the missionaries, and sends them off. The text does not say that it is the church that sends them (even less a missionary committee). It stresses the fact that "they [were] *sent on their way by the Holy Spirit*" (Acts 13:4). The Holy Spirit calls and sends; but the church does not only manage logistics. In fact, once the mission was completed "they sailed back to Antioch, where they had been committed to the grace of God for the work they had now completed. On arriving there, they gathered the church together and reported all that God had done through them" (Acts 14:26–27). The church commended the missionaries to the grace of God, and it doubtless remained mobilized in prayer for them; and after the trip, it received the report of their work. Barnabas and Saul knew that they had been chosen by the Holy Spirit; however, they gave an account of their mission to the church. Mission is not separated from the church; it is jointly with the church that the Holy Spirit sends men and women in the world to carry the good news of Jesus Christ. The fact that mission, as wanted by Christ, left the bosom of the church and become almost exclusively the business of the missionary societies, thus reducing the church to the only role of material and financial support, is a regrettable shift.

CONCLUDING THEOLOGICAL AND METHODOLOGICAL POSTSCRIPT

The Holy Spirit gave birth to the church at Pentecost. This church is the body of Christ of which he is the head, and it is at the same time the house of the living God. These three assertions lead to the following conclusion: the church has a Trinitarian foundation. This biblical truth calls for a fresh perspective on our approach to the theological task in Africa. It was on the basis of this logic, that the participants at an International Conference on the Future of the Evangelical Theology in French-speaking Africa adopted a number of recommendations on what should be the focus of an African Christology. One of these recommendations stipulates that African theology should "promote a Christology which leads to ecclesiology [because] a Christology without close ties to the Church . . . gives an incomplete vision of the work [of Christ]."[1] I submit that this judgment should be extended to the Holy Spirit and the church as well. If this is done, such an approach will make room for Christology, pneumatology and ecclesiology to be treated in an integrated fashion instead of three juxtaposed and disjointed disciplines. I believe that it is to such a task that Paul invites us when he pleads for "the unity of the Spirit" (Eph 4:3–7).

Needless to say that such an approach necessitates a relinquishing of the Cartesian spirit which has influenced much of traditional theological reflection and which has often led to an artificial truncation of the unitary message of salvation. While the church-Spirit separation may vary in severity in standard theological treatises, such a disjunction is always prejudicial to the functioning of the church, since the church cannot exist without the Holy Spirit. Additionally, the truncation of the two doctrines is detrimental to pneumatology as well, since it can easily lead to a view of the Spirit which sees him simply as a diffuse power which is bereft of a concrete sphere of action when its mission in the world is described.

Evolving as it is in a context which pushes it to redefine its nature, and to rediscover the true meaning of its mission, the African Church needs to be the sphere of operation of the dynamic Spirit if it is to respond to the daunting ills that afflict the African continent. If the church is a bearer of the good news, what does this good news really mean for a continent where armed conflicts, which always result in throngs of refugees, poverty, diseases, the violation of human rights, educational deficit, and so many other evils which threaten daily the wellbeing of human beings? Or, which church for an area always in search of more spirituality? More still, which church for a society where sorcery, fetishism, magic, demon possessions fill the agenda of pastoral action? It must be a church that is consciously a pneumatic community which functions in the fullness and empowerment of the Spirit. African theology should seek to redefine theology with a view to regaining its unity, and recovering its cash value in the here and now.

At a time when Western theology shows signs of the loss of breath, for having existed too long in a disembodied form with an overemphasis on an ever-increasing erudition, if theology is to benefit the church, it needs

---

1. The Declaration of Bangui, "The Future of Evangelical Theology in French Speaking Africa."

a renewal which will come from a faith sustained by a simple reading and listening of the Holy Scriptures under the illumination of the Holy Spirit.

8

The Church as Liberated and Liberating Community: A Primer for a Latin American Ecclesiology

Dario Lopez (Peru)

INTRODUCTION

THE PURPOSE OF THIS chapter is to examine the relation between the Holy Spirit and the church in the Latin American context. With this purpose in mind, within the sections which follow, we examine whether evangelical churches in our time follow the missionary route carved by Jesus and continued by the first Christian communities. There is a particular concern to understand the nature and mission of the church as a liberated and liberating community, anointed and sent by the Holy Spirit to declare the good news of the kingdom in every sphere, whether social, cultural, political, economic, or religious.

The first section examines the liberating mission of Jesus and how that liberating mission was understood by the earliest Christian communities empowered by the Holy Spirit. A particular focus is to determine whether the two main themes, the universal nature of the love of God and the preferential love for the poor and the marginalized, appear as the characteristic signs of his comprehensive mission.

Building on the previous discussion about the liberating mission of Jesus and the witness of the first Christian communities, the second section the examines whether Latin American evangelical churches, under the impulse of the Spirit and as a visible sign of the presence of the kingdom of God in history, have understood their calling to be communities of life that love life and strive for a full and dignified life for each and every human being.

The last section summarizes our perspective on the main theme while taking into account previous arguments; it also examines to what degree Latin American evangelical churches, anointed and empowered by the Holy Spirit, are liberated and liberating communities, rather than justifiers of repressive and corrupt governments or of religious organizations that have simply acquiesced to the prevailing system.

THE CHURCH IN THE NEW TESTAMENT

Luke tells how Jesus, after being baptized, "full of the Holy Spirit, left the Jordan and was led by the Spirit into the wilderness . . ." (Luke 4:1 [TNIV here and throughout]). Luke relates in addition that after the temptations (Luke 4:2–23), "Jesus returned to Galilee in the power of the Spirit" (Luke 4:14) and began to teach in the synagogues (Luke 4:15). A bit after this, Jesus reveals his messianic platform in the synagogue of Nazareth (Luke 4:16–19). One is bound to notice that on this occasion, using a passage from the prophet Isaiah (Isa 61:1–2), Jesus begins his messianic pronouncement with these words: "The Spirit of the Lord is on me . . ." (Luke 4:18).

What did Luke wish to communicate with all this information about Jesus? From all the information that Luke presents about the beginning of the itinerant preaching ministry of Jesus, one can deduce that the mission of the Messiah was a liberating mission carried out in the power of the Spirit. Concerning this matter, Rene Padilla insists that:

> From the perspective of the synoptic gospels, Jesus is preeminently a man anointed by the Holy Spirit to fulfill the ministry that God had entrusted him. . . . Various passages in the New Testament explicitly establish the relation between the Spirit, as the protagonist, and the events by which Jesus accomplishes the redemption: his incarnation (Matt 1:18; Luke 1:35), his ministry

(Luke 4:18), his crucifixion (Acts 9:14), and his resurrection (Rom 1:4).[1]

A reading of the various documents of the New Testament corroborates in effect that the liberating mission of Jesus, like the mission that he commended to the disciples after his resurrection, was a liberating mission in the power of the Holy Spirit.

What was the message of Jesus? To whom was this message directed? And which community was formed in the obscure, marginal Roman province of Palestine? During his missionary travels through the cities and hamlets in Galilee and other regions of Palestine (Luke 8:1; Mark 1:39; Matt 4:23), Jesus of Nazareth, by the power of the Spirit, set about forming a new community that is both a bearer of life and a defender of life. It was a new community that in its social composition and in its norms and lifestyle emerged as a radical alternative to the surrounding society. In the words of John Yoder:

> in a society characterized by very stable family ties held together by religion, Jesus is here calling into being a community of *voluntary* commitment, willing for the sake of its calling to take upon itself the hostility of the given society . . . .[2]

In this community of voluntary commitment, the poor and those excluded from society were treated as whole, worthwhile human beings, as designated recipients of the good news of salvation, and as active subjects in the collective task of extending the kingdom of God throughout diverse social, political, cultural, and religious frontiers.

Who were the poor and the excluded with whom Jesus of Nazareth was associated? They were individual human beings with concrete needs, such as the tax collectors (Matt 9:9–13; Luke 19:1–10), lepers (Matt 8:1–4; Luke 17:11–19), women (Matt 8:14–17; 9:18–26; Mark 12:41–44; Luke 7:11–17; John 4:42), the sick (Matt 9:1–8; 12:9–14; 14:34–36), children (Matt 19:13–15), and the Samaritans (Luke 17:15–19; John 4:1–12). This is in complete harmony with the messianic platform Jesus set out in the synagogue at Nazareth (Luke 4:16–19), and that he reaffirmed in the answer that he gave to the messengers from John the Baptist (Luke 7:18–22). This preferential option of Jesus for the poor of the land would provoke, as time went on, serious conflicts between Jesus and the leaders of the established religion (Matt 9:3; 12:14; Mark 2:6–7, 16; 3:3; Luke 5:30; 13:14).

---

1. Padilla, "El Espíritu Santo y la misión integral de la iglesia," 115–47.
2. Yoder, *Jesús y la realidad política*, 37.

The actions of Jesus in favor of poor and excluded persons had, in addition, a close relation to the good news of the kingdom of God that Jesus proclaimed in various places (Matt 9:35; Mark 1:38–39; Luke 4:42–44; 8:1). The kingdom of God was already present. Jesus himself, in his person and by his ministry, manifested it (Mark 1:14–15). The destiny of the poor and the excluded began to be transformed, just as the Virgin Mary had promised in her messianic canticle (Luke 1:52–53). A new reality was introduced into history—a new reality that the angel, sent to poor, marginalized human beings like the shepherds in the hills of Judea, called "good news of great joy that will be for all the people" (Luke 2:10—a new reality that the elderly Simeon and Anna identified as the advent of the time of liberation longed for and invoked by the holy ones of Israel, Luke 2:25–32, 38).

Jesus' answer to the messengers from John the Baptist listed concrete actions liberating oppressed persons with words that related his messianic identity, showing that the kingdom of God had invaded history (Luke 7:20–22). For Jesus, the presence of the kingdom of God meant a direct confrontation with forces of darkness that disfigured and distorted the purpose of God, that is to say, all human beings should live full and dignified lives as creations of God. This is evident in his response to those who accused him of casting out demons by Beelzebul, the prince of demons (Luke 11:15). "But if I drive out demons by the finger of God, then the kingdom of God has come upon you" (Luke 11:20; cf. Matt 12:27).

In light of this rapid reading of the Gospels, one can affirm the new society that was gestating. Note that the liberating mission of Jesus of Nazareth by the power of the Holy Spirit included the excluded, called into question the social and cultural guardians of exclusion, and upheld the dignity of the poor and the oppressed. In addition, this new reality bore witness to the impartial and gracious love of God, to the leveling effect brought about by the proclamation of the good news of salvation, and to the open confrontation with the anti-kingdom forces that had provoked the public announcement of the good news of the kingdom of God.

What else is affirmed in the other New Testament documents about these same themes? How was the good news of the kingdom expanded into other regions of the Roman Empire by the testimony of disciples who were empowered, impelled, and sustained by the Holy Spirit?

Luke, in his account of the missionary practice of the primitive church empowered, impelled, and sustained by the strength of the Holy Spirit, records that the church followed the example of Jesus with regards to his concern for the poor and the outcast. The primitive church, full of the Spirit, had a clear personal and collective preoccupation with the poor and the outcast (Acts 2:44–45; 3:1–10; 4:34–37; 6:1; 9:36, 39; 11:28–30; 20:35). During its missionary advance under the direction of the Spirit, breaking with the religious and cultural characteristics of Jewish society (Acts 10:28), the Hellenistic Jewish converts to the Christian faith—like Philip and other anonymous missionaries—proclaimed the gospel among the despised gentiles (Acts 8:8; 11:19–20). This fact is important because, according to the Jewish religious and cultural patrons, the gentiles formed a part of the world of the excluded. Nevertheless, owing to the personal and collective testimony of the Hellenistic Jews empowered by the Holy Spirit, the Gentiles, originating from the diverse social strata of the Greco-Roman world of the first century, formed a part of the community of disciples that were established in various points of the Roman empire (Acts 13:42–43, 48; 16:14, 27–34; 17:4, 34; 18:8; 1 Cor 1:26–28).

Following the example of Jesus, the kingdom of God was also the message that the earliest church proclaimed when it extended across the length and breadth of the Roman Empire (Acts 14:22; 28:23), and it was the teaching that was transmitted to the first communities of disciples that were formed in diverse settings (Rom 14:17; 1 Cor 4:20; 6:9; 15:24; Gal 5:21; Eph 5:5; 2 Thess 1:5; Heb 12:28; Jas 2:5). The announcement of the kingdom of God, whose center was the appearance of Jesus of Nazareth, a Jew crucified by the imperial power as *Kyrios* and as *Cristos* (Acts 2:36; 11:17; 15:26), had five ingredients: Christ incarnate, crucified, resurrected, exalted, and coming King (Acts 3:13–16; 4:10–12, 33; 7:55–56; 10:36–43; 13:27–38).

The Pauline correspondence also records that the churches with which Paul had written communication had a genuine concern for the poor and the defenseless (Rom 15:25–28; 1 Cor 16:1–4; 2 Cor 8:1–16; Gal 2:10; Eph 4:28; Phil 4:10–20; 1 Tim 5:10; Titus 3:14). It also shows that Paul transmitted to the new disciples the gospel that he himself had received (1 Cor 15:1–4); a good news related to the announcing of the kingdom of God, as Paul himself confirmed in his farewell to the elders of the church of Ephesus (Acts 20:25), and in various of his letters (1 Cor 6:9; Gal 5:21; 2 Thess 1:5). The Pauline letters also point out that the appearance of Jesus as *Kyrios* and *Cristos* was central to the *kerygma* that was transmitted to the churches that were established outside the Jewish world by Paul and by anonymous missionaries like those who preached in Antioch of Syria (Rom 5:11; 7:25; 1 Cor 1:10; 5:4; 2 Cor 1:2; 8:9; Gal 1:3; 6:14; Eph 3:11; 5:20; Phil 2:11; 3:20; Col 3:24; 1 Thess 3:11; 5:23; 2 Thess 1:1–2, 12).

The Pauline correspondence also gives notice concerning other very valuable themes, sketching a rough picture of a church as liberated and liberating by the power of the Spirit. As Samuel Escobar points out:

> from the time of the New Testament the Church appears as a new community that rises in contrast to the surrounding society. . . . [T]he epistles and the book of Acts offer additional material that reflects the alternative practices of this community, with respect to the use of money, power, sex, attitude before the authorities, and diverse forms of social solidarity.³

That is how it is in effect, since the Pauline corpus is very clear that the church is a new humanity in Christ Jesus (Eph 2) and that the practice of good works (1 Tim 6:18; Titus 3:8, 14) constitutes a distinctive note of being a follower of Jesus of Nazareth: "For we God's handiwork, created in Christ Jesus to do good works, which God prepared in advance for us to do" (Eph 2:10).

The concern for the poor and the outcast, as well as the prophetic criticism of those who oppressed them, is present in the Epistle of James (Jas 2:1–26; 5:1–6). What is more, the references to the kingdom of God that appear in the other letters of the New Testament, although with less frequency than in the Pauline correspondence, indicate that it was not a rare or peripheral theme for the communities of disciples to whom these letters were directed (Jas 2:5; 1 Pet 1:11; Heb 11:28). Likewise, as in the case of the Pauline communities, the presentation of Jesus of Nazareth as *Kyrios* and *Cristos* formed part of the kerygma that the churches received—the churches that were sent the letters of James, Peter, and Jude (Jas 1:1; 1 Pet 1:3; 2 Pet 1:8, 14, 16; 2:20; 3:18; Jude 4:21).

The other theme that stands out when the New Testament documents are examined is the presence of the Holy Spirit anointing and granting gifts to the agents of the mission, in order for them to carry out the ministry *(diakonia)* that the resurrected Christ had entrusted to them. As mentioned earlier, Jesus was full of the Holy Spirit before beginning his ministry, and in the power of the Holy Spirit began to preach the good news of the kingdom of God in the cities and hamlets of Galilee and in other regions (Matt 4:23–25; Mark 1:39; Luke 4:14–15). Then the disciples were empowered with the Holy Spirit to broadcast the Good News of salvation in Jerusalem, in all Judea and Samaria, and to the ends of the earth (Acts 1:8).

The Gospels give testimony as well that Jesus, by the power of the Holy Spirit, healed the sick and liberated the demon possessed (Matt 4:23–24; Mark 1:32–34; Luke 4:40–41). Luke, for his part, records in the Acts of the Apostles that the first Christian missionaries, in addition to publicly proclaiming the gospel in different places, performed signs, wonders, and prodigious works in the name of Jesus (Acts 2:43; 5:12; 6:8; 8:4–7). And he

---

3. Escobar, *Tiempo de Misión*, 123.

makes clear that these signs, wonders, and prodigious works had to do with the healing of the sick (Acts 4:22; 5:12–16; 8:4–7; 9:32–35). The Gospels and Acts of the Apostles also indicate that all this constituted a concrete sign of the breaking in of the reign of God into history.

The missionary experience of Jesus and of the first Christian missionaries indicate, then, that the proclamation of the good news of the kingdom of God by the power of the Holy Spirit was accompanied by concrete signs of the active power of God in human history. In light of this reality, we should not be surprised that in our time Pentecostal churches and believers affirm that that experience remains in effect:

> The healings, miracles, and liberations done in the power of the Spirit signaled the struggle of the Kingdom of God against the kingdom of darkness, the struggle of life against the signs of death. This fight did not conclude at the end of the first century, but rather rages on today. It is to be expected that the Lord's church will participate in the fight by the power of the Spirit. Every sick person healed, every possessed person liberated, every anguished person comforted is the triumph of the Kingdom of God.[4]

In relation to the presence of the Holy Spirit in the churches, when St. Paul writes his epistles, he also discusses the gifts that the Holy Spirit imparts to believers (Rom 12:4–8; 1 Cor 12:1–11, 27–31; Eph 4:11). Even though no case refers to a hierarchical order of the gifts or an exhaustive or detailed treatment of the same, nevertheless, what is clear is the that the Triune God grants diverse gifts to the church fellowship in order to carry out the mission entrusted to them by the power of the Holy Spirit. From the perspective of Noberto Saracco:

> The diversity of charisms aims at taking into account the different needs. From another perspective, it reflects God's will that in his Kingdom even the most insignificant things should be done according to the order of the new creation in Christ and by the power and authority of his Spirit. . . . The bishop and deacon, the evangelist and the one who distributes alms reflect nothing

---

4. Saracco, "La Iglesia y el Espíritu," 43. Saracco also points out the reductionist vision that has characterized many Pentecostal churches and believers, introducing, in his critical commentary, a corrective note that the Pentecostals ought to heed: "We ought also to recognize that those who frame their ministries in the dimensions that we have just expressed, tend to leave aside other characteristics of the mission, such as the struggle for justice and peace. Those who operate this way revert to mutilating and limiting the Lord's redeeming purpose. A life that under the pretext of being spiritual dares to turn its back to these realities, betrays the Lord's Spirit. Here also we need the fullness of the Spirit and his power." Ibid., 83.

more than distinct expressions of the same Spirit. There are no qualitative differences among them, only functional differences. The charismatic organization of the community presupposes on her part both an openness and a disposition to the work of the Spirit.⁵

An attentive look at what actually occurs on the worldwide religious stage, on which the Pentecostal movement occupies an outstanding place, affirms the accurate commentary by Samuel Escobar with respect to the reasons for the vigor and dynamism of these churches that believe in the present reality of the gifts of the Spirit:

> The popular churches of the Pentecostal type that have grown in Latin America often incarnate the notes of the missionary dynamism of Moravians and Pietists better than other evangelical churches that consider themselves guardians of the Protestant heritage. . . . The Pentecostal movement is a contextual and popular expression of the Protestantism of the sixteenth century, arisen in a world of poverty in North America and Latin America alike.⁶

On this same theme, the putting into practice of the gifts of the Spirit in the life and mission of the Pentecostal churches, René Padilla expresses the following:

> One of the secrets of the fantastic numerical growth of Pentecostalism in Latin America is undoubtedly [indubitably] its emphasis on the lay leadership. The ordination of men and women to pastoral ministry, with or without much theological preparation, is common in Pentecostal circles. The priesthood of all believers is not an abstract principle, but rather a living reality without which it is not possible to explain the Pentecostal phenomenon.⁷

This emphasis on the lay leadership in the Pentecostal movement, as well as the ordination of men and women to pastoral ministry, with or without a formal theological preparation, cannot be explained apart from the belief these churches have about the person and work of the Holy Spirit, who gives gifts and who accompanies the people of God in their mission, in the distinct contexts in which they find themselves.

---

5. Ibid., 76.
6. Escobar, *Tiempo de Misión*, 98, 100–101.
7. Padilla, "La nueva eclesiología en América Latina," 221.

What then should characterize a church that is full of the Spirit and that carries out its mission under the influence of the Spirit? From the examination of the New Testament documents it may be inferred that a church full of the Spirit that is driven by the Spirit, as a liberated and liberating community, called to love life and to defend it, has five concrete characteristics that mold her mission in the world. These characteristics are her kerygmatic nature—inclusive, leveling, empowering, destabilizing, and prophetic.

What implications for her integral mission, as a liberated and liberating community full of the Spirit, does each of these characteristics have? What implications for the social and political dimension of her mission as a liberated and liberating community are inferred from her kerygmatic nature—inclusive, leveling, empowering, destabilizing, and prophetic?

1. Her kerygmatic nature. The church as a liberated and liberating community, full of the Spirit and which carries out her mission in the power of the Spirit, has a public truth to proclaim: the good news of the kingdom of God. The nucleus of this public truth is the appearance of Jesus of Nazareth—incarnate, crucified, resurrected, exalted, and coming King—as Lord and Messiah. It is a public truth that does not need to accommodate itself to the subaltern interests of religious leaders or politicians, nor need it sell itself at auction, as if it were an item of merchandise subject to the offer and the demand of the ever-changing contemporary religious market.

2. Her inclusive nature. This is a reality visibly expressed in her social composition. This is particularly so because in the church, as a liberated and liberating community, one finds persons from diverse social, political, cultural, and religious contexts. This is a characteristic that goes against the current the social, cultural, and religious patrons (guardians/sustainers) of exclusion and marginalization commonly as "normal" in asymmetrical societies, such as those in Latin America.

3. Her leveling nature. This is a clear sign of the social inversion that the presence of the kingdom of God brings with its arrival. In the church as a liberated and liberating community and as a visible sign of the presence of the kingdom of God, all the differences of race, sex, age, and economic status that dominate the surrounding society must disappear—inequalities condemn hundreds of defenseless human beings to social ostracism.

4. Her empowering nature. The church is a pneumatic community. As a pneumatic community, today as yesterday, she needs the fullness and power of the Spirit to continue with the liberating mission of Jesus. No

disciple and no church can carry out the mission of proclaiming the good news of the kingdom of God without the presence of the Spirit who gives power to serve and to affirm life in a climate of death and violence.

5. Her destabilizing nature. The announcement of the kingdom of God, with words and with concrete deeds of liberation of the poor and the excluded, constitutes a political criticism of the kingdoms of this world and an announcement that their end has come. The mere presence of the church as a liberated and liberating community, with its values and its lifestyle radically distinct from those that prevail in the surrounding society, destabilizes and dismantles the messianic pretentions of those who presume to have the final word in history.

6. Her prophetic nature. The church as a liberated and liberating community full of the Spirit, does not fit into the surrounding society, and so becomes extremely uncomfortable for those accustomed to exercising political and religious power despotically. This converts the church into an alternative society that, due to countercultural character, emerges as a community of active resistance to the predominant religious and political system.

So it was yesterday, and so it must be the same in our time if she faithfully follows the missionary practice of Jesus of Nazareth anointed by the Spirit, and of the primitive church that was born under the umbrella of the Spirit and expanded, empowered and impelled by the Spirit. Samuel Escobar hits the nail on the head, when, referring to the popular evangelical churches that extend through length and breadth of Latin America, he says the following:

> the missionary vigor of the Latin American popular evangelical churches in the twentieth century comes from the impulse of the Holy Spirit, that finds [churches] willing to recognize that the Spirit gives gifts to all and to structure themselves to permit the manifestation of the impulse of the Spirit.[8]

In light of the missionary practice of Jesus and of the primitive church, as well as the Pauline correspondence and the other documents of the New Testament, it is clear that the churches as liberated and liberating communities empowered by the Spirit, have to be a counterculture that affirms and defends human life and dignity as a gift from God. In that sense, the practice of good works oriented to the common good and the active resistance to the

---

8. Escobar, *Tiempo de Misión*, 98.

practices of death by the nominal powers (politicians, meddlesome mediators, military leaders, and religious leaders) are two concrete ways to love and to defend life, especially a life of dignity for the poor and the excluded of society.

If the churches of our time follow this missionary course under the impulse of the Spirit, it should not surprise them that those who have in their hands political, mediating, economic, military, and religious power feel threatened by the church's message, and try to silence, persecute, and exterminate her. This occurs particularly when they realize that the churches see themselves as communities of active resistance to the politics of death imposed by the temporal authorities and implemented by their political operatives and their religious legitimizers.

THE EVANGELICAL CHURCHES IN LATIN AMERICA

From the examination of the New Testament about the nature and mission of the church forged by Jesus of Nazareth and expanded by the primitive church under the impulse of the Spirit, one infers that a liberated and liberating community, animated, sustained, and impelled by the Spirit, was more than a simple voluntary association of persons that shared common religious interests and practices. In light of this intimate relation between the Holy Spirit and the church, one can better understand the following words of Samuel Escobar, with respect to the mission of the church in the world:

> The historians, anthropologists, and sociologists make studies about the migration of communities or peoples, and movements, or the cultural penetration and changes of religious affiliation. What turns out to be difficult for them to explain is the dynamism that moves the believers to share their faith, especially when they gain no advantage and sometimes must endure persecution. What we Christians believe is that in this continual crossing of frontiers, the Holy Spirit impels the church to complete the mission for which God formed it, and she thus realizes the purpose of redeeming love, revealed and made real by Jesus Christ.[9]

That is how it is in effect. The presence and testimony of the Latin American evangelical community is not explained solely by the sacrificial efforts of national and foreign missionaries. Behind these missionaries, some known and some anonymous, is the sovereign action of the Holy

---

9. Ibid., 10.

Spirit. The Spirit that calls, sends, and enables human beings of flesh and bone in order for them to spread the good news of the kingdom of God in concrete realities of oppression, exploitation, injustice, sickness, violence, and death.

The evangelical community has more than one hundred years of presence and witness in Latin America. Because of her accelerated numerical growth in recent decades, she has gone from a religious minority persecuted by the Roman Catholic religious majority and ignored by politicians, social scientists and the media, to the primary religious minority and the second religious force in all the nations of the region. Despite the differences that exist in polity and in worship styles, the various evangelical churches are also kerygmatic, inclusive, leveling, empowering, destabilizing, and prophetic, as were the first communities of disciples according the testimony of the New Testament.

What characteristics do contemporary Latin American churches have? Do they walk in the integral missionary way created by Jesus of Nazareth and raised up by the primitive church within the diverse social, political, cultural, and religious contexts in which they proclaimed the good news of the kingdom of God by the power of the Holy Spirit? How does the church express her kerygmatic, inclusive, leveling, empowering, destabilizing, and prophetic nature, as liberated and liberating communities full of the Spirit and sent into the world by the power of the Spirit?

In the first place, the Latin American evangelical churches are heterogeneous, as much by their origin and theology as by their liturgy, polity, location in the context of mission, occurrence, social composition, and numeric size.[10] Nevertheless, beyond their diversity, they share a common theological foundation that identifies them as evangelical, despite their differences of origin and doctrinal emphasis. [11]

10 Miguez Bonino identifies four faces that, from his point of view, comprise Latin American Protestantism: the liberal face, the Evangelical face, the Pentecostal face, and the "ethnic face." Miguez Bonino, *Rostros del Protestantismo Latinoamericano*. He also points out that in Latin America "Protestant" and "Evangelical" have generally been synonymous terms. Ibid., 6. In my case, I prefer the term Evangelical. About this, Samuel Escobar points out that "The majority of these 'Protestants' in Latin America prefer to call themselves *Evangelicals*.... The preference for the term 'Evangelical' indicates a historical reality that is important to remember. The majority of the missionaries that came to preach from the ranks of Protestantism belonged by their convictions and their vocation to a wing of a special sector of the European or North American Protestant world. It is the sector that is customarily called 'Evangelical' and that defines itself as conserving fundamental doctrines and as strongly evangelistic and missionary in practice." Escobar, "Que significa ser evangélico hoy?" 15.

11 The following are, according to Samuel Escobar, the distinctive notes of the evangelical identity in Latin America: The theological heritage of the Reformation,

Some Latin American evangelical churches are tied to the Protestantism of transplantation or immigration, like the Lutheran churches in southern Brazil and Chile that came with migratory movements and established themselves to serve the immigrant communities. Others are the result of independent and interdenominational missionary movements that gave origin to national denominations like the Peruvian Evangelical Church. In addition, one finds in Latin America, churches that are the result of missionary effort of denominations like the Methodist Church, The Church of the Nazarene, the Presbyterian churches, or the Baptist churches. And there are also widely extended in Latin America the Pentecostal denominations of foreign origin like the Assemblies of God or The Church of God, as well as the Pentecostal churches of national origin like the Pentecostal Methodist Church in Chile or the Pentecostal Church of Jesus Christ in Peru.

In the second place, the majority of the Latin American Evangelical churches, and the ones that have grown the most numerically, are the popular churches.[12] These churches are found in the poorest and most oppressed zones of the great urban centers and the rural areas, and have linked very well with the social and spiritual hopes of the poor and excluded persons of Latin America. The social composition of these churches, with their poor and migrant majorities, their participatory and festive liturgy, and the active participation of lay leadership, among other visible characteristics, demonstrate their popular character. According to Samuel Escobar:

> Much of the methodology, the liturgy, the style, of these churches reveal precisely the popular origin of their membership and of their leadership. In that sense they are truly contextual even though they have never theorized about contextualization.[13]

This is the case, for example, of the diverse Pentecostal denominations that together represent the most vigorous, dynamic, and growing sector of the Latin American Evangelical community. For any attentive observer of the Latin American religious map, it doesn't appear strange or exaggerated to recognize that the Pentecostal denominations are fundamentally churches of popular origin, constitute the immense majority of the Evangelical population in this region of the world, and are the churches that have a sustained and accelerated numeric growth.

In the third place, the Latin American Evangelical churches are inclusive and leveling. This reality can be observed in the majority of the

evangelizing passion, personal piety, an Anabaptist stance, a Puritan ethic, and the social dimension of the gospel. Escobar, "Que significa ser evangélico hoy?" 15.

12. Escobar, *Tiempo de Misión*, 79.

13. Ibid., 90.

Evangelical churches quite independent of their economic setting. Nor is it merely a characteristic of the popular churches such as the Pentecostals. Even in the churches located in the middle class zones, one observes the growing presence of immigrants and poor families that come from low income neighborhoods. The same thing occurs in the few Evangelical churches that have been established in the upper class zones. In all these cases, one notes a heterogeneity in the attendance at the worship service; nevertheless, the same does not always occur when it is a matter of leadership positions, in which case one observes a preference for persons from upper and middle classes.

In the fourth place, the Latin American Evangelical churches are missionary churches. The verbal proclamation of the gospel, using diverse media such open air preaching or the handing out of evangelistic tracts, is one of their outstanding traits. It is this way because, for any Latin American Evangelical church, beyond her doctrinal emphasis and her particular history, to be Evangelical necessarily implies sharing one's faith with other people. In that sense, every believer is converted into a missionary that has a testimony to share with her relatives, neighbors, and colleagues.

During recent years there has developed, in addition, a growing missionary consciousness connected to transcultural missions. Denominational and interdenominational missionary agencies have formed in the last two decades, and the number of Latin American missionaries that are now found in other regions of the world is increasing. What is more, as a result of the immigration process, many Latin Americans that went to the countries of Europe or to North America in search of better economic opportunities, because they had a faith to share, made themselves missionaries along the way. As Samuel Escobar has underscored:

> Among the thousands of Latin Americans that go to other parts of the world in voluntary or obligatory exile, there is a small but significant number of Evangelicals that carry their enthusiast faith and share as they move forward.[14]

With respect to the theme of the mission one has to signal, nevertheless, that one of the most notorious deficiencies of the Latin American Evangelical churches, owing to having concentrated mainly on the verbal proclamation of the gospel, which they considered the supreme and singular task of the church, has been her fairly rare (or non-existent) participation in the public life of Latin American. A radical separation from the world based on a very bad understanding of the church-world relation, with

---

14. Ibid., 35.

its correlative of passivity, indifference, and silence in the face of critical matters such as the violation of human rights and the scandalous poverty in which millions of Latin Americans live, minimized their missionary presence in these lands.

The majority of the Latin American churches persistently preach about Christian hope; nevertheless, they find it difficult to commit themselves to social and political actions oriented to the common good. This may explain why, three decades ago, Orlando Costas affirmed the following about this problem:

> To speak of hope for a new world without involving oneself in the means for making it a better place to live is to deny the very same hope; certainly it is an escape toward a vague and otherworldly abstraction that paralyzes the transforming force of the eschatological mission of the gospel and ends up making the status quo sacred. To have the hope that the world will be redeemed and not take any redeeming action in the world is a blasphemy.[15]

Although this situation has changed a little in recent years,[16] nevertheless, there is still a need to continue reflecting theologically about the social and political responsibility of the churches and of Evangelical believers, with the conviction that the defense of human dignity and the struggle for social justice are legitimate forms of living in the Spirit and concrete expressions of the social dimension of holiness. This contextual theological reflection is necessary and urgent, particularly, because in the fragile Latin American democracies marked by diverse forms of institutionalized injustice, those who usurp the political and economic power trample with impunity the human dignity of the poor and the oppressed, among whom are found thousands of members of the Evangelical churches. In that necessary and urgent process it would be very helpful to keep in mind proposals of holistic mission like those by Samuel Escobar, for whom:

---

15. Costas, "La vida en el Espíritu," 17.

16. At present, portions of the Evangelical community have realized that the defense of human dignity in the critical social and political realms forms a part of the holistic mission of the church and constitutes a legitimate way of living in the Spirit. Other portions of the Evangelical community, in this period of gradual dismantlement of the lawful democracy, have understood that the defense of the State that is ruled by law represents a form of giving witness to its love for life. The same can be affirmed with respect to the increasingly visible presence of Evangelical women who, now thrust into social movements, fight day by day together with women of other religious confessions against poverty and the lack of opportunities in a closed-door society that has condemned the poor to the rubbish bin of history.

> In one broad sense the term *mission* has to do with the presence and the witness of the Church in a society, the form in which the Church is a community whose members incarnate a way of life according to the example of Jesus Christ, the worship that the community publically offers to God, the service given to meet human needs that the community undertakes, and the prophetic function of confronting the forces of evil that destroy people and societies.[17]

From this succinct characterization of the Latin American Evangelical community, comparing it with the first section of this chapter, one can affirm that there still exist vessels connected to the missionary purpose of Jesus and the missionary experience of the primitive church. The Latin American Evangelical churches are also (to a greater or lesser degree) kerygmatic, inclusive, leveling, empowering, destabilizing, and prophetic.

With regard to the four primary characteristics of a church full of the Spirit—kerygmatic, inclusive, leveling, and empowering—there are no major problems. The Latin American Evangelical churches, whatever their denominational identity, are kerygmatic, given they preach the good news of the kingdom of God in season and out of season in the diverse realities in which they find themselves. They have a heterogeneous social composition that demonstrates their inclusive nature. In a good number of these churches one notes a leveling nature in the growing presence of a mixed lay leadership comprised of men and women, of diverse social and cultural backgrounds. And in the churches from a lower class background one clearly notices that when the good news of the kingdom of God reaches the poor and excluded of society, it produces a radical transformation in their lives that converts them into full-time missionaries among their families, in centers of work and of study, and in their neighborhood. In other words, the Holy Spirit empowers the poor and excluded, granting them gifts (charisms) to fulfill the ministry (diakonia) that has been entrusted to them.

It is in the other two characteristics of the church full of the Spirit (destabilizing and prophetic) that one still notes certain deficiencies that must be attended to if there is a desire to have greater presence and more frequent input in public life. As has been pointed out at various points, the problem owes in a good part to the exaggerated emphasis that was placed on the verbal proclamation of the gospel, in disproportion to the social and political responsibilities of the believers, that had as a final product churches and believers alienated from the context of mission, and who thus became, as it were, strangers in their own land.

17. Escobar, *Tiempo de Misión*, 10.

What are the challenges for this time, particularly if there is a desire to radically change the public face of the Latin American Evangelical churches? Assume a church full of the Spirit that walks impelled by the Spirit: what must be taken into account in a region where poverty and extreme poverty, social and cultural exclusion, infant malnutrition, inadequate access to basic utilities such as water and electricity, and violence against women, children, and adolescents, among other forms of institutionalized injustice, are tolerated or permitted?

FINAL WORDS

If, as Orlando Costas proposes, "a sign of the messianic era is the outpouring of the Spirit of God upon everyone as a redeeming power permanently in the heart,"[18] and if the messianic age has not yet ended, but rather remains in effect because Christ continues being the Lord, it must then be affirmed that the power and the impulse of the Spirit has not left the church. The Spirit still animates, sustains, and leads the church so that it does not cease to proclaim the good news of the kingdom of God. It must be thus because as Saracco says:

> The Church is the people of the Spirit. It is, as much by the presence of the Spirit in her bosom, as by the fact that her origin is in the work of the Holy Spirit. . . . [T]he Church is also the people of the Spirit because in her there is the Spirit of the Lord. Certainly this was one of the most important promises that Jesus left his disciples (John 14:15–31). The resurrected Christ lives within the Church through the Spirit.[19]

Anchored in this conviction, the evangelical churches and the evangelical believers of our era should not forget that, following the missionary model of Jesus and of the primitive church, their first churches were liberated and liberating communities whose missionary focus was concentrated on the sectors that society treated as throwaways. In that missionary soil are sunk the roots of our history. The "subversive memory," highly uncomfortable for the Evangelical sectors who have been converted into addicts of the values of the consumer society and the religious legitimizers of corrupt and unjust governments that oppress thousands of human beings, must be the missionary key that drives us to love life and to defend it. A "subversive memory" should be irrevocable for those who have encountered face to face

---

18. Costas, "La misión como discipulado," 12.
19. Saracco, "La Iglesia y el Espíritu," 71–72.

the God of life and the Spirit of life. Even though being faithful to that "subversive memory" may mean, as the recent history of Latin America testifies, risks for the physical security of the disciples, persecution and martyrdom, because, "to be an authentic disciple of Jesus Christ in our continent today means not only willingness to run the risk of social scarring and shame, but also of torture and death."[20]

Without ignoring that concrete reality of violence and death, the Latin American Evangelical Church as a liberated and liberating community that has spoken a resounding yes to life must take seriously the present and the future of all the poor and the oppressed that suffer directly the consequences of institutionalized violence or of legalized violence. And for that very reason, she cannot and should not remain quiet for a moment, because, among other reasons:

> To believe in the Resurrection means also to defend the life of the most vulnerable in society. To seek the Lord among the living leads to committing oneself to those who see their right to life permanently violated. To confess the Resurrection of the Lord is to affirm life in the face of death. . . . There is no affirmation of life without passing through death, without confronting it. . . . The message of the Resurrection of the Lord and ours along with his is clear: life, and not death, is the ultimate word in history.[21]

The gospel of the kingdom is good news for the poor and the oppressed, and it would be a betrayal of the God of life to keep to remain silent or permanently indifferent, when thousands of human beings are sacrificed daily to satisfy the contemporary idols of today, whether technology, nuclear arms, material prosperity, a certain model of exclusionary economics, or ideologies.

To affirm the kerygmatic nature—inclusive, leveling, destabilizing, empowering, and prophetic—of the church, as a liberated and liberating community, we are obliged to love life and to oppose directly to every form of violence. Even more, to confess Christ incarnate, crucified, resurrected, exalted and coming King, must make us live as members of an alternative community to the surrounding society—an alternative that has but one Lord and yields to nothing else.

To struggle actively so that the poor and the oppressed live with dignity, as human beings created in the image of God, does not constitute a task belonging exclusively to the theologies of liberation, nor is it a concern

20. Costas, "La misión como discipulado," 51.
21. Gutierrez, *El Dios de la vida*, 54.

solely preoccupying social activists linked to human rights organizations, nor a theme merely linked to the ideological interests of the political left. It is a legitimate dimension of the Christian witness that desires to be faithful to the God of life and, for that very reason becomes a concrete form of life in the power of the Spirit.

This is the message that the church, as a liberated and liberating community, must proclaim and incarnate in her life and witness, no matter the historical reality in which she finds herself, giving witness to the God of life. The corollary of this countercultural missionary action becomes a direct disengagement from the values and the practices of death that characterize the surrounding culture. It is a detachment that converts the members of churches into persons who trouble and who are dangerous to the system. It is a church-formed counterculture that by her presence and her witness announces the end of all the human empires and of all earthly lords.

This is the missionary path that a church must follow that lives under the impulse of the Spirit and acts by the power of the Spirit. It is a missionary road, with its ruts carved out by Jesus of Nazareth, followed by the primitive church, as well as by the communities of disciples who dared to be faithful to the example of their Lord and Savior down through history. This must be the unmistakable mark of the church in which the Liberator Spirit, a Spirit who calls, empowers, and sends forth in mission, who is present like a living flame that keeps fresh the spiritual life of the community of the kingdom of God, that like the primitive church proclaims boldly at all times:

> Now, Lord, consider their threats and enable your servants to speak your word with great boldness. Stretch out your hand to heal and perform signs through the name of your holy servant Jesus. (Acts 4:29–30).

PART 4
Eschatology and Mission

9

An Eschatologically Driven Missiology for Holistic Engagement with African Realities

Abel Ngarsoulede (Chad)

INTRODUCTION

THE DEBATE OVER ESCHATOLOGY in Africa boils down to two great schools of thought: the school of John Mbiti and the school of Byang Kato. According to Mbiti, the African does not believe in futuristic eschatology[1] because his concept of time is oriented toward the past. For his part, Byang Kato insists that Africans do believe in the kind of futuristic eschatology described in Scripture. We have here a battle over the direction of African eschatology: is it retrospective or prospective?

These divergent positions by themselves justify the need for research in the field of eschatology in Africa. But beside this, there are other reasons that justify such task. They include, among other things, the changing and

---

1. Petersen, " Eschatology," 575–79. The term eschatology comes from the Greek word *eschatos* which means "last" or "final"; it is the biblical doctrine which deals with the last things or the last days. It can also mean the end of history and the ultimate destiny of humankind. See Cook, "Eschatology in Early Judaism," 290–308.

temporary nature of our world, the urgency of Christian mission, and the prospect of the imminent return of Jesus Christ.

Eschatology is such a complex subject that we cannot pretend to cover all its facets in the scope of a short chapter. In light of this, we will limit the scope of our study to the following three issues.

- First, we will seek to ascertain if there is an eschatology in the African religions.
- Second, we will attempt to determine the meaning of mission in the African context.
- And third, we will endeavor to show how biblical eschatology and Christian mission might be linked in the African context?

In our attempt to explore these areas of inquiry, we will make use of the works that have already been produced on the theme of eschatology in Africa, both by African thinkers and non-African theologians. Methodologically, in each section of the chapter, we will consider the views of others on the issues, and then draw our own conclusion at the end of the discussion. I need to point out that, in the first part of the chapter, I will present the results of a survey that I conducted in N'Jamena, Chad, among government officials on various aspects of eschatology. My hope in using the survey is to shed some light on the debate that has been sparked by the contending positions mentioned above with respect African eschatology.

ESCHATOLOGY IN THE AFRICAN CONTEXT

Eschatology in the African Traditional Religions

John Mbiti strongly argues that the notion of eschatology does not exist in African societies because the concept of a distant future is elusive to Africa. In his article "New Testament Eschatology and the Akamba of Kenya," Mbiti conducts a linguistic analysis of the concepts of "time" and "history" and comes to the conclusion that: "There is no concrete verb tense to express something happening beyond two years from now."[2] This leads Mbiti to affirm that the concept of futurity is not a notion that is shared by Africans. He goes on to argue that: "There are, however, events in the rhythm of nature, such as day and night, seasons of rain and dry weather, birth, marriage and death, that are 'fixed' and must always happen. But, there is nothing in

---

2. Peterson, "Eschatology." The term "mission "comes from the Greek *apostole* which means "sending" or "commission". It speaks of the main task that Jesus Christ entrusted to the church in the world which is to make disciples of all nations and to bring souls captive to the obedience of Christ.

an eschatologically driven missiology 183

the conceptualization of the people to suggest that this rhythm would ever be broken, interfered with, radically changed or brought to an end."[3]

Mbiti is so adamant about the peculiarity of the African perspective on eschatology that he denies seeing references to the future even in African proverbs and myths. "There is no African myth about the future, as far as I know,"[4] he says. He downplays any idea of eschatology in African societies. He writes: "Both linguistically and mythologically there is no action in traditional African thought that the world will ever come to an end. The rhythm of nature ensures an endless continuity of human life and the world. What comes to an end is really what is eventually removed from the present period of time to the past."[5] Mbiti argues that the Ndebele people bury their dead with their personal possessions so that the departed will not be classified as poor in the other world.[6] According to him, the idea behind this practice is the African linear view of life. In African societies, he explains, life is viewed as a continuum. Mbiti clarifies that: "for most [African] people, the other world is geographically 'here'; it is only separated from us by its invisibility to humans' [eyes]."[7] He goes to add that: "The majority of Africans do not expect any kind of judgment or reward beyond the grave."[8]

On this issue, many African thinkers follow Mbiti's lead. They use the same language as him, or language similar to his own. Parrinder, for instance, supports Mbiti's position, when he states that "The African worldview is life-affirming; a philosophy of vitalism or dynamism lies behind many [African] attitudes and actions. . . . Because of this life-affirming character, African religion covers the whole of life."[9] This means that in the African context, the traditional conception of life does not view death as the end of the life story. For the African, life continues in the land of the dead which is populated with departed ancestors and with other spirits who serve as mediators between God and humans. Raymond Ogunade agrees with this idea, as well. He says, "In African Religions there is no hellfire. Wicked people, according to the Yoruba, are confined to *Orun-Apaadi* (heaven of potsherds). Death does not put an end to the human life. The good people continue to live in the ancestral realm, as ancestors."[10] According to this concept, physical death

3. Ibid.
4. Ibid.
5. Mbiti, "New Testament Eschatology in an African Background," 456.
6. Mbiti, *Religions et Philosophies Africaines*, 161.
7. Ibid., 169.
8. Ibid.
9. Parrinder, *Africa's Three Religions*, 233–34.
10. Ogunade, "African Eschatology and the Future of the Cosmos." https://unilorin.

is only a transition from one world to another. Ogunde goes on to say that, "There is no permanent end in African Eschatology. There is continuous creativity going on; the end of one's life leads to another life, as we have seen death being a transition into another form of life."[11]

In the same vein, commenting on Albert Camus, Johan Denegaar states that "the idea of the immortality of the soul is used as an escape from the trials of life."[12] According to Denegaar, a human's life is full of trials that need to be overcome in order to give life meaning and value. To use other criteria such as salvation in the hereafter is an excuse that downplays peoples' responsibility for their lives here on earth. According to Mugabe, there is no hell after this present life. For the African, hell is the barren woman at home who does not bear enough children to carry the family name.[13]

Many who uphold traditional African social values agree with Mugabe's view on eschatology. Eloi Messi Metogo, for instance, who conducted research among students in several African countries some twenty years ago, found that many young Africans not only denied the existence of life after death, they also said that there is neither hell nor paradise.[14] Indeed, he found that for them, even belief in God was of secondary importance. In fact, Metogo found that, to many youths, the idea of eschatological salvation which is based on belief in God was simply incredible. According to Metogo, for many African youths, religion which typically provides the practical underpinning for belief in the hereafter was reduced to mere morality. Finally, Metogo concludes by pointing out for African youths, religion is concerned with happiness in the afterlife, not in this world.[15]

The problem with Mbiti's perspective on religion in general and on African eschatology in particular lies in its exaggerated anthropocentrism and pronounced universalism. According to Mbiti, the African people's intrinsic religiosity provides them all with the possibility of salvation.[16] But it seems to us that those who register agreement with Mbiti's theology do not seem to have adopted a sufficiently critical stance vis a vis his position to realize the difficulty that such a theological position poses. If, in fact, there is no concept of eschatology in the African religions and cultures because of

edu.ng/publications/raymond/Journal%20of%20Arabic%20and%20Religious%20Studies.htm (accessed July 29, 2011).

11. Ibid.
12. Denegaar, "The Changed View of Man," 56.
13. Mugabe, "Salvation from African Perspective," 241.
14. Metogo, 109.
15. Ibid., 118.
16. Mbiti, *Religions et philosophies africaines*, 9.

African's alleged linear and retrospective view of life, this very fact itself renders the missionary effort in the continent justifiable and indeed necessary. For, as Paul asserts, God has set a day for judging the living and the dead with justice by the man he has appointed, and he proved to everyone who he is by raising him from the dead; and this man is Jesus (Acts 17:31–32). Indeed, the patience that God has demonstrated with respect to the end of history is to provide the opportunity for all to repent in order that they might be saved (2 Pet 3:9).

In the context of his critique of Mbiti's culturally laced perspective on New Testament eschatology, Byang Kato puts forth an entirely different position. In stark contrast to Mbiti, Byang Kato argues that Africans do have a keen awareness of the future. Appealing to his own field research, Kato asserts that Africans believe *both* in life after death *and* in hell. He writes, "I conducted a survey in 1967 in Igbaja, Nigeria, among some 500 college students and discovered that nearly 90 percent found Christ through a message concerning [his] second coming."[17] If correct, Kato's assertion means that despite the perspective of the Mbiti-led school on the belief of Africans regarding the inexistence of hell, there is a significant percentage of Africans who believe in its existence and are concerned about protecting themselves from that painful future by availing themselves of the salvation that Christ provides. Besides showing that the Mbiti school does not reflect fully the view of Africans on eschatology, Kato turns to the New Testament to buttress his stance. He concludes his critique of Mbiti's perspective with the blunt assertion that: "The reality of heaven and hell is a fundamental teaching of Biblical Christianity."[18]

As part of our examination of the above positions on African eschatology, we offer a case study as an illustration. It is an extract of the results of the research I conducted for my doctoral thesis from September 2009 to January 2010 with some fifty employees in N'Djaména, Republic of Chad, Africa. The employees were all functionaries of the state and were drawn from the Muslim, the Roman Catholic, and the evangelical communities.

Case Study of N'Djamena

The choice of persons for the research was based on the fact that they were hired because they were intellectually competent and were educated in the Western educational system. They were all exposed to the influence of foreign ideas in the area of metaphysics and the rigors of modern thought. It

17. Kato, *Theologial Pitfalls in Africa*, 77.
18. Ibid., 85.

was assumed that given their intellectual and cultural background, these functionaries would be able to resist the influence of modernity. In the collection of the data, we adopted the approach of semi-directive conversations and the method of free flowing interview. These methods allowed us to gather a wealth of information on the subject.

The basis of our eschatological affirmations is the sacred book of one of the revealed religions, namely, the Bible. Based on Scripture, Christianity affirms that life after death comes from God himself, but humans must choose that life. The Bible says, "This day I call heaven and earth as witnesses against you that I have set before you life and death, blessings and curses. Now choose life, so that you and your children may live" (Deut 30:29). Elsewhere, we read this declaration, "I am the way and the truth and the life. No one comes through the Father except through me" (John 14:6). Among other biblical witnesses on this subject is that of the Apostle John who says "For God so loved the world that he gave his one and only Son, that whoever believes in him shall not perish but have eternal life.... Whosoever believes in him is not condemned, but whosoever does not believe stands condemned already because he has not believed in the name of God's one and only Son" (John 3:16, 18). In another text, the same author writes: "Blessed and holy are those who have part in the first resurrection. The second death has no power over them" (Rev 20:6). Christian beliefs and preaching are both anchored in these words.

The Existence of Judgment and of Hell

Based on what we said above, the question we asked our interviews was this: "Do you believe in a judgment day and in hell? If not, what do you say?" The answers given to this question vary from a firm yes to an hesitating affirmation. There is no answer that denied the reality of a final judgment and hell for the wicked. For some, belief in hell and a final judgment at the end of history is based on the fundamental premise of the existence of God. For others, the brevity of life and the character of the world prove there is judgment and hell. For still others, this truth is taught by the Holy Books, such as the Quran and the Bible. But despite the sense of powerless before a sovereign God and the certainty that one day they will appear before him for judgment, people still choose to live their lives as they please. A Roman Catholic adherent states: "I say, even if there is doubt, we must believe that there is a God and that God is omnipresent; one day he will judge the living and the dead."[19] The ignorance of the time when final judgment will take

---

19. Interview No. 39, January 11, 2010, 1:13 p.m.

an eschatologically driven missiology 187

place does not erase in the mind of one interviewee the fundamental conviction of its veracity: "yes, there will be a judgment one day. Will the world come to an end before the day of judgment, or not? I don't know; but judgment day will come one day. This is in keeping with God's foreknowledge."[20]

The belief in the existence of hell and paradise is shared and supported by several respondents. Similarly, the view that people will be judged by God according to the way they lived their lives on earth is also held by many of the interviewees. A Muslim summarized his perspective as follows, "yes, there is a hell and there is a paradise; God will apply judgment according to what each person has done. Everyone will bring his or her deeds before the throne of God, and if those deeds are good, men can hope to enter paradise, however, if one acts against God's will, hell."[21] According to another Muslim the following law that guides human life will also guide divine judgment: "God will judge us according to our acts on earth because there is a book of inner rules that says how to live in society."[22] In the mind of one of the interviewees, the knowledge that people will be judged by their deeds is joined to the conviction that they will appear before God in judgment. "According to the Quran, if my behavior is conformed to Islamic faith, I will see him one day. On the day of judgment, He [God] will seat down and we will come before him to give an account for our good or bad behaviors."[23] Two Muslim interviewees said the same thing: "The history of humankind will end and everyone will have his or her end one day,"[24] said the first one. "And beyond that history, there is paradise and hell. To access paradise, one must believe in God and respect religious values: being honest with people, with oneself and with God, don't do evil,"[25] said the second. This narrative views a moral life and religious ethic as the condition of access to God. According to these affirmations the belief that history will end one day is very strong.

The people interviewed had no doubt about judgment day. However, the lack of assurance dominated the mind of many of the interviewees. Such is the case of that evangelical Christian who shows uncertainties about the future although he acknowledges the likelihood of meeting God: "The day when Lord returns, it can be in different ways, it could be through death, or I may still be alive when Jesus Christ returns, there will be a meeting there.

20. Interview No. 10, September 29, 2009, 9:40 a.m.
21. Interview No. 42, January 11, 2010, 2:45 p.m.
22. Interview October 1, 2009, 9:30 a.m.
23. Interview No. 45, January 12, 2010, 12:14 p.m.
24. Interview No. 46, January 12, 2010. 12:14 p.m.
25. Interview No. 48, January 13, 2010, 1:05 a.m.

So, it's up to the Lord to decide."[26] The mind of another evangelical Christian is clear: "God will send to hell those who sin; and me I want to be on his side because I don't want to go to hell." In stark contrast, incertitude filled the mind of this Muslim: "The Quran" he says "teaches us to do good deeds, everything that the prophet Mohammad and the Hadiths said. If you do all these things God can bring you to his paradise, but if you do not do them, he will send you to hell."[27]

These statements show how strongly questions concerning life after death and particularly questions about the end of the world dominated the thoughts of the interviewees—but in different ways. As the responses to the survey show, people are certain about meeting God but at the same time they are uncertain about many eschatological questions particularly, the assurance of salvation. They weighed the conditions of access to the afterlife and the criteria that will be used for final judgment.

The Possibility of Life After Death

To the question, "Do you believe in life after death?", we received diverse responses. Two main themes surface from these responses: the awareness of meeting God, and the understanding of the other world. The first seems to derive from the respondents' religious upbringings, and the second from their inability to control the future. With respect to the world beyond some equate it with paradise, while others view the other world and paradise as two different realities. Some understand the other world as a life with God or eternal life, while others speak of a future life.

Some interviewees expressed clearly their convictions on the existence of life after death at the end of history. An adherent to Roman Catholicism said "One day this world will cease to be and we will meet our God, whether you are Muslim or Christian."[28] "For me, this supreme being, I am on my way to meet him. It is Christianity that will allow me to meet the God that I am looking for,"[29] said another Roman Catholic. Another Muslim, joined in: "Yes, there is a life after death, according to our faith."[30]

The respondents use a variety of terms and expressions to refer to the reality of life after death. For another Roman Catholic in his thirties, this is salvation: "Yes, there is salvation beyond life. The day when Christ will

26. Interview No. 15, October 1, 2009, 12:25 p.m.
27. Interview No. 29, January 5, 2010, 2:37 p.m. and No. 40, January 7, 2010, 1:30 p.m.
28. Interview No. 12, October 1, 2009, 7:23 a.m.
29. Interview No. 6 September 21, 2009, 8:40 a.m.
30. Interview No. 32, January 7, 2010 4:30 p.m.

return, he will give us salvation if we are pure."[31] An evangelical woman calls it "eternal life,"[32] while a thirty year old Muslim who derives his belief from the Quran speaks of "paradise"[33]—a statement supported by other respondents.[34] Another Muslim interviewee expresses his conviction like this: "I strongly believe there is paradise and a world beyond. To access it, according to the teachings of the Quran, one must not commit major sins; such as crime or beating your mother, etc."[35] However, the same interviewee expresses his doubts concerning the access to the enjoyment of that paradisiacal life. He says "one can wish to enter paradise, but what God decides can be very different."[36] Concerned about the reality of life the other world, a sixty year old Muslim man shows his hesitation and worry: "I think there is something that is awaiting me in life beyond death, but I don't know where it is; I don't know; I often question myself because I always have conflicts with my personality."[37]

The acknowledgement of the reality of life in the other world is shared by many of the respondents. A Roman Catholic woman vehemently declared: "Yes, I am a believer! I believe in God, there is life after death."[38] For others while the conviction of life after death is there, the condition to access such a life proves elusive and is a cause of anxiety. According to one Muslim, entrance into the afterlife is conditioned on the personal effort that one makes: "yes, there is life after death, it is certain. And to have access to it the conditions are numerous and difficult. But we need to do our utmost to meet those conditions."[39] One person candidly expresses his agony about not being accepted or received by God in the other world. In the belief that the accumulation of efforts would earn him salvation, he is busy producing the maximum effort on earth to secure the outcome he desires.

Looking at the attitudes and the responses of the respondents as a whole on eschatological issues, I see three different and uneven groups. The first and largest group consists of those who are certain about the existence of life after death and have no doubt that they will go to paradise. The next group (also next in size) consists of those who are certain about the existence of life after

---

31. Interview No. 39, January 11, 1010, 1:13 p.m.
32. Interview No. 10, September 29, 2009, 9:30 a.m.
33. Interview No. 22 October 7, 2009, 3:13 p.m.
34. Interview No. 29 January 5, 2010, 2:37, and No 26 January 5 2010, 8:35 a.m.
35. Interview No. 50, January 13, 2010, 2:12 p.m.
36. Interview No. 50
37. Interview No. 43, January 12, 2010, 8:27
38. Interview No. 46, January 12, 2010, 1:15, p.m.
39. Interview No. 27, January 4, 2010, 10:26 a.m.

death, but they are not sure they can access it. They think that their access to eternal life is up to God because he is sovereign and he does what he wants. In the view of Roman Catholic, "Salvation is not open to anyone, because it is God who chooses. It is God who calls and saves, when you believe in his name, he saves you."[40] In her view, life in eternity is a reality, but entrance into that eternity depends on the sovereign will of God. When it comes to the nature of eternal life or eschatological salvation, all form of concrete representation proves elusive. The last group consists of those who are certain of the existence of life after death but they burden themselves a great deal with the personal efforts they must make in order to enter that life. This group appears skeptical about the possibility of life itself.

The perplexity surrounding the nature of the other world causes anxiety in the hearts of the respondents. For some, the future life is synonym to paradise, and the beyond is the place where that life will be lived. One interviewee said: "There are two lives: the actual and the future life, that is, paradise in the yonder."[41] According to a Muslim who was in his fifties, the yonder is another viable reality: "for me, the yonder is another world that you will see after life on earth. The characteristics of this life are peace, bliss, absence of crime and banditism. One has access to it after death."[42] Many interviewees share the conviction that this world is temporary, ephemeral, but the effort to live the blessed life, either in the beyond or in this temporary life, is the responsibility of the individual.

With respect to the opposing views on African eschatology, our research in N'Djamena shows that all the interviewees acknowledge the existence of life after death and they that this life is located in the beyond—in another world. Some respondents hope to live that life one day. Others acknowledge it, but are indifferent about it, either because they don't feel called to it, or because it is too far away. Only on the manner of representing life in the hereafter do we observe divergence of opinions among our respondents. Some spiritualize it; others materialize it.

The analysis of the views expressed on the existence of final judgment, hell, life after death are summarized with the use of strong terms. Respondents use expressions such as "to meet God," "meeting with God," "earn paradise," "obtain salvation," "obtain eternal life," "be near God or the side of God," "the day of judgment," "the final judgment," "give an account," "hell," "the future life," "another world," etc. These statements of faith came from the majority of the respondents who, as we indicated, came from different

---

40. Interview No. 36, January 8, 2010, 8:06 a.m.
41. Interview No. 42, January 11, 2010, 2:55 p.m.
42. Interview No. 46, January 12, 2010, 12:15 p.m.

religious traditions and Christian confessions. This seems to suggest that, contrary to the view of Mbiti and his followers, the belief in metaphysical realities and a futuristic eschatology of the sort found in Scripture and defended by Kato is largely adhered to by adherents of both Muslim and Christian faith. If there is a resurrection from the dead and a judgment, it follows that there is the reality of another world away from this tangible world. In traditional African thinking, the earthly life is viewed in continuity with the life beyond the grave into which one is transitioned through death. After death, another life goes on in an immaterial body in the world of invisible beings—the community of the ancestors. From the views expressed by our interviewees, we conclude that the concept of time and history—past, present, and future—is very much part of the belief system of the Africans. In regard to biblical eschatology, what weighs on the hearts of our interviewees is the fear of not seeing God, of going to hell, and the uncertainty surrounding access to the life after death. For Africans, the belief in life after death is not a matter of philosophical speculation. It informs one's conduct and behavior, and influences the way one's relates to God in the here and now.

MISSION IN THE AFRICAN CONTEXT

The Concept of Mission in the African Traditional Religions

"Mission is a contested concept," states Alan Le Grys.[43] According to him this has been the case from the inception of the Christian community to this day. He observes that with regard to the African context, the concept of "mission" is of biblical and theological origin. God has his will for humanity. But the power of sin on humans prevented them from living with integrity before God and in accordance to his norms. That is why God sent his prophets to his people and to the kings of Israel to teach, exhort, and warn them about his judgment. Armed with the same concern when God realized that these human messengers were insufficient and ineffective to the missionary task, he sent his Son to the world to die on the cross in order to redeem lost souls and to provide them a way to his eternal kingdom. God the Holy Spirit now mediates Christ to his church to keep her in the ways of God and lead her to his kingdom.

This concept of mission does not exist in the traditional African religions because these religions do not have a norm to uphold that's universal in scope. Neither do they have a concept of final judgment before the throne of God for which people need to prepare one way or another. In the African

---

43. Le Grys, *Preaching of the Nations*, 169.

religions, human suffering is caused by the wrath of the mediating spirits that exist between men and the gods or by the wrath of the gods themselves. African cosmology does not foresee an end to history. Instead, it envisages a continuity of life, or better, a renewal of life cycle. It believes firmly that physical life goes on in the world of the ancestors who are considered living and organized. This explains the absence of the concept of mission in African cultural categories.

Foreign Missions in Africa

The great commission given by Jesus to his church has inspired Western Christians to take the gospel to Africa. Christian missions have brought significant change to the continent in the sociocultural, educational, and economic domains. The missionary effort has also contributed to the socio-political changes that have occurred on the continent. Yet, despite these achievements, Africans have typically attributed the ineffectiveness of the gospel in their own lives to Western missions. According to B. J. Van der Walt : "The process of secularization . . . started early in the history of Christianity. It is not the 'world' which is guilty of this in the first place. Christianity itself has sowed the seeds. Modern secularism is simply the harvest which has been yielded by the infected seeds."[44] Van der Walt thinks that the worldview that the missionaries took to Africa was not a biblical worldview. He believes that secularization and secularism are the results of a Christianity that failed to take into account the worldview and culture of the people in the way it communicated the gospel to them. In the view of Van der Walt, what Western missionaries brought with them was a kind of pietism—a Christianity that negates the world. That is why the gospel message did not touch the various dimensions of the lives of the people. They brought to Africa a gospel coated with the Western worldview and Western culture. According to him, the clash of the two worldviews has caused the gestation of secularization in the lives of many Africans, as is evident in their privatization of religion. The clash plunges others into outright secularism.[45] Van der Walt thinks that this situation applies to the continent as a whole, particularly the fostering of a vision of life that is becoming increasingly anthropocentric.

Fabien Eboussi Boulaga levels the same criticism at the Western missionary effort in Africa. In his critique, Boulaga argues that Western metaphysics and natural reasoning, which served as the intellectual basis

44. Van der Walt, *The Liberating Message*, 20.
45. Ibid.

for the missionary discourse in Africa, failed to make use of African cultural categories in the communication of the Christian message. Because the language was not understood by the indigenous people, the metaphysical discourse fell on deaf ears. Consequently, the Christian God that was proclaimed through that message did not receive a radical welcome in the hearts and lives of the individuals.[46] Even those who embraced him did not break with their tribal gods to whom they continued to show allegiance.[47]

Addressing the case of Nigeria, Abiola Dopanu does not sound differently from Boulaga. According to Dopanu, the Yoruba elites (and their view is fairly representative)[48] viewed Christianity as the incarnation of Western culture behind the mask of religion. He thinks that Western education was a powerful and effective tool used by Christians to challenge traditional African beliefs considered sacred by African leaders and people alike. Christianity, he charged, has condemned and destroyed the beliefs and practices of the traditional religions along with their symbols. To support this contention, Dupanu relates the following words which were spoken by the first missionary to the land of the Yoruba.: "I believe our converts sincerely give up all worship of false gods. . . . Moreover, some converted adherents to Yoruba Religion composed songs to ridicule the Traditional Religion and to demonstrate the uniqueness of Christianity."[49] To this we must add the introduction to Africa of Western medicine and Western technology that undermine the use of traditional healing methods by the Yoruba people.

The participants in the research we conducted in N'Djamena display similar sentiments on the role of Christianity in Chad. They show that the Christian mission did not take into consideration the cultural peculiarities of the Chadian people. This is what renders the gospel ineffective in their lives. A consequence of this superficial and partial missionary endeavor in the continent has been the rise of secularism and pluralism.

---

46. Boulaga, *Christianisme sans fétiches*, 52–56.

47. Ibid.

48. To many Africans who belong to the elite who have lived with people from the West and who have experienced Western culture in the West, Christianity is seen as an enemy of African culture. For explains the hostility that some African intellectuals have shown vis a vis Christian faith and to the church itself in certain places on the continent.

49. Dopanu, "Secularization, Christianity and the African Religion in Yorubaland," 146–47.

Secularism and Pluralism in Africa

Some socially mobile Africans explain away the concept of eschatological salvation and consider it illusory. They are suspicious of the reality of another world and the idea of the ultimate destiny of humans before God seems inimical to their progress on the earth. This explains why some choose religious alternatives that place less constraint on their consciences. This outlook provides the explanation for the rise of secularism and pluralism on the African continent.

With respect to secularism, many African intellectuals and students who are exposed to other cultures have become less and less inclined to believe that the Bible is true. In their eyes, Scripture is more like a myth or an ordinary book. These intellectuals promote interpretations that suit their taste and alternative religious beliefs that accord with their ideologies. A large portion of the elite, including a high percentage of young Africans, does not display a disciplined theological mind. Increasingly, the idea of a God who makes promises regarding the future is considered incredible. For some, experience is paramount. Many Africans who are influenced by secularization do not view the end of history through biblical lenses and according to the Christian view of God as loving, compassionate and good. Some take the view that God is not that interested in the nature of human actions to inflict punishment on them for committing these actions.[50] Aylward Shorter and Edwin Onyancha observe that secular values have reached deep into the various dimensions of the lives of all the social strata of African society. The current growth in the number of African Christians does not seem to stem the simultaneous development of de facto secularism on the continent.[51] In fact, according to secularism, there is no authority whose word has the power to elevate the hearts of humans to a horizon higher than the physical sphere.

How about pluralism? Here let us observe that the emergence on the continent of various religious forms as well as the several new spiritualities was motivated by two things. On the one hand, there is the fact that people's experience with God and the world are diverse; on the other hand, there is also the fact that people nurture the hope to find the true source of fulfillment in the here and now. But as we saw earlier, the idea of eschatological salvation is doubted by secular intellectuals. They want healing, self-liberation, and a life worth living in the here and now.

---

50. Moser, "Religious Skepticism," 108–28.
51. Shorter and Onyancha, *Secularism in Africa*, 27–28, 34–36.

With all this in mind, how do we reconcile eschatology and mission in the African landscape? The following section of this chapter will seek to address this question.

ESCHATOLOGY AND MISSION IN THE AFRICAN PERSPECTIVE

Biblical Eschatology and Christian Mission: Challenge for the Church in Africa

Naturally, doubt and even skepticism can invade the heart when one considers the future from God's perspective (2 Pet 3:3–5). As we've seen many Africans, particularly the intellectual elite, tend to adopt this outlook. When one adds to this the allurement of pluralism and the tendency of African societies to look for instant salvation in the here and now, we can conclude that, on several levels, eschatology and Christian mission will remain a challenge for the church in Africa.

One dimension of the challenge is temporal and spatial in nature (Mark 16:15). The nations of this world plan their activities in space and time. In some places, secular organizations have already put on their agendas the projects they will tackle for 2050. For the church, Africa remains a huge field to win for the Lord; there are still many African tribes that are yet to be reached with the gospel in their contexts and in particular situations. In the great commission of the Matthew 28:19, the participle *porenthentes* translated by "going" that Jesus uses to indicate the ordering of the missionary task, is an aorist passive that can be rendered in French by the imperative, when we consider the tense of the main verb of the verse. In addition to the missionary mandate that it conveys, *poreuomai* conveys the idea of distance, duration, and continuity. This brings to the fore the temporal and spatial aspect of the challenge that we are highlighting here.

Another aspect of the challenge is material and financial (2 Cor 8:5). The Lord promises his presence as a resource that is available on a permanent basis for the fulfillment of the missionary task. When we look at missionary work in Africa, we can say that the dependence of the African churches on foreign aid delays and adversely affects the quality of the missionary effort on the continent. If African mission is to be effective in every tribe and everywhere on the continent, the financial and material means needed for this task must be generated in Africa and by Africans. African churches have the human resources and the gospel, which is the content of mission. However, they do not contribute honestly to the work of God. They seem to find it difficult to free their financial and material means in order to make them available for the fulfillment of the missionary mandate on the continent. In this area, the challenge is yet to be faced in order that the imminent return of Christ may be announced to every African.

The third challenge is ethical in nature. In two different contexts, Jesus spoke the same word to his listeners. (1) To the Greeks who wanted to see him because of his fame, he said: "If someone wants to serve me, let him follow me" (John 12:26). (2) Following his resurrection, he said to Simon Peter: "you, follow me" (John 21:22). During his entire mission in the world, Jesus Christ lived a fully human life—but without sin. (Heb 2:17). His life was a beacon for those who were following and listening to him. His life as a missionary on earth seems to suggest that much emphasis needs to be placed on the life of sanctification that missionaries ought to live. If some authors and respondents highlight the flaws in the approach adopted by Western missionaries, this provides the opportunity for African missionaries to avoid these errors in their own missionary endeavors. The complacent lifestyle adopted by certain African missionaries due to the pressure of their own contexts and the exigencies of modernity adversely affect the relevance and the integrity of their message. Yet, the Bible says clearly that without sanctification, no one will see God (Heb 12:14). Notice that, because of the absolute holiness of God, the urgency of mission is implied in the obligation for the missionary to live of sanctification. The fact that Jesus is central to the conduct of the missionary mandate in Africa must inform the ethic of missionaries in every nook and cranny of the African continent. In view of the imminent return of Christ, every missionary is called to follow Jesus Christ and to be a model of virtue wherever he or she is placed.

Biblical Eschatology: Vector of Christian Mission in Africa

In the face of the skepticism mentioned earlier, and the African's penchant for the things of the earth, and all the challenges mentioned above, we contend that biblical eschatology must be the vector or the driving force of Christian mission in Africa. The preoccupation of the human heart with this world was manifest (perhaps as an omen of modernity already present in the first century) in the question, (apologetic in nature), that Pilate put to Jesus in naivete, jealousy, or ignorance: "'Are you the king of the Jews?' he asked our Lord" (John 18:33). In response Jesus says bluntly "My kingdom is not of this world my kingdom is not from here" (John 18:36–38). Jesus' discourse was intended to help Pilate understand that his kingdom was not a political kingdom; rather it was a kingdom of truth. Jesus was not disregarding the reality of the kingdom in the midst of which he was fulfilling his mission; instead, he wanted to elevate the mind and heart of Pilate to a kingdom which was higher than his limited and visible worldly kingdom; he wanted to direct his gaze toward the kingdom of God. Moreover, conscious of his mission and the preoccupation of the human heart, the Lord prays to the Father: "I am no longer in the world; they are in the world, I am going to you" (John 15:19; 17:6ff). Jesus' answer to Pilate implies the existence of two worlds: the physical or the created order and the kingdom of God that is beyond this historical world. This clearly affirms the existence of a world below and a world beyond this world.

As the mediating agent of creation and the recipient of the Father's authority by virtue of his victory on the cross, Jesus Christ is the head of all kingdoms—the kingdoms of this world and the kingdom above. Both the sacred and the secular, the material and the immaterial fall under his authority. All power and authority in heaven and on the earth belongs to God. The sacred and the secular fall under his authority; the immaterial universe and the material universe are subject to his authority. Voluntarily and temporally, he allows humans to reign in the earthly kingdoms—but always under his control. By virtue of his victory over all powers and principalities at the cross and his victory over death and hades, "the here below," and "the beyond" are under his dominion. The task of theology is to penetrate the logic of the Christian story with a view to presenting clearly the distinction that exists between "the here and now" and the world beyond. Theology must explain to all the adherents of the African religions and the dwellers of African societies the eschatological message of salvation that God alone offers to people in Jesus Christ. Moreover, theology must challenge its public to invest in the world beyond, without being insensitive or indifferent to the material needs of the individual in this present world. For God is interested in the total wellbeing of humans—in their holistic salvation.

That is why it is necessary to contextualize the gospel message. A holistic mission which seeks to transform the mentalities and the social condition of the people is also necessary. Joining the debate on eschatology in Africa, Englebert Mveng argues that we must help the African break free from his present alienation so that he may free himself, fulfill his potential and contribute to the different areas of thought and creativity.[52] Ultimately, this mission must seek to bring Africans to share the conviction that according to Scripture this world will pass away and that they need to take their refuge in Christ so they may enjoy the glorious life in the new world promised by God at the end of history.

---

52. Mveng, *Théologie, libération et cultures africaines*, 141.

10

Prophecy and Preaching in the Last Days in John's Revelation: A Reflection on the Ministry and Mission of the Church in South-East Asia

Tony Siew (Singapore)

WHAT IS THE MISSION and activity of the church in the last days? In the first part of this chapter I will investigate the nature of the church's mission during the End-times according to the book of Revelation, and in the second part I will offer some reflections on how the church in South-East Asia could do ministry and mission as the Day approaches.

JOHN'S CALL TO PROPHESY AGAIN

John, the author of the book of Revelation believes that prophecy and preaching will be the mainstay of God's servants in the last days. In one of the most remarkable visions in the middle section of the book, John saw himself eating a little scroll and having consumed it, he was told that, "You must again prophesy about many peoples and nations and tongues and kings" (Rev 10:11). John is thus re-commissioned to prophesy to the nations. The temporal context of this vision is made clear in the following narrative (Rev 11:1–13). Immediately following the re-commissioning, John is commanded to measure the temple and those worship in it as the nations will come and trample the holy city for forty-two months (Rev 11:1-2). While the holy city is being trampled, God will send his two witnesses to *prophesy* for 1,260 days (Rev 11:3). John's commission to prophesy again and the two witnesses' prophecy seem to be connected in some ways as the close proximity of the two texts suggest. This eschatological period of forty-two months or 1,260 days is crucial in that it sets John's and the two witnesses' prophesying in the last days before the coming of the kingdom of God (Rev 11:15). As this period of three and a half years ends in 11:13–14, the seventh trumpet sounds in 11:15 signaling the arrival of the kingdom of God on earth.[1]

Thus, there will be prophecy and preaching in the period called the Great Tribulation (cf. Rev 7:14) when the nations trample on the holy city and the beast rules the world for three and a half years (Rev 13:5). As the Great Tribulation is mentioned in Revelation 7, it is probable that John sees the events of the Great Tribulation unfolding with the sounding of the seven trumpets in Revelation 8 including the events of the final three and a half years in Revelation 11–13.[2] The period of three and a half years is only found in chapters 11 to 13 of Revelation (11:2, 3; 12:6, 14; 13:5). It is seen as the Danielic period of "a time, times and half a time" before the End comes

---

[1] Ben Witherington III comments thus: "The reference to forty-two months comes from Daniel and is just another way of rendering the period of three and a half years, that final penultimate period before the end of history." Witherington, *Revelation*, 158.

[2] While it is true that from John's perspective the saints are already suffering tribulation at the time of his writing (1:9; 2:10, 22), the reference to the great tribulation here at 7:14 refers to a future period when the seven trumpets begin to sound (Rev 8) until the dawn of the kingdom of God (cf. 11:15). Concerning the phrase "the Great Tribulation" in 7:14, Brian K. Blount comments, "The combination of the article and the adjective 'great' suggests that this is not just any tribulation but the great time of distress that would accompany the ushering in of God's Day of Judgment and Salvation (see Dan, esp. vv. 14)." Blount, *Revelation*, 154. John could have also alluded to Jesus' teaching of "the Great Tribulation" in Matt 24:21 which takes place when the abomination of desolation is set up in the temple (Matt 24:15) coinciding with the trampling of the Temple's outer courts and the holy city (Rev 11:12). David Aune comments that, "the articular phrase ... 'the great tribulation' is anaphoric and assumes that the readers know the final tribulation or period of woes that will introduce the eschaton, first mentioned in Dan 12:1 ... and thereafter part of the series of events associated with the arrival of the eschaton in early Judaism and early Christianity ... ." Aune, *Revelation 6–16*, 473.

where the saints will suffer great persecution and many will fall or martyred for the sake of their faith in Christ (cf. Rev 12:14, echoing Daniel 7:25; 12:7). The events of the Great Tribulation of the three and a half years are narrated by John from Revelation 11:1 until the beginning of chapter 14 where the Lamb returns to Mount Zion in triumph with his 144,000 companions (Rev 14:15). Significantly, the vision of an angel *preaching* the eternal good news (Rev 14:67) begins a new section of Revelation after the events of the three and a half years of Revelation 11:13. Apart from 14:6, the only other word for "preaching the good news" in Revelation is found in 10:7 as follows: "but that in the days of the trumpet call to be sounded by the seventh angel, the mystery of God, as he preached to his servants the prophets, should be fulfilled."

PROPHECY AND PREACHING

What is prophecy? What is preaching? It is submitted that prophecy and preaching the good news are intricately linked in Revelation. As God preaches or announces the good news to his servants the prophets (Rev 10:7), they in turn will *prophesy* as John (Rev 10:11) and the two witnesses (Rev 11:3) are commanded to do. The content of the proclamation in 10:7 is not specified except for the fact that when the seventh angel sounds, the mystery of God would have been fulfilled. Within the context of Revelation 10, the mystery of God is contained in this little book/scroll given by the angel to John, who having digested it is called forth to prophesy again. It is significant to note the word *"palin"* (again) indicates that John is entering a new phase of his prophesying.[3] He has prophesied concerning the things that are and the things that are to come (Rev 1:9), now he is re-commissioned to prophesy *again*. The mystery of God that is to be fulfilled consists of the events of the Great Tribulation of the last three and a half years leading to the dawn of the kingdom of the Lord and his Christ which John goes on to narrate in Revelation 11:13.

JOHN AS PROPHET

Although John never calls himself a prophet, he nonetheless thinks of himself as a prophet. First, John calls his book "the words of prophecy," and

3. As Pierre Prigent remarks that the adverb, *"palin"* suggests that John's prophecy from 10:11 "would thus be a new prophecy which distinguish itself from that which is expressed in the preceding chapters of the book of Revelation." Prigent, *Commentary on the Apocalypse of St. John*, 336.

these prophetic words consist of the things that are about to come to pass shortly (1:13; 22:19). Towards the end of the book of Revelation, John is addressed by an angel in this manner: "I am a fellow servant with you and your brothers, and with those who keep the words of this book. Worship God" (19:10a). And he said to me, "Do not seal up the words of the prophecy of this book, for the time is near" (Rev 22:9).

The words of Jesus at the end of Revelation further confirm that John is not alone in his prophetic ministry: "I, Jesus have sent mine angel to testify to you [plural] these things in the churches" (Rev 22:16). David Aune has shown that the "you" in the plural form refers to the *prophets* who receive the words of the prophecy and convey them to the churches. Thus in the book of Revelation, John is seen as the leading prophet within the fraternity of his brother prophets.[4]

Prophecy signifies things/events that are (present) and also the things that are yet to come to pass (future), and the act of prophesying by John and his fellow prophets in Revelation is to convey these things and future events to the church and through the church to the rest of the nations on earth. This is evidenced by the fact that John is commanded to write about "the things which must soon take place" (Rev 1:1). Significantly, John is commanded to "write the things which you have seen, and the things which are, and the things which will take place after these things" (Rev 1:19). I take "the things which are" to refer to the events mentioned in the seven letters and "the things which will take place after these things" as referring to future events after the events of the seven churches.[5] Further, after the seven letters to the seven churches are penned, John is caught up in heaven and is told that he would be shown "what must take place after these things" (Rev 4:1).[6]

---

4. Aune, "The Prophetic Circle of John of Patmos and the Exegesis of Revelation 22:16," 103–16. So also Fiorenza, "Apocalypsis and Propheteia: Revelation in the Context of the Early Christian Prophecy," 105–28. For a discussion of "Prophet and Prophetism" in Revelation, see Prigent, *Commentary*, 79–84.

5. Gregory K. Beale is correct to remark that, "The meaning of v 19 is crucial since it is usually understood to be paradigmatic for the structure and content of the whole book." Beale, *The Book of Revelation*, 216.

6. The question of how we understand prophecy in John's Revelation has been debated by many scholars throughout the ages but as far as this paper is concerned, Revelation 1:19 and 4:1 suggest that from the perspective of John, most of the things that he has seen and heard are to take place in the future *after* the events of the seven churches (especially Rev 6 onwards).

THE FORM OF PROPHECY

The nature of prophesying is described in John's *prophecy* to the seven churches. John's seven letters to the seven churches are given in the form of prophecy. The first words, "*Thus says . . .*" in each of the seven letters has John speaking by way of prophecy like an Old Testament prophet.[7] Each of the seven letters also starts with a specific and distinctive characterization of Jesus followed by the first person's address to the angel of the church in question: "*I know . . .*" (Rev 2:2, 9, 13, 19; 3:1, 8, 15). It is as if through the prophetic words of John given in writing, Jesus is speaking directly to the churches. In the inaugural vision of Rev 1, John sees Jesus, one like a Son of Man in the midst of the seven lampstands (Rev 1:13), the seven lampstands symbolizing the seven churches (Rev 1:20). What John saw and heard from Jesus, he *prophesied* to the seven churches accordingly.[8]

Thus, John posits that in the last three and a half years the activity of prophesying will be prevalent in the church as he sees himself as an end-time prophet (Rev 10:11). And this task of prophesying is exemplified in the last days by the two witnesses who will prophesy for 1,260 days (Rev 11:3).[9] Further, these two witnesses are explicitly called the two prophets (Rev 11:10) and their proclamation in those three and a half years as "the days of their prophesying" (Rev 11:6).

THE CONTENT OF PROPHECY

It would be useful to John's readers if John had explained the content of the two witnesses' prophecy. At best we see John equating prophecy with testimony as 11:7 seems to indicate: "When they have finished their *testimony*, the beast that ascends . . . ." We may well ask what constitutes the content of their testimony or prophecy in those 1,260 days. All that we can garner from the prophecy and testimony of the two witnesses is that their activity of prophesying leads to torment for the inhabitants of the earth (Rev 11:10). It appears that the two witnesses' prophecy is so fiery, perhaps literally (Rev 11:5)[10] and metaphorically in that it pronounces judgment and

---

7. So Prigent, *Commentary*, 157.

8. Leonard L. Thompson notes that, "Each of the seven messages that he [John] dictates takes the form of a prophetic pronouncement . . . ." Thompson, *Revelation*, 62.

9. The future tense of the verb, "they will prophesy" in 11:3 is significant to locate the activity of the two witnesses as unfolding in the future from the perspective of John's writing in the late first century C.E.

10. There is considerable debate on how the sign, "fire coming out of their mouth" in 11:5 is to be interpreted. A literal interpretation can be supported with reference to

condemnation on the dwellers in the world who are bent on idolatry and worship of the Beast and rebellion against God. In the Hebrew Bible, prophecy is often associated with judgment as Jeremiah the prophet declares: "The prophets who preceded you and me from ancient times prophesied war, famine, and pestilence against many countries and great kingdoms" (Jer 28:8). John's re-commissioning as a prophet to the nations and kings (Rev 10:11) could have been patterned after Jeremiah's calling as "the prophet to the nations" (Jer 1:5). Moreover, in the first four seals of Revelation 6, John also prophesies concerning war (second seal), famine (third seal), pestilence (fourth Seal), which accords well with the biblical prophecy cited by Jeremiah. One other significant parallel between Revelation 10:11 and Jeremiah 28:8 is that John is called to prophesy against "many kings" while a typical prophet according to Jeremiah prophesies against "great kingdoms."

PROPHECY AND PREACHING THE GOOD NEWS

We have noted that the verbal forms of "preaching" or "preaching the gospel/good news" in the active voice are found only in Revelation 10:7 and 14:6.[11] The angel with the eternal gospel begins a series of visions of three angels making Revelation 14:6–13 a distinct unit within the book of Revelation. What is interesting about the first angel of 14:6 is that he has this eternal gospel to preach to those who dwell on earth—to every nation, and kindred, and tongue and people.[12] This four-fold description of the inhabitants of the earth is also found in John's re-commissioning although the latter's formulation has "kings" at the fourth element together with peoples, nations and languages (Rev 10:11). The content of this eternal Gospel preached by the angel is defined as follows: "Fear God, and give him glory for the hour of his judgment is come: and worship him that made the heaven, and earth, and the sea, and the fountain of waters" (Rev 14:7). Again, the four-fold

---

the prophet Elijah who called fire down from heaven to consume the two companies of fifty soldiers sent to capture him (2 Kgs 1:10–12). A metaphorical or spiritual interpretation can be argued if John echoes Jeremiah's experience of God's word: "Therefore thus says the LORD, the God of hosts: Because they have spoken this word, behold, I am making my words in your mouth a fire, and this people wood, and the fire shall devour them" (Jer 5:14).

11. Stephen Smalley notes that "the active voice of the verb is rare, and is found in the New Testament only at Rev. 10.7 and Rev. 14.6." Smalley, *The Revelation to John*, 361.

12. As Edmondo F. Lupieri correctly notes, "This is the only appearance of the term, 'gospel' in the book, and the only appearance of the phrase, 'eternal gospel' in the whole of the NT." Lupieri, *A Commentary on the Apocalypse of John*, 223.

dimension of creation is given here as the spatial and cosmic order over which the Creator reigns. This four-fold created order is not fortuitously mentioned at this juncture but serves as a literary device that links the angelic proclamation with the first four trumpets that affected the earth, the sea and the fountain of waters and the heaven/sky (Rev 8:7–12). It appears that the angel's preaching of the eternal gospel coincides with the judgments unleashed under the Trumpet series.

To fear God and give him glory means to repent from sinful deeds and worship the one true God. As severe as the Trumpet judgments are, they are intended to lead the inhabitants of the world to repentance (Rev 9:20–21). At the conclusion of the sixth trumpet/second woe, the remainder of the dwellers in the holy city repented at the sight of the two witnesses being resurrected and ascended into heaven accompanied by an earthquake for they "gave glory to the God of heaven" (Rev 11:12–13).[13]

WHO ARE THE TWO WITNESSES OF REVELATION 11:1–13 AND THE ANGEL OF REVELATION 14:6?

We have attempted to show that John portrays several activities as taking place by God's emissaries in the final period before the coming of the kingdom of God. The two witnesses of Revelation 11 are said to prophesy and the angel of 14:6 is said to preach the eternal gospel to all the inhabitants of the world. Who are these two witnesses and who is the angel of Revelation 14:6? John's readers would have wished that John could be more explicit in his description of the two witnesses as he identifies them as the two olive trees and the two lampstands that stand before the Lord of the earth (Rev 11:4). The imagery of the lampstands seems to suggest that the two witnesses are representatives of churches as the seven lampstands in Revelation 1 are said to symbolize the seven churches (Rev 1:20). Hence, many scholars take the two witnesses as symbolizing the corporate church in its testimony and prophecy to the world.[14] However, the two witnesses are not only identified as the two lampstands but they are *first* identified as the two olive trees in 11:4. The symbol of an olive tree is not interpreted in

---

13. Richard Bauckham argues that the prophetic ministry of the two witnesses brings about the conversion of nations. See Bauckham, "The Conversion of the Nations," 274.

14. Ian Boxall, after discussing the various interpretations of the two witnesses as individual prophets concludes that, "it is perhaps better, then, to view them as the representative figures of the prophetic ministry of the Church." Boxall, *The Revelation of Saint John*, 164. For a detailed discussion on the identity of the two witnesses, see Siew, "The Identity of the Two Witnesses and the Two Beasts," 214–50.

Revelation. The allusion by John to Zechariah's vision of the two olive trees standing one on the left and the other on the right of a lampstand is almost certain. In Zechariah 4, the two olive trees represent Zerubbabel the governor and Joshua the high priest as the two leaders of the people of God in the post-exilic community. By using this imagery of the two olive trees, John is probably indicating that the two witnesses are the two leaders of the people of God, the church in the last days. As leaders, the two witnesses are also the representatives of the church in her testimony to the nations before the End comes. Further, as the two witnesses are also called the two lampstands as well as the two olive trees, John is conveying a double-identity for the two witnesses as two individuals (olive trees) as well as the church corporate (lampstands). As the two individual prophets, they are given power to perform certain powerful signs (Rev 11:56), but they are also part of the church in its prophetic witness to the world in the last 1,260 days.[15]

The angel of Revelation 14:6, on the other hand, is probably to be interpreted as the heavenly representation of what is happening on earth. It is only here in Revelation that an *angel* is said to be "flying in mid-heaven." Elsewhere, an *eagle* is said to be flying in mid-heaven proclaiming the last three woes (Rev 8:13). The angel of 14:6 and the eagle of 8:13 are arguably linked as they are the only entities said to be flying in mid-heaven with *messages* to announce.[16] At least we can conclude that if there is a correspondence between the angel and the eagle, the angel of 14:6 preaches this eternal gospel at the time of the last three woes announced by the flying eagle which are the final three trumpets leading to the establishment of God's kingdom on earth.

As the heavenly angel preaches the eternal gospel in the sky, the saints preach it on earth.[17] Like the two witnesses of Revelation 11, the angel with the eternal gospel is another imagery of the church's preaching activity in the

---

15. It is unlikely that John is saying that every member of the church can perform the signs mentioned in 11:5–6. The whole church is called to witness to Jesus, but only the two individual prophets can perform the powerful signs at the end time.

16. Prigent comments thus: "The first angel [14:6] flies at the zenith: the message he is going to proclaim must be heard by the entire universe, like the eagle who foretold of the three disasters (Rev 8:13)". Prigent, *Commentary*, 438. In Rev 19:17, birds are said to be flying in mid-heaven ready to eat the flesh of the kings and soldiers gathered at Armageddon. Brian K. Blount rightly observes that, "The description [angel of 14:6] calls to mind both the eagle flying in mid-heaven at 8:13 and the birds flying in mid-heaven at 19:17. In both those cases the flights occur in the context of God's graphic judgment against the idolatrous inhabitants of the earth. . . . The angel is a visible reminder that God is preparing a powerful and just response." Blount, *Revelation*, 271–72.

17. This accords well with the apocalyptic worldview of John that whatever happens in heaven affects what goes on in the world or conversely what happens on earth is a reflection of heavenly realities.

last days. The conflict in the last days is intense—one on side is the appearance of the two beasts of Revelation 13 who commit gross blasphemies in making the world's populace worship Satan and the sea-beast (Rev 13:1–5), and on the other side is the appearance of God's two witnesses proclaiming the worship of the one true God who will come to judge the world.

THE WORD OF GOD AND THE TESTIMONY OF JESUS CHRIST

One further clue as to the content of prophecy and preaching is found in the phrase used by John to describe why he was exiled at the island of Patmos for he "bore witness to the word of God and to the testimony of Jesus Christ" (Rev 1:2). I agree with David Aune that it is possible that the *kai*, joining the "word of God" and "the testimony of Jesus Christ" is epexegetical: i.e., "the word of God" is further defined by the phrase "the witness of Jesus Christ."[18] And specifically, the testimony borne by Jesus is the prophetic word given to John through an angel.

John is called to be a witness in the manner of Jesus who is said to be "the faithful witness" (Rev 1:5). Bearing witness to the Word of God and the testimony of Jesus could land one into trouble with the political authorities in John's time. Likewise, in the last days when the beast rules the world, any prophecy or preaching against idolatry or worship of the beast will be dealt with severely. Thus, it is said that the beast that ascends from the abyss will make war against the two witnesses and kill them (11:7; cf. 13:7). In the vision of the dragon and the woman of Revelation 12, the dragon is said to make war on the rest of the seed of the woman, on those who keep the commandments of God and bear testimony to Jesus (12:17). The saints on earth bear testimony to Jesus and obey the commandments of God rather than the decrees of the beast or that of his right-hand man, the land-beast (Rev 13:11–18).

In the last days, it is a question of submission and worship. Does one submit and worship the beast or worship God? It is also a question of action or inaction. Does one keep silent for safety's sake or declare one's allegiance to Jesus and unmask the pretension of the beast? At the center of the pivot

---

18. David Aune also notes that the phrases, "the word of God" and "the testimony of Jesus" are closely associated or virtually equated (1:2, 9; 6:9; 20:4). Aune, *Revelation 1–5*, 19. For a discussion of this important phrase, "the word of God and the testimony of Jesus," see Trites, *The New Testament Concept of Witness*, 155–64; Sweet, "Maintaining the Testimony of Jesus," 101–17; Lampe, "The Testimony of Jesus is the Spirit of Prophecy (Rev 19:10)," 245–58; Wallis, *The Faith of Jesus Christ in Early Christian Traditions*, 163–74.

of Revelation 12, the key to the victory of the saints is stated thus: "They conquered him [the devil/beast] by the blood of the Lamb and by *the word of their testimony*, for they loved not their lives unto death (Rev 12:11). On earth, the saints are defeated by the beast (they are conquered and some are killed), but ultimate victory belongs not to the beast but to those who dare profess Christ in their mouth with the word of their testimony.

THE TESTIMONY OF JESUS IS THE SPIRIT OF PROPHECY (REVELATION 19:10)

Another passage may shed further light on the meaning of the phrase "the Word of God and the testimony of Jesus" and on how Jesus' testimony is linked to prophecy. Towards the end of the book of Revelation, John is commanded to write down what he saw: "These are the true words of God" (Rev 19:9). John fell down to worship the angel who commanded him, but he was rebuffed by the angel with these words: "You must not do that! I am a fellow servant with you and your brethren who hold the testimony of Jesus. Worship God. *For the testimony of Jesus is the spirit of prophecy.*"[19] The command to "worship God" in 19:9 is also found in the angel's proclamation in 14:6–7 which reiterates that the message of the gospel includes the affirmation that God is to be worshipped and no one else. But the enigmatic verse of 19:10 has many commentators scrambling for answers as to how it should be interpreted. Robert Thomas suggests that the verse may have the sense of "He who has the spirit of prophecy will convey Jesus' testimony."[20] While the Greek syntax of 19:10 may support Thomas' explanation, nevertheless reversing the order of words may not yield the desired result. I interpret 19:10 to mean that the testimony borne by Jesus is the prophetic spirit in the sense that what Jesus testifies to the angels of the churches is also what the prophetic Spirit is saying to the churches as shown by the prophecies of John to the seven churches (Rev 2–3). The Word of God in John's Revelation is defined as the testimony of Jesus Christ and what is spoken by Jesus is *prophetic* for it is thus inspired by the spirit of prophecy.

---

19. The genitival phrase, "the testimony of Jesus" can be understood as both subjective and objective genitive: "the witness by and to Jesus." So Beale, *The Book of Revelation*, 947. In Rev 19:10, the subjective genitive is probably intended by John, giving the sense of "testimony given by Jesus."

20. Thomas, *Revelation 8–22: An Exegetical Commentary*, 377.

SUMMARY

We have attempted to establish that in the last days, a number of personages are given messages to deliver to the church and to the world. The author, John, prophesies to the seven churches (Rev 2–3) and is called to prophesy again (Rev 10:11) and this prophecy appears to be taken up by the two witness-prophets in the last 1,260 days. An eagle flies in mid-heaven announcing three woes/last three trumpets to sound (Rev 8:13) in the period of the Great Tribulation while an angel also flying in mid-heaven preaching the eternal gospel to all and sundry (Rev 14:6–7). John also sees the saints conquering their enemies by the words of the testimony (Rev 12:11) and the rest of the children of the woman subjected to the persecution of the dragon because they keep the commandments of God and hold to the testimony of Jesus (Rev 12:17). All these entities or symbols in one way or another represent the prophetic ministry of the church on earth. John sees the church rising in the last days with boldness prophesying of the things to come as well as declaring the eternal gospel which is to fear and worship God and that judgment is to come upon all those who reject this gospel (Rev 14:7). Ultimately, prophecy and preaching comes from God for God himself announces his mystery to his servants the prophets until it is all fulfilled in God's pre-determined time (Rev 10:6–7).

THE CHURCH IN SOUTH-EAST ASIA: A REFLECTION ON MINISTRY AND MISSION

As the events of the End-time still lie in the future, it is not easy to take the events which I have described above and apply them in the present context of ministry and mission in South-East Asia (SEA). Out of the ten or eleven countries that made up SEA with a population of 600 million people, I have only visited five and preached in four countries, namely, Indonesia, Thailand, Malaysia, and Singapore where I am now based.[21] South-East Asia is not a monolithic or mono-cultural entity. Within one country there

---

21. ASEAN is a political grouping of ten countries—Myanmar, Thailand, Laos, Cambodia, Vietnam, Malaysia, Brunei, Singapore, Indonesia, and the Philippines. The eleventh country which can be listed geographically as belonging to the South-East Asian region is East Timor. When I was doing research on this paper, the only article written from an Asian inter-cultural perspective that I know of is one by Khiok-Khng Yeo, "Hope for the Persecuted, Cooperation with the State, and Meaning for the Dissatisfied," 221. In his essay, Professor Yeo who was born and raised in Sarawak, East Malaysia writes concerning his experience in China and does not touch on South-East Asia at all.

could be up to 100 or more different ethnic groups such as in Indonesia and Myanmar. My home state, Sabah (formerly British North Borneo) in Malaysia has some thirty-five ethnic groups with the Kadazan-Dusuns, being the major tribal group. I am Chinese by race, born and bred in Malaysia, and became a Christian in New Zealand, where I read law and theology. Before I moved to Singapore in 2008, I spent more than a decade in full-time ministry among the Kadazan-Dusuns in my home state, using the Malay language as a medium of worship and preaching. My background and experience as a Christian and minister of the gospel living in South-East Asia may not be typical of an ethnic Chinese in Malaysia given the fact that many ethnic Chinese Malaysians do not speak Malay well nor do they have much involvement with the indigenous peoples of the land. With my limited experience and knowledge of the variegated cultures, peoples and nations of SEA, I will, therefore, write of what is more familiar to me, that is the context of Malaysia and Singapore within which most of my ministry has been conducted.

Singapore is related to Malaysia in many ways, historically, politically and culturally. Singapore used to be part of Malaysia when Singapore together Sabah and Sarawak joined Malaya to form Malaysia on 16th September 1963. In less than two years due to political and racial tensions, Singapore left Malaysia and became an independent nation on 9th August 1965. Malaysia and Singapore since the latter's independence experienced different levels of development so that Singapore by the late 1990s has gained developed nation status with a GDP per capita of about US$50,000 p.a., whereas Malaysia is considered a developing nation with a varying degree of development across the thirteen states of the Federation with a GDP per capita of US$8,500 p.a.[22] Both countries have written Constitutions that provide for the freedom of religion within certain legal limits and constraints.[23] Malaysia is seen by some as an Islamic country though the Constitution only

---

22 The latest figures given by Mr Lee Kuan Yew writing for Forbes Asia Magazine (26th March issue) in "The world is truly a global village" has Singapore's GDP per capita at US$50,123. This short essay is reported in Straits Times (17th March 2012), at p. A38. Mr Lee Kuan Yew is the founding Prime Minister of Singapore from 1959–90. Singapore's economic success story for the past twenty years is without peers in Asia.

23 The Constitution of the Federation of Malaysia provides for religious freedom as per Article 11. (1): "Every person has the right to profess and practise his religion and, subject to Clause (4), to propagate it . . ." Clause 4 (4): "State law and in respect of the Federal Territories of Kuala Lumpur, Labuan and Putrajaya, federal law may control or restrict the propagation of any religious doctrine or belief among persons professing the religion of Islam." The Constitution of the Republic of Singapore's Article 15 (1) states: "Every person has the right to profess and practise his religion and to propagate it" which is somewhat qualified by Article 15 (4): "This Article does not authorise any act contrary to any general law relating to public order, public health or morality."

provides that "Islam is the religion of the Federation."[24] Politicians from opposite sides of the political spectrum argue whether Malaysia is a secular state or an Islamic state. Singapore, on the other hand, does not have an official religion except that like in Malaysia, Singapore is equally sensitive regarding inter-racial and inter-religious harmony between various races in the country, emphasizing tolerance and mutual respect towards all religions. Within this political-religious milieu of Malaysia and Singapore, the gospel is preached and the Christian faith propagated in varying degree of success and progress. According to the 2010 census, Singapore's percentage of Christians per population has grown from 14 percent in 2000 to 18 percent in 2010, and Malaysia's Christians constitute less than 10 percent of the total population, with the majority of Christians living in the two East Malaysian States of Sabah and Sarawak.[25]

As John's Revelation suggests, the preaching of the gospel will become increasingly more difficult in the last days. The state will become less and less tolerant towards Christians until the appearance of the beast that will persecute anyone who dares challenge his supremacy and his desire for deification (Rev 13). When the time of the Great Tribulation comes, any proclamation of the Christian faith will stand the risk of censure to the point of imprisonment and martyrdom. While the opportunity of preaching the gospel is still relatively free in most SEA countries, it is important to take advantage of this openness to win souls for Christ and strengthen the faith of believers.

Christian leaders are especially challenged in two respects as far as church-state relations are concerned. On the one hand, the members of the church who are also citizens of a state are bound to honour its political leaders as Scripture commands (Rom 13:1–7; 1 Pet 2:13–14; Titus 3:1). But on the other hand, Christians are called to be bold in using the present opportunities and all available avenues to preach the gospel as freely and as widely as possible.

Second, Christian leaders in Malaysia and Singapore will need all the courage and wisdom to exercise the prophetic ministry envisaged by John of Revelation of the End-time church. Despite certain prohibitions, legal or cultural that appear to restrict the propagation of the gospel to certain groups, Christian leaders cannot maintain their silence as the eternal gospel

---

24. Article 3 (1): "Islam is the religion of the Federation; but other religions may be practiced in peace and harmony in any part of the Federation."

25. See Department of Statistics Singapore at http://www.singstat.gov.sg/ (accessed 15th March 2012). Malaysia's statistics are only an estimate as religious affiliations of citizens are considered sensitive classifications and official or unofficial accounts may not tell the whole story about the actual numbers of religious adherents.

in Revelation 14:6–7 is to be announced to all peoples from all nations, languages, and tribes. Propagating the Christian faith even in all wisdom may lead to certain repercussions, but as the book of Revelation shows, suffering, tribulation, and persecution is part and parcel of the cost of following the Lamb that was slain before the foundation of the world. This does not mean that Christian leaders should not exercise caution when it is called for. Restraint, tolerance, and mutual respect towards others could well be just as effective an evangelistic tool as confrontational preaching that may be offensive and a stumbling block. There is no justification to antagonize any person, race, or religion unnecessarily with our actions or words. If the mission of the church in SEA is to advance further, I believe there are three things that need our serious attention and prayerful consideration.

DEMOGRAPHICS & LANGUAGES

First, preaching is done in the language or languages of the people to whom the gospel is directed. Preaching can only be well received and understood by the masses if the vernaculars of the target people groups are used. Out of 600 million population in SEA, almost half (270 million) speak the Malay language in Malaysia (28 million), Indonesia (240 million), Brunei and parts of southern Thailand. Despite some differences in the language spoken by Malaysians and Indonesians, Malaysia's Malay and Indonesian are essentially the same language. In Singapore, since the introduction of bilingualism policy in the late 1970s, only a fraction of non-Malay Singaporeans can now speak Malay.[26] Yet, Singapore is surrounded by its closest neighbors, Malaysia, Brunei and Indonesia with Malay the dominant language in these countries.[27] If Singaporean Christians are to do mission in their own backyard, they need to learn and speak Malay well. Singapore's *Samaria* is

---

26. Singapore's bilingualism policy has it that all Singaporeans learn English as the primary language of instruction and a second language, usually the student's mother tongue. As for Chinese Singaporeans, the two languages learnt are English and Mandarin/Chinese whereas the Singaporean Malays learn English and the Malay language. Singapore's population of 3.9 million (citizens and permanent residents excluding those on work permits) is made up of three main ethnic groups—Chinese (73%), Malays (14%), and Indians (10%). For a fascinating account of Singapore's bilingualism policy, see Yew, *My Lifelong Challenge: Singapore's Bilingual Journey*.

27. Malaysia's population of 28 million people is made up of three main races—Malays (60%), Chinese (25%), and Indians (11%). Chinese Malaysians used to number up to 40% of the total population in the 1970s, but due to various factors, economic, social and political there has been an exodus of Chinese Malaysians migrating to other countries in the last two decades. The problem of brain drain in Malaysia has been recognized by the government recently.

Malaysia and Indonesia. Churches in Singapore should prayerfully reflect whether they have done enough in their Samaria before going to the ends of the earth on mission.[28] Likewise in Malaysia, with most ethnic Chinese choosing Chinese-stream schools instead of the national school system, a majority of Chinese Malaysians cannot speak Malay well. Ministry and mission to the indigenous peoples of the land who speak Malay will be hindered if language barriers persist.[29]

Another phenomenon in the demographic shifts in populations within South-East Asia is the growth of migrant workers in Singapore and Malaysia. In Singapore, more than 1 million out of 5.3 million people living in Singapore are here on work permits or long-term social visas. For instance, there are some 200,000 maids in Singapore, mostly from Indonesia and Philippines. Christian families that have maids can minister to their own maids if they act with justice and kindness towards their maids and respect basic employees' rights of a day's rest in a week, knowing that both employers and employees have one Master in heaven (Col 4:1).[30] There are large numbers of other peoples from South-East Asia working in the construction sector, road works, factories, hospitality and tourism services and retail sectors. Some local churches have taken up the challenge to reach out to the foreign workers but much more can be done.

In my home State of Sabah, out of 3 million people, an estimated number of undocumented immigrants totaling up to half a million people, mostly from southern Philippines and Indonesia have now taken up residence in the state. This is a serious political and security issue as almost a quarter of the state's population may have entered the state illegally. To make matters worse, some of these immigrants may have obtained Malaysian citizenship all too easily through some dubious legal means.[31] The church

---

28. Obviously, a large segment of Singaporean Christians are English-speaking which makes Singaporean churches strategically placed for world mission, especially to the English-speaking Western world which has become a mission field in the last twenty or thirty years in view of the decline of Christianity in the West.

29. It must be said that an increasing minority of Chinese Malaysians speak good Malay and Christian leaders in Malaysia as a whole must embrace the national language if mission within Malaysia is truly nation-wide, embracing all people groups.

30. "Masters, treat your slaves justly and fairly, knowing that you also have a Master in heaven" (Col 4:1).

31. Sabah State's politicians have been pushing for the Federal government to set up a Royal Commission of Inquiry into this problem. See the statement dated 29th Oct 2011 by the Deputy Chief Minister of Sabah, Tan Sri Joseph Pairin Kitingan who is also the President of Parti Bersatu Sabah (PBS), a coalition party within the ruling National Coalition: http://www.pbs-sabah.org/pbs3/html/news/2011/291011-bernama.html (accessed 16th March 2012). The Royal Commission of Inquiry has since been set up and is now in the process of carrying out its investigations. See the report on the

in Sabah could shun these migrants and treat them as a security risk and does nothing to promote their welfare, material and spiritual or the church could see its role as a channel of blessing and compassion, which is to reach out to these immigrants with the good news, a harvest field right at our doorsteps while at the same time as responsible and civic-minded citizens doing its part in helping the authorities to overcome this serious political and security problem.

SOCIAL MEDIA, INTERNET, & GLOBALIZATION

Second, churches need to utilize and take full advantage of the technological advances of the twenty-first century. Singapore is the second most-wired nation in Asia after South Korea. More than 77 percent of the population has access to the Internet.[32] More than half the population reads and interacts with blogs, Facebook and other social media regularly. Yet, the Christian community appears to be slow in using this new media to propagate the Christian faith. Rev. Canon Terry Wong has written convincingly that there is much to be gained if churches, pastors and theologians are fully conversant with the explosion of Information technology (IT).[33] It is imperative that Christian leaders harness this new technology for the work of the church and her mission to the world. Canon Wong laments the lack of investment on IT and communications staff in many churches and Christian institutions in Singapore.[34] He goes on to say that "the church should not relegate IT issues to technicians and hobbyists. Leaders, pastors, theologians and thinkers need to give leadership to these matters."[35] I can't agree more.

For example, there are only a handful of blogs written by scholars and theologians in Malaysia and Singapore. Blogging is taken up with relish by many Malaysians and Singaporeans alike but it is rare to see biblical scholars and theologians engaged in the new media. Perhaps, it is the risks involved in stating your positions or beliefs in the public domain that has hindered many from even considering starting a blog on Christian and theological

---

progress of the RCI from Sin Chew Daily dated 21st Jan 2013 at http://www.mysinchew.com/node/82181 (accessed 21st January 2013).

32. According Internet World Stats at http://www.internetworldstats.com/asia/sg.htm (accessed 15th March 2012). South Korea has 81 percent internet penetration as of 2010. For a discussion on how Information technology (IT) has impacted the nation and society in Singapore as a whole, see Arun Mahizhnan's essay on "Networked Society in an Intelligent Nation," 409–21.

33. Wong, "The Church Ministry in a Digital Age," 53–59.

34. Ibid., 58.

35. Ibid., 59.

matters. Again, the angel flying in mid-heaven of Revelation 14:6–7 comes to mind. The angel preaches the gospel far and wide announcing in the air (sky) to all concerned. What better way is there today to broadcast the gospel to the widest possible audience in real time if not through the Internet using various forms of online media?[36] I am not going to preach the gospel to all the 200 countries of the world in my life-time. Yet through blogging in recent years I have reached tens of thousands of people in more than seventy countries that have accessed to the Internet. The size of the online audience is only limited by the availability of Internet access and possible censorship by some countries. The forces of globalization march on. Beside the Internet, frequent travel from one country to another within South-East Asia is made possible with the rise of low-cost carriers in the region. Bringing the gospel to a neighboring country has never been easier or cheaper.

UNITY OF THE CHURCH AND UTILIZATION OF RESOURCES

Third, the unity of the church of Jesus Christ must be our priority. The mainline churches have been established in Malaysia and Singapore for over 100 years. In the past decades many more independent churches have sprouted in Malaysia and Singapore. Some of these independent churches have become mega-churches with 10,000 members or more.[37] In Malaysia, my home denomination of Sidang Injil Borneo (SIB) has over 1,000 congregations, mostly among the indigenous peoples of Sabah and Sarawak but is also growing among the Chinese in West Malaysia.[38] In the book of Revelation, the churches are seen as one church (seven churches in Asia Minor representing the universal church) and the two witness-prophets are the leaders of the end-time church. It is important, therefore, for Christian leaders in South-East Asia to work together and develop greater and more

---

36. I blogged at http://cherubim77.blogspot.com/ from May 2006 to April 2012 and more than 100,000 page-views have been recorded from July 2010 to April 2012. Since Sept 2012, I have been blogging at http://cherubim777.blogspot.com.

37. According to a survey by "The Christian Post" online Singapore edition, there are 570 registered Protestant churches in 2010. See The Christian Post's article dated 22nd Jan 2012 at http://sg.christianpost.com/dbase/church/2422//1.htm (accessed 16th March 2012).

38. The Wikipedia entry on Sidang Injil Borneo cites a report that SIB has 500,000 members. This figure is far too high and active membership is probably in the region of 250,000 as of 2011 (Sabah—100,000; Sarawak—150,000; West Malaysia—8,000). See http://en.wikipedia.org/wiki/Sidang_Injil_Borneo (accessed 17th March 2012).

effective networks of ministry and mission than what is evident today to better serve the vast number of unreached peoples of the region.

Working together often means pooling and maximizing our resources instead of reduplicating what another church is doing on its own. Churches can share premises used for worship and save costs as some churches are doing. What a waste of resources if a multi-million dollar building is only used once or twice a week by one single congregation? Local seminaries could have inter-loan library facilities with one another.[39] Exchange programs between faculty members and students could be arranged to share the faculty's expertise and resources and above all project Christian unity among the larger Christian community. As Singapore's seminaries take on many students from SEA countries, theological institutions play a strategic role in training and educating pastors and mission workers in the region.[40]

Singapore as one of the wealthiest nations in the world simply cannot look after her own interests only without also considering the interests of the neighboring countries that are much poorer. Churches within SEA must bear one another's burden as the body of Christ and the family of God (e.g., Paul's collection from gentile churches to help the poor in Jerusalem). Coming from a decade-long ministry among the indigenous churches in Borneo with limited financial resources, I can't be more amazed at the wealth of most churches in Singapore. It is not unusual for an average size congregation of 300–400 members to have more than a million-dollar annual income. Imagine if only 10 percent of that income goes to mission to Borneo (Singapore's *Samaria*) and multiplied that by 500 churches, one will have S$50 million a year for mission to neighboring countries in SEA.

CONCLUSION

The challenges in the last days are immense and the task is great but if we look to the God of heaven, we will receive grace and mercy to be used by him to preach the good news of the imminent arrival of the kingdom of God. As we see the time of distress coming upon us, it is incumbent on us to work while it is still day for when the night comes no one can work (John 9:4). We shall take every opportunity to share the gospel of eternal life so that everyone who believes in Jesus Christ may worship and glorify the God of heaven and earth and enter into eternal bliss of the New Jerusalem (Rev 21:1–7).

---

39. There are twenty-one seminaries/colleges offering some kind of theological education in Singapore listed in *A Guide to Churches & Christian Organizations in Singapore 2011–2012*, 346–49.

40. I have taught students from all the countries of ASEAN except Laos and Brunei in the past four and a half years.

11

Sino-Theology: Recapitulation and Prospect[1]

Chen Yuehua and Wu Dongri (China)

SINO-CHRISTIAN THEOLOGY IS NOT a systematic theology *per se*, but an ongoing academic movement that is committed to the investigation and research in the Christian faith in the Chinese language (汉语, *Han Yu*). Sino-Theology started in the 1980s and was initiated by Chinese intellectuals from the academic fields of the humanities and social sciences. Since the mid-1990s, this movement has been facilitated by the Institute of Sino-Christian Studies in Hong Kong, which also coined the now widely accepted term "Sino-Christian Theology" (汉语神学, hereafter "Sino-Theology"). The Institute has played a key role in the movement ever since. For over a decade now, many scholars who are outside the circle of traditional ecclesiastical theology have participated actively in this movement and have produced numerous publications for the consumption of the Chinese society. Their achievements have also attracted considerable attention and generated unprecedented discussions

---

1. We would like to thank Prof. WANG Xiaochao and Prof. CHOOG Chee Pang. They read the draft and gave constructive advice for improvement. Certainly, the responsibility for any remaining flaws and errors are ours.

on Christianity in Chinese academic circles both at home and abroad. However, the movement, being *extra ecclesiam*, has also raised the question of its "legitimacy," as it enjoys its autonomy as an academic discipline independent of the organized church and traditional theology.

This chapter aims to provide an outline of Sino-Theology and its main issues. It will analyze the essence of Sino-Theology, briefly review its history, and, by clarifying its boundaries with ecclesiastical theology, attempt to identify its major themes and characteristics. Based on these preliminary works, we will look further at the tension in the relationship between the divine and the human, together with its implications for the theoretical innovation of Sino-Theology and its future direction. Finally, three projected trends of Sino-Theology will also be put in their respective contexts and perspectives. They are: (1) The establishment of Sino-Theology as a respectable academic discipline. (2) Sino-Theology's interaction with Chinese ecclesiastical theology. (3) Sino-Theology's development into a public theology and its effects on Chinese society and culture.

THE EMERGENCE AND DEVELOPMENT OF SINO-THEOLOGY

Broad and Narrow Definitions

The principles and framework of Sino-Theology are spelled out in its first declaration. In 1994, the Institute of Sino-Christian Studies (ISCS) flew the flag of "Sino-Christian Theology" by reviving its journal *Tao Fong* (*Logos & Pneuma*) and by adding a Chinese subtitle to it, which literally means "an academic journal of Sino-Christian Theology."[2] In the first issue, the "Words on the Re-publication" clearly set out the original aims of Sino-Theology:

First, Chinese Christian theology must draw from the rich resources of Chinese culture, history and thought as well as social experience in forming a Chinese theology with a distinctive Chinese philosophical and cultural flavor. Second, a Christian theological discipline must be construed within Chinese academic thinking which could engage in meaningful dialogues with Confucianism, Daoism and Buddhism as well as modern trends of thought. Only then could Chinese Christian theology become a formative element of the larger Chinese cultural and philosophical system. Third, being an open and inclusive movement, its participants should regard themselves as fellow-members of the community of Chinese (*Han Yu*) scholars of

---

2. However, its official English name is written as *Chinese Journal of Theology*.

religion, be they from the mainland, Taiwan, Hong Kong, South-East Asia or North America.³

From the very beginning this journal has become a very important platform for Sino-Theology studies.⁴

Later on, as Sino-Theology became increasingly related to other academic disciplines, the original term, "Sino-Theology," needed to be defined both in its broad and narrow sense. In its broad sense, the term refers to any Christian theological literature written in the Chinese language, the earliest piece of which can be traced back to the Tang Dynasty, in a book entitled *The Stele about the Spread of Persian Nestorianism in China*, written by a Syrian Nestorian Presbyter. This was first pointed out by Professor He Guanghu, who regards Sino-Christian Theology as a native-language theology that "employs the life experience and cultural resources expressed in this native language, and which serves the users of this language."⁵ In this broad sense, the Sino-Theology movement is merely a continuum of a long tradition.

In its narrow sense, the term refers to the phenomenon of theological investigation and academic work which is based on the humanities and social sciences and which was produced in the aftermath of the inauguration of China's Reform and Open policy in the late 1970s—a phenomenon which was totally new and which fell outside the Chinese ecclesiastical tradition.⁶ Professor LIU Xiaofeng, an advocate of this understanding of the term, insists that this is a kind of study within the context of the humanities, which is very different from that of the church. A noted commentator writes that "LIU is not arguing against non-Christian theologies, neither is he ignoring previous and existing Christian theologies; rather [he is] calling for a Christian theological investigation from a new perspective."⁷ It was certainly not the intention of the pioneers of the movement to introduce a new type of systematic theology to the Chinese culture.

However, it is still difficult to explain what Sino-Theology is by sheer definition. While enjoying wide acceptance, the twofold sense mentioned above is not without problems. As Professor WANG Xiaochao recalls:

---

3. ISCS, "On the Re-publication" (cited directly from its official English version).

4. *Logos & Pneuma* was accepted to Arts & Humanities Citation Index (A&HCI) in 2007, and it is the only instance in Hong Kong, the third accepted Chinese academic journal all over the world. This is an approval for its academic quality and also a symbol for Sino-Christian Theology to be valued by Chinese academic circles as well as the world.

5. HE, "The Ground and Significance," 89.

6. Although this article mainly focuses on this narrow sense and restricts its scope to the specific historical period, the broad sense should be kept in mind.

7. WANG, "Understanding and Doubts," 43.

"During the first ten years of the development of Sino-Theology . . . determining what its definition was and who should be its researchers have been a most disputed problem."[8] However, while the debate continues, attention to the controversy has been diminishing.

Who are the Researchers of Sino-Theology?

Leaving the "what" problem, we now come to the "who" issue. It is perhaps proper to start with the phenomenon of the so-called "Cultural Christians". In the 1980s some leaders of the Hong Kong churches noticed that in some circles of Mainland China, there were scholars who were intellectually well disposed toward the Christian faith. As most of them were not "church members" in the technical sense, a rather strange term, "Cultural Christians," was created to distinguish them from ordinary Christians. But this somewhat intriguing and even sensitive label immediately generated discussion and debate in the Chinese academia both at home and abroad.[9]

The "Cultural Christians" are mostly attached to the universities and research institutions but not to the church or related religious organizations. They have all a sympathetic understanding of Christianity, and are keenly interested in theological reflection. Some scholars feel quite comfortable with their identity as "Cultural Christians." LIU Xiaofeng was one of those who highlighted their "conversion" and argued that "Cultural Christians . . . are intellectuals who have a conversion to individual faith," since, in his view, "only the one who believes in Christ could be called a Christian."[10] However, some scholars who have been identified with this group regarded it only as a label which has been superimposed on them by certain scholars in the Hong Kong Christian academia without evidence and sufficient explanation.[11] They argue that since a sympathetic understanding does not require the confession of faith, it is not proper to call them "Christians." And if a scholar is, in fact, a Christian, the adjective "cultural" would be redundant. All this seems to imply that the expression "Cultural Christian" does not necessarily indicate that the researchers identify themselves with Christianity.

Beside the identity issue, another question arises: Who should be the researchers of Sino-Theology? The varying responses given to this question show that religious belief continues to be an important issue in China.

8. WANG, "Some Considerations," 167–81.
9. Cf. ISCS, *Cultural Christian*, v.
10. LIU, "Phenomenon," 57.
11. AN, "Who," 36–37, also cf. HUAI, "Review," 51–52.

The more conservative thinkers tend to hold the view that only believers, or "Christian scholars," should work in the field of Sino-Theology. Others, however, question the wisdom of such a narrow and exclusivist position. They fear that this position will reduce the scope of Sino-Theology, resulting in the weakening of the academic standing and the social function of Christianity. Further, they argue that this runs the risk of turning Sino-Theology into a mere apologetic enterprise, which would be a departure from its the original intention.[12] Those who take a more inclusive position want Sino-Theology to reflect a diversity similar to that of other academic disciplines.

The debate goes on, but it is gradually diminishing in the face of the hard won fruits of arduous scholarly labor. Generally speaking, Sino-Theology is now recognized as being basically an academic investigation without the presuppositions of religious belief. More and more participants and outsiders have come to accept the reality that anyone, believer or not, can participate in the discipline. It is, therefore, very different from ecclesiastical theology, which commonly emerges from the church and is done for the church. By contrast, Sino-Theology is open to everyone with an interest in academic theological reflection, or in the search of a spiritual meaning of life.[13]

The Present State of Sino-Theology

From its formative period to its relatively mature stage, Sino-Theology has never been a system of rigid theology, but an academic movement involving Chinese scholars all over the world. In September 2005, at its third roundtable symposium on Sino-Christian Theology, the ISCS declared that Sino-Theology had entered a stage of "One Flag, Various Expressions."[14] The ISCS noted, in particular, the diversity of its participants and the multiplicity of their research interests, subject matters, and approaches. Sino-Theology scholars have come to recognize the wide scope of Sino-Theology as a respectable academic discipline which, nonetheless, operates under one single "flag." As uniformity and consensus are not their primary concerns, scholars continue to respect and even welcome differences. They enjoy their academic

---

12. Cf. WANG, "Some Considerations," 167–81.

13. WANG, "On Three Characteristics of Sino-Christian Theological Studies." http://www.iscs.org.hk/Common/Reader/News/ShowNews.jsp?Nid=770&Pid=9&Version=0&Cid=18&Charset=iso-8859-1. (accessed April 2, 2013).

14. WANG, "Some Considerations", 167–81.

autonomy and feel very comfortable with differing expressions. In so doing, they are able to yield some fairly encouraging results in the process.[15]

This academic movement does not have a set of rigorous theoretical standards or a detailed developmental blueprint. Its participants have formed an open academic community, not a closed organization. A leading scholar of the movement, Professor LI Qiuling, once confessed in a meeting of the ISCS that "we are inclined to treat Sino-Theology as a shared undertaking, not as a parochial faction. In a relatively broad sense, we regard it as a free study of Christian theology outside the institutional church."[16]

In its broad sense, Sino-Theology seeks to accommodate Chinese ecclesiastical theology while not intending to construct a new theology in addition to it. As Wang says: "Sino-Theology is a platform for a diversity, that does not seek to establish a theological school that can represent China."[17] But a question still remains: How then is Sino-Theology distinguished from the native theology developed by modern Chinese churches, or other theologies in China? In other words, how does it continue to retain its own legitimacy and uniqueness in the Chinese academy?

DISTINCTIONS BETWEEN SINO-THEOLOGY AND ECCLESIASTICAL THEOLOGY

Context and Theological Paths of the Chinese Church

Beginning in the early nineteenth century, Western colonial powers brought Christianity to China in large scale. In light of this, the famous educationalist Chiang Monlin created a well-known metaphor: "Christianity conspired with commercial operations backed by warships, so that in the memory of the Chinese people, this religion that preaches 'love of others as love of self' also becomes the tool of the invaders. Buddha came to China riding on a white elephant, while Jesus Christ [came] on a flying cannonball."[18] This created a difficult historical predicament for Christianity in China, and puts the Chinese church in an embarrassing situation vis a vis the wider culture. Thus, the main concern of the Chinese church has been to rid itself of that negative image in China, as well as the impression of Christianity as being a "foreign religion." The hope is to make Christian faith more acceptable to the Chinese people. But this requires a theology that seeks "to reflect,

15. WANG, "On the Influence", 45–56.
16. LI, "A Historical Reflection", 1–2.
17. WEN, *On the Transformation and Transcendence*, 169.
18. XI, "The Fate," 3.

expound, and serve the native people's religious belief."[19] Accordingly, a Chinese theology, which seeks to respond to Chinese culture, society and politics, generally follows two paths: Indigenization and Contextualization. The former attempts to integrate Christian theology into traditional Chinese culture, while the latter seeks to engage Christian theology with China's contemporary socio-political realities and dynamics.

In the early twentieth century, theologians who first proposed the indigenization of Chinese theology included such figures as ZHAO Zichen, WU Leichuan, WU Yaozong, and XIE Fuya, who had high regard for the socio-ethical values of Confucianism. They tried to use Confucian ideas as the vehicles to express Christian faith in the Chinese context. They did so with the hope of bridging the gap between their Christian commitment and their national identity. Since late Qing Dynasty, Chinese nationalism had been dominant in the thinking and consciousness of Chinese intellectuals. As such, the indigenization of the Chinese church and its theology was considered important to Chinese nationalism.[20]

Since the early 1950s, the effort to indigenize Chinese theology has been gradually replaced by the effort to contextualize it. In the New China, Chinese society takes Marxism as its national ideology in both theory and praxis. Consequently, contextualized theology becomes a serious response to this new socio-political situation. In the decades that followed, WU Yaozong tried to bring Chinese ecclesiastical theology in alignment with the new socio-political situation.

After the enactment of the Reform and Open policy in the late 1970s, the development of a high-level academic theology was placed on the agenda of the official Chinese church as a matter of priority. The late leader of the Chinese Protestant church, Bishop DING Guangxun, once said that the construction of a Chinese ecclesiastical theology was "the most fundamental and the most crucial step the church needed to take if was to find a new lease on life in the post-Cultural Revolution era."[21] At the same time, Chinese intellectuals were becoming increasingly interested in Christianity. Sadly, at that time, the official Chinese church was not in a position to meet the needs of that inquisitive "elite," due in part to a lack of a theologically literate intelligentsia.

In that new environment, and confronted with unprecedented challenges, Chinese ecclesiastical theology faced the twofold task of helping the church to take root in Chinese society and to meet its many practical needs.

19. HE, "The Ground and Significance," 89.
20. HUANG, "Modernity," 182–214.
21. DING, "On the Development," 4–5.

In light of this, issues of indigenization, "Sinicization," and other related concerns continue to be most important and relevant in the context of a new socio political culture.[22]

The Themes and Theological Path of Sino-Theology

Since its inception, Sino-Theology has been in search of new possibilities in theology, and has pursued this outside the confines and scope of contemporary Chinese ecclesiastical theology. Its pioneers have made special reference to China's social and intellectual culture the focus of their investigation. If ecclesiastical theology and other possible "theologies" can be regarded as "Chinese" theology, the following declaration by the proponents of Sino-Theology clearly indicate that this new theological movement was consciously and deliberately taking a new path and direction: "It is assumed that besides the paths of the traditional church, and under the present particular situation of China, there is a possibility for the development of academic Christian studies with a humanist character and based on Chinese humanist tradition, and which could eventually exert its influence on Chinese society and culture."[23]

While the goal of Sino-Theology was sufficiently clear from the outset, its paths were far from being free of controversy.[24] LIU Xiaofeng, for example, felt strongly that Sino-Theology should distinguish itself from Chinese ecclesiastical theology, and be independent even of the tradition of Western theology. For this to happen, he argues that the researchers should first face the "Christ event" in their own personal experience, and from that encounter (which Liu calls "the ideal form of Christian theology") embark on the path of Sino-Theology. If LIU can rightly be regarded as a "Cultural Christian," it is not too difficult to understand why his path can stand apart, not only from Chinese ecclesiastical theology, but also from the academic study of Christianity conducted by Chinese humanists who have accepted the ideas of the Enlightenment.[25] The adjective "Sino-", which refers specifically to the written Chinese language, did not constitute the essence of Liu's "ideal theology." It was only used to indicate that the theology expressed in and through that language was paralleled to Greek theology, Latin theology, or other existing

---

22. WANG, "Understanding and Doubts," 48.
23. YEUNG, *Preliminary Studies*, viii.
24. For more detail, see CHOONG Chee Pang, "Studying Christianity."
25. LAI, "Types," 3.

theologies. LIU's ultimate intention was to rid theology of its "Sinicization," which was the goal set by the organized church of modern China.[26]

HE Guanghu, also a leading figure of the movement, argues that rather than replacing ecclesiastical theology, Sino-Theology should work with its methodologies of indigenization and contextualization.[27] In HE's more "conservative" opinion, Sino-Theology should inherit and make good use of traditional Chinese theological resources, and break new grounds from there. His view is, therefore, very different from LIU's more radical position. For HE, "Nearly all theologies are written in the theologian's own native language. The revealed Word must be expressed in human languages in order to be understood and received by human beings. Therefore, language is a necessary vehicle of theology. Each and every language can be used to express Christian theology. Accordingly, for HE, "Sino-" means that Sino-Theology is a "native-language theology."

In HE's opinion, indigenization is directed toward a particular nationality, and thus weakens the universal dimension of theology. By the same token, contextualization can also be in danger of being too context-bound. Chinese language users are not only in the native land, nor are they in one and the same context. Sino-Theology should seek, therefore, to transcend the constraints of indigenization and contextualization.[28]

Basic Characteristics of Sino-Theology

Besides the issues discussed above, there is the question regarding the basic characteristics of Sino-Theology. We observe three leading characteristics.

Professor WANG thinks that Sino-Theology can best be described as "non-church, humanistic, and cross-cultural."[29] Considering the changes that occurred in the Chinese academia since the inauguration of China's Reform and Open policy, it is reasonable to suggest that without its "non-church" characteristic, Sino-Theology could hardly be acceptable to Chinese academics, and consequently, able to exert an appreciable influence on Chinese society.[30] In keeping with David Tracy's three divisions or the three publics of Christian theology (university, church, and society), Sino-Theology has taken the universities and other academic institutions as its main spheres of activity. Also, in contrast to Western universities where aca-

26. WANG, "Understanding and Doubts," 43.
27. HE, "The Ground and Significance," 97.
28. HE, "The Methods," 101.
29. WANG, "On the Influence," 49 and cf. WANG, "On Three Characteristics."
30. WANG, "On the Influence," 45–56.

demic theology is studied in departments of theology, in China, it is often conducted in close connection with other disciplines, especially in religion and philosophy.³¹ As such, it is virtually detached from the institutional church of China in its operation and activities. This is understandable in the context of modern China. As Professor LI Xiangping explains: "the institution of the Chinese church is almost the same as any administrative sector in Chinese politics and economics, and is embedded in its basic structure."³² There is, therefore, no way for Sino-Theology to fit in within this structure comfortably. "Sino-Theology isn't the result of the church's reflection, but of the reflection on the church."³³ The Reform and Open policy has allowed the Chinese people to express their religious belief with relative freedom. The concerted effort of scholars of different disciplines has enabled Sino-Theology to create a whole new public theological space, which allows it to makes inroads into Chinese academia and society.³⁴

Another important feature is the humanist nature of Sino-Theology. LIU Xiaofeng has argued that historically, theology has tried to place the church in the context of humanity. Sino-Theology has now put such a great emphasis on that humanist dimension that "its form and pattern are determined by its dialogical relation with the humanities and social sciences."³⁵ This stems from the fact that most of the participants in Sino-Theology tend to have roots in the humanities and social sciences before embarking on religious studies, including Christianity. This background makes it much easier for Sino-Theology to find general acceptance in the Chinese academia, and enables it to find a place in the highly institutionalized educational system of China.³⁶

Lastly, a cross-cultural feature is fully embodied in Sino-Theology. Academically, this is an advantage since it frees Sino-Theology from the need to abide by the commitments of one or more specific theological traditions. As LIU says, "There is no sequence in listening to the Logos, although it could take a particular written form. The history of both Eastern and Western Christian thoughts is 'the pre-history' of Sino-Theology. Sino-Theology must enter this pre-history and inherit its various traditions."³⁷ HE believes Sino-Theology can provide the much-needed stimulus, creativity, and in-

---

31. XIE, *Public Theology and Globalization*, 36.
32. LI, "Sino-Christian Theology," 63.
33. Ibid.
34. Ibid.
35. LIU, "Sino-Christian Theology," 36.
36. WANG, "On the Influence," 48.
37. LIU, *The Sino-Christian Theology*, 91.

spiration to Chinese culture for its renewal and enrichment. Because of this, much theologically creative work is expected of Sino-Theology beyond mere translation of works produced in other places. "It needs both succession and development, both maintenance and openness."[38]

From what has been said so far, it is sufficiently clear that the path of Sino-Theology is markedly different from that of the traditional theology of the institutionalized church. Its objectives, its cadre of researchers, its scope and audiences are all different. Its autonomy and academic approach, as well as its humanist orientation, allow it to serve a constituency that is much larger than the institutionalized church. In light of this, Sino-Theology has, in reality, become a "public theology."[39]

THE DIALECTICAL RELATIONSHIP BETWEEN THE DIVINE AND THE HUMAN

Ontic Christology

LIU Xiaofeng once defined his Sino-Theology as "an individually-oriented existential theology." He sought to formulate a subjective Christian theology, which seeks to break away from the rhetoric of national theology, and thus, frees itself from the national grand narrative to make room for a primarily existential experience.[40] In the view of LIU, the relationship between Chinese culture and Christianity must not be construed as a dialogue between Chinese and Western cultures, but as a conversation about existential ontology. His slogan is "to straightly face the Christ event."[41] In other words, according to LIU, Sino-Theology should return to the issue of individual life, and encounter there the "absolute spirit" of Christ, rather than a Western or Chinese spirit. In his "Ontic Christology," LIU holds that the gospel of the Christ event should confront, first and foremost, our existential experience.[42] In this context, the time factor is secondary since there is no need to be concerned with the question as to who arrived at the truth first.[43] LIU is, therefore, critical of any indigenizational or sinicizational framework.

38. HE, "The Methods," 101.
39. Cf. LI, "A Historical Reflection," 2.
40. LIU, "Sino-Christian Theology," 42.
41. Some of LIU's terminologies were invented by himself and therefore hard to be translated into English. They are vague even for Chinese scholars, cf. LAM, Jason T. S., "Issues," appendix, 254–55.
42. LIU, "Sino-Christian Theology in the Modern Context."
43. LIU, "Sino-Christian Theology," 42.

For, if the essence of theology is "to straightly face the Christ event," the real concern should be human existence, humanity, and modernity.[44]

LIU's overall approach to Sino-Theology could be said to be existential and Barthian. He argues that in its ideal form, Christian theology is first and foremost, "God's Word itself"; it is something that God alone possesses. Secondly, the Christ event is the "historical revelation of God himself," and every historical theology has its own particularity and limitation both in terms of its national language and national experience.[45] As such, Sino-Theology should not be too preoccupied with "man's words." Its main task is to express "God's Word" directly.[46]

LIU's Ontic Christology could also be regarded as "individualistic."[47] As he explains, "the gospel of the Christ event primarily speaks to the individual's existential experience rather than national ideology. . . . Christian theology arises from a person's encounter with God in his concrete existence, rather than the result of any national ideology."[48] As such, the rejection of traditional Chinese culture, including Confucianism, Taoism, and Buddhism, is both logical and necessary. In the end, the person who has a personal encounter with God's Word is no longer a person of his old community and historical background, but a totally new individual.[49]

LIU does not focus on contrasting Chinese and Western cultures. Rather, his concern is on how Christianity and all other cultures ought to relate. He criticizes both the Chinese culture and the Western Enlightenment mindset for its penchant toward, among other things, nihilism. He is interested neither in the rights and wrongs of Chinese and Western cultures, nor in the dynamics of their relationships. Regardless of the culture, his concern is the individual and the existential dimensions of the Christian faith.

The Word of God and the Words of Human Beings

In contrast to LIU, Chinese scholars who regard Christianity as an alien culture feel strongly that Sino-Theology must respond to Chinese culture and its present problems. In their view, the Divine Word does not exist in a vacuum but has to be recorded and expressed in human words, whether in the Chinese or other traditions, in which an individual person finds his

44. WANG, "Methods and Paths," 137.
45. LIU, "Sino-Christian Theology."
46. LI, "A Historical Reflection," 1–2.
47. AN, "Who," 36–37.
48. Ibid.
49. LI, "A Historical Reflection," 1–2.

or her being and existence. Chinese language, like any other language, is a human language. When a language is employed to express God's Word, it is immediately confronted with the cultural background from which it originates. Christian faith, being a religion from an alien culture, would immediately feel the tension as soon as it enters into dialogue with traditional Chinese culture.

Some scholars are critical of LIU's position for allegedly disengaging the Chinese culture from Christian faith. They point out that the "Christ event" was recorded and expounded first in Greek and subsequently in other human languages. It is, therefore, impossible and unrealistic for it to detach itself from human culture, be it Chinese or otherwise. No theology can exist meaningfully in a vacuum.[50] Even the canonization of the New Testament was fixed within specific cultural contexts in the course of several centuries. Similarly, they argue that the researchers of Sino-Theology have been brought up in their own particular culture. Hence, "one should not leave behind his/her own nationality and tradition . . . it is impossible for one to face the Christ event only with his/her individual existential experience."[51]

God's Word must be translated into human words in order to be understood. The history of the Bible itself bears witness to its "translatability." As Professor YANG Huilin has argued: "The New Testament was not written in the mother tongue of Jesus Christ . . . [Here], there is no substantial difference between the Chinese language and its Western counterparts."[52] In other words, when facing the Divine Word, the Chinese language and other human languages are on the same footing. The Divine Word places limitation on its interpretations by human words, which can only *approximate*, but never quite *reach* it.[53] As one scholar has said, "By its very nature, Christianity always challenges and disturbs its host culture."[54] Scholars who are engaged in Sino-Theology are aware that human words have a particular cultural context, and that in every culture, the Divine Word is revealed only partially and imperfectly. Sino-Theology must continue to "listen" to the Divine revelation and learn from other cultures. Sino-Theology should also accept the reality that the Chinese language, the individual's existential experience, and the cultural resources are only theological tools and means, but not the end itself.[55]

50. HE, *He Guanghu's*, 86.
51. LI, "A Historical Reflection," 1–12.
52. YANG, "On Sino-Christian Theology," 680.
53. Ibid.
54. Ibid.
55. HE, "The Methods," 99.

YANG sees the relationship between God and humanity in Sino-Theology largely in terms of communication and dialogue between the human and the "Wholly Other." It is a humbling epistemological act on the part of the human person.[56]

From what has been surveyed so far, it becomes sufficiently clear that the Sino-Theology movement first began partly as a reaction to the Western-centeredness of the theological enterprise. While LIU is rightly critical of the Western dominance of theology, he does not say how Chinese theologians should deal with the Western theological tradition.[57] At the same time, his own proposal may be too individualistic and idealistic for Sino-Theology.

"Man" (人) in Chinese can refer to a person individually, people corporately, or a nationality. Sino-Theology is concerned with all three. In light of this, LIU's theology seems individualistic and thus oblivious to the communal dimension of humanity. As an inclusive movement Sino-Theology should serve all users of the Chinese language (*Han Yu*), regardless of backgrounds, just as the Apostle Paul did in his evangelistic effort: "I have become all things to all people" (1 Cor. 9:22).[58]

Multiple Approaches

The themes and topics that appeared in the journal *Logos & Pneuma* in the past twenty years have clearly shown that scholars of Sino-Theology have not been entangled merely in metaphysical or epistemological discussions, but have engaged in in-depth investigations on the relationships that exist between the divine and the human. The approaches they've taken in this important search may be summed up under three broad categories:

(1) Translation and introduction of noted Western theologians, both ancient and modern, to the Chinese milieu. Ancient theologians include Latin fathers such as Augustine and Aquinas; Greek fathers such as Origen and Gregory of Nyssa; and modern thinkers including the likes of Karl Barth, Paul Tillich, Dietrich Bonhoeffer, Wolfhart Pannenberg, Jürgen Moltmann, John Hick, and David Tracy. Sino-Theology has a very open and unbiased attitude in the selection of the Western theologians it engages. Although individual scholars have their own research preferences, the emphasis has always been on the influence of the theologians and on their contributions to contemporary Chinese society and the academy. For example, eschatology has been a relatively alien and incomprehensible subject to Chinese

56. YANG, "On Sino-Christian Theology," 693.
57. WANG, "Understanding and Doubts," 47.
58. Cf. HE, "The Methods," 101.

culture. Professor LAI took up the challenge to make it intelligible to the Chinese audience through the use of Paul Tillich's interpretation of the Kingdom of God.[59]

(2) The second approach focuses on dialogues between Christianity and Chinese native religions and thoughts, especially Confucianism and Chinese Buddhism. For Chinese scholars, the main concern is not comparative studies of religions *per se*, but the construction of Sino-Theology. This is evident in the choice of comparative religion as the theme of an entire issue of the journal *Logos & Pneuma*. In this connection it is worth noting that following the lead of John P. Keenan, some scholars have discussed the possibility of constructing a "Mahāyāna Theology" with thoughts and ideas from Mahāyāna Buddhism.[60]

(3) A third approach centers on uncovering and gathering resources in the long history of Chinese indigenization efforts. On the occasion of the 400th anniversary of Matteo Ricci's death, *Logos and Pneuma* published a special issue in memory of the famous Jesuit missionary. A re-examination of China's own history has clearly shown that the relation between the divine and the human has, in fact, been present in the Chinese tradition, although Chinese cosmology was quite different from its Christian counterpart.[61]

The ongoing work of the scholars of Sino-Theology is a process by which these thinkers become increasingly conscious of, and more assertive about, their new academic identity.[62] It is this shared identity that has held them together as an academic community, and which provides them with sufficient room and freedom to pursue their individual research interest in a variety of ways.

PROSPECTS AND DEVELOPMENTAL ORIENTATIONS OF SINO-THEOLOGY

The Construction of Sino-Theology as an Academic Discipline

Professor ZHUO Xinping of the China Academy of Social Sciences recognizes the influence that Sino-Theology has had on the Chinese academy. However, he is also aware that Sino-Theology's body of work and academic

---

59. LAI, Pan Chiu, "Tillich's Interpretation," 43.

60. TANG Andres S. K., "Rethinking of Mahayana Theology," 124.

61. See HE, "Being vs Nothingness" and ZHANG Qinxiong, "'Between God and People.'"

62. Cf. LAM, *A Polyphonic View*, "A Typological Consideration," and *Narrative, Tradition, Faith*.

position have yet to be fully recognized and respected in the Chinese academia and in the Chinese society as a whole.⁶³ In recent years, as the fruits of scholarly research increase and the range of study expands, Sino-Theology has sought to morph into a kind of "Sino-Christian Studies."⁶⁴ However, as a discipline the standing of Sino-Christian Studies is ambiguous and vague as is evident in its definition, its interdisciplinary character, its methodologies, and academic infrastructure. At this juncture, it appears that the construction of a Sino-Theology faces at least three tasks. First, it needs to clarify the distinction between Sino-Theology and the academic study of Christianity. Second, it needs to sharpen its status vis-à-vis ecclesiastical or traditional theology. And third, there is the need to make Sino-Theology a more recognizable and better defined academic discipline.

At the moment, Sino-Theology is widely regarded as an interdisciplinary discipline in the humanities and social sciences, which include literature, history, philosophy, religion, political science, sociology, cultural studies, and biblical studies. It is, therefore, broadly based.⁶⁵ HE Guanghu thinks that Sino-Theology consists of three basic components. They are: philosophical theology, moral theology, and cultural theology.⁶⁶ Having said that, it is still not clear what form Sino-Theology should take organizationally and functionally. One thing seems sufficiently clear, however. Under the present socio-political conditions, it is neither possible nor desirable for Sino-Theology to become a "divinity school" or a "department of theology." It seems more feasible for it to be a kind of synthetic "liberal education" that would include theological knowledge.⁶⁷ In the foreseeable future, therefore, it is far more likely that Sino-Theology will remain an academic discipline in the broad context of interdisciplinary studies of the humanities and social sciences.

On the contents of Sino-Theology's research programs, Professor ZHANG Qingxiong's *Categories of Christian Theology* could be taken as a useful reference. The book consists of seven chapters: God, Revelation, Creation and Protection, Humanity, Sin and Evil, Christ and Salvation, End and Hope. The final chapter is "the definition of religion and approach to its understanding."⁶⁸ It looks quite like any traditional "systematics" textbook, but its approach is unmistakably academic and humanistic. Professor

63. ZHUO, "Academic Theology," 153.
64. LAI, "Religious Studies," 155.
65. WANG, "On Three Characteristics."
66. HE, "The Methods," 108–9.
67. Cf. LAI, "Religious Studies," 153–72.
68. ZHANG, *Categories*, 351.

WANG Xiaochao suggests, however, that some kind of introduction should be added to it. He goes on to further suggest the following: (1) definition and principle of theology, the relationship of theology and philosophy, the relationship of theology and other disciplines, the methodology and the classification of theology, the unique features of theological thinking, the task and methodology of Sino-Theology, the unique vision of Sino-Theology; (2) the core belief of Christianity and the Christian Bible, brief history of Christianity, world Christianity, Chinese Christianity, the Christian classics, basic doctrines of Christianity, creeds and confessions; (3) the relationship of Christianity and culture, the public value of Christianity, church and society, and so on.[69] He thinks that all these areas should be covered by Sino-Theology. If he is right, this is an enormous task which will require the involvement of the whole academic community, not just the participation of a few scholars.[70]

Interaction between Sino-Theology and Ecclesiastical Theology

From the very beginning, leading scholars of Sino-Theology have been sensitive to the issue of the relationship between church-based theology and the new form of academic Christian studies with its humanist perspective.[71] While the two may overlap in the range of subjects they cover, their complementary roles have been recognized and welcome.

Although Sino-Theology is not church-related, it is nonetheless concerned with issues of importance to the church. These include the Bible, history, tradition, faith, and spirituality. It is keenly interested in tapping the spiritual resources of Christian thought and the Christian tradition, even as it seeks breakthroughs in Chinese culture itself, to identify new ways of dealing with the social problems of modern China. The Chinese corporate church as a whole, as well as individual Christians have benefited from its insights. Its vibrancy and dynamism are particularly evident in the Chinese academia. Its reception has generally been warm and positive, as it continues to interact with the universities, churches, and society. Particularly noteworthy here is the fact that a growing number of Christian scholars have joined the ranks of those engaged in the discipline of Sino-Theology.

The non-church character of this brand of theology allows it that to enjoy the freedom and space that it would not probably enjoy were it to operate within the confines of the organized church. Yet paradoxically,

---

69. WANG, "Some Considerations," 167–81.
70. WANG, "Understanding and Doubts," 53.
71. YEUNG, *Preliminary Studies*, viii.

Sino-Theology's disengagement from the official church of China has enabled it to play a more effective role in positioning the church to help shape direction of civil society in the country.[72] Sino-Theology duly acknowledges the traditional role of the Chinese church in matters religious and ecclesiastical, including the running of seminaries for the training of priests and pastors. However, with regard to culture, the humanities and social sciences, and the academic world, Sino-Theology seems better positioned to exert a greater influence on modern Chinese society. And, because they are rooted in the academic community, Sino-Theologians are better poised to communicate Christian ideas and concepts more intelligibly and effectively, not only to the academia but also to the public at large. It is actually not far-fetched to conceive the possibility of Sino-Theology generating renewal and transformation in the theological thinking of leaders the organized church.[73] Sino-Theologians believe that through their communication and interaction with diverse modes of thought the Chinese people might gain a more informed view of Christianity, and in so doing, become more open to Christian faith. Such an approach resonates well with China's open policy reform as well as with the accelerating modernization and globalization of the present age. It is hoped that both individually and corporately, participants in Sino-Theology would remain committed to serving the Chinese society and contributing to the well-being of the Chinese church. It is only in so doing that it will eventually become a credible "public theology" in modern China.[74]

Looking Ahead

The concern of Sino-Theology for China's public good is inherent both in the objective that it sets for itself and in its response to the expectation of Chinese society. Leaders of the movement have long felt the need to escape the ivory tower of academia, as well as the inner experience and struggles of the individual, in order to face head on China's pressing social issues and problems. This awareness was further sharpened as scholars became embroiled in interdisciplinary research. Realizing the great potentials of Sino-Theology's impact and influence on China's public sphere, WANG Xiaochao feels that Sino-Theology should elevate profile and become more vocal about its concerns for the pressing issues and problems of contemporary Chinese

---

72. WANG, "Some Considerations," 167–81.
73. Ibid.
74. XIE, "'Social' or 'Theological,'" 83.

society.⁷⁵ This seems also to be the feeling of HE Guanghu as he ponders the prospect of Sino-Theology. HE says "the situations of contemporary Chinese life are puzzling, complicated, tough to deal with, and are socially very serious."⁷⁶ He sees here an opportunity for Sino-Theology, since, in his view, China's social issues and problems have a theological dimension, and thus call for an appropriate theological response.⁷⁷

In this connection, it is correct to say that Sino-Theology's socio-political concerns echo the concerns of Western socio-political theology.⁷⁸ One thinks of the stance taken by a group of German theologians toward Nazi Germany and Hitler's massacre of the Jews. These theologians were convinced that their Christian faith and theology compelled them to stand on the side of the weak and helpless. While the war experience of the United States was very different from that of Germany, American theologians became strong advocates, and even activists for justice in the socio-political realm, both during and after the war. The Niebuhr brothers are good examples of this. In their response to the post-war situation, they raised critical questions about democracy, market economy, science and technology, and modern education. Sino-Theology could well learn from the experiences and insights of German political theology and American public theology.

It has been suggested that for a credible academic activity to occur, the personal belief of the Sino-Theologians should not be taken as a presupposition. It should be "suspended" to ensure the objectivity that is required in serious studies and research.⁷⁹ If this is true, it seems that in the foreseeable future, academic institutions such as the universities will most likely remain the places where Sino-Theology will be done. This seems only natural, as most participants in the discipline are found in the various disciplines of the universities.⁸⁰ The "non-church" character of Sino-Theology must be maintained in all its public activities and pronouncements.

Judging from the number of the users of Chinese language alone, Sino-Theology deserves the attention and concern of the world community. In the opinion of Professor HE Guanghu, "A very large portion of the human population's need for theology can only be satisfied by Sino-Theology, and a very significant amount of its resources and composite elements could only be provided by Sino-Theology itself. The significance of Sino-Theology can

---

75. WANG, "On the Influence," 47.
76. HE, "Trends," 70.
77. HE, "The Present and Prospect," 2.
78. YANG, "Introduction," 20.
79. WANG, "On the Influence," 45–56.
80. Ibid.

hardly be overestimated."[81] While Sino-Theology is mainly committed to meeting the needs of Chinese language users, as a theology of China's "mother tongue", it will also make a contribution to the world community at large.

REFERENCES

AN, Ximeng. "Who is Cultural Christian?" *The Religious Cultures in the World*, no. 1 (2000): 36–37.

CHOONG Chee Pang, "Studying Christianity and doing theology extra ecclesiam", in *Christian Theology in Asia*, edited by Sebastian C. H. Kim, Cambridge: CUP, 2008, pp. 89–109.

DING, Guangxun. "On the Development of Three-self Patriotic Movement of the Protestant Churches in China." *Tian Feng: the Magazine of the Protestant Churches in China*, no. 1 (2000): 4–5.

HE Guanghu, "Being vs Nothingness: A Challenge to the Compatibility of Chinese Religious Philosophy with Christian Philosophy?" *Logos & Pneuma: Chinese Journal of Theology*, no. 12 (2000): 165–85.

HE, Guanghu. "The Ground and Significance of the Chinese Language Theology." In *He Guanghu's Self-selected Works*, 85–97. Guilin: Guangxi Normal University Press, 1999.

HE, Guanghu. "The Methods and Approaches to the Chinese Language Theology." In *He Guanghu's Self-selected Works*, 98–111. Guilin: Guangxi Normal University Press, 1999.

HE, Guanghu. "The Present and Prospect of 'Christian Theology in Chinese' in the Academic Community in Mainland China." No pages. Online: http://www.iscs.org.hk/Common/Reader/News/ShowNews.jsp?Nid=806&Pid=3&Version=0&Cid=191&Charset=gb2312.

HE, Guanghu. "Trends of Chinese Scholars in Christian Studies in the Turn of the Twentieth and Twenty-First Century." *Logos & Pneuma: Chinese Journal of Theology*, no. 29 (2008): 53–75.

HE, Guanghu. *He Guanghu's Self-selected Works*. Guilin: Guangxi Normal University Press, 1999.

HUAI, Renlian. "Review on 'Cultural Christians'." *The Religious Cultures in the World*, no. 4 (2004): 51–52.

HUANG Ruicheng. "Modernity of Nationalism and Chinese Christian." In *Correlating Chinese and Western Culture*, edited by Wang, Xiaochao and YANG, Xinan. Guilin: Guangxi Normal University Press, 2006.

ISCS, ed. *Cultural Christian: Phenomenon and Argument*. Hong Kong: Institute of Sino-Christian Studies, 1997.

ISCS. "On the Re-publication of *Logos & Pneuma*." *Logos & Pneuma: Chinese Journal of Theology*, no. 1 (1994): 8–9.

LAI, Pan Chiu. "Religious Studies, Theology and Sino-Christian Studies." *Shan Dao Journal* 12, no. 2 (2009): 153–72.

LAI, Pan Chiu. "Tillich's Interpretation of the Kingdom of God and Chinese Christian Eschatology." *Logos & Pneuma: Chinese Journal of Theology*, no. 9 (1998): 43–74.

---

81. HE, "The Ground and Significance," 97.

LAI, Pan Chiu. "Types of Chinese Theology and Developing Paths." In *Preliminary Studies on Chinese Theology*, edited by YEUNG, Daniel H. N. Hong Kong: Institute of Sino-Christian Studies, 2000.

LAM, Jason T. S., *A Polyphonic View on Sino-Christian Theology*. Beijing: China Religious Culture Publisher, 2008.

LAM, Jason T. S., "A Typological Consideration of Sino-Christian Theology." *Logos & Pneuma: Chinese Journal of Theology*, no. 23 (2005): 165–84.

LAM, Jason T. S., "Issues concerning the 'Linguisticality' of Sino-Christian theology." *Logos & Pneuma: Chinese Journal of Theology*, no. 17 (2002): 229–57.

LAM, Jason T. S., *Narrative, Tradition, Faith: A Search for the Social Identity of Sino-Christian Theology*. Hong Kong: Logos and Pneuma Press, 2010.

LI, Qiuling. "A Historical Reflection on Sino-Christian Theology." *Newsletters of Institute of Sino-Christian Studies*, no. 2 (2005): 1–2.

LI, Xiangping. "Sino-Christian Theology: Invisible Church and Public Faith." *Logos & Pneuma: Chinese Journal of Theology*, no. 32 (2010): 57–69.

LIU, Xiaofeng. "Sino-Christian Theology in the Modern Context." *Logos & Pneuma: Chinese Journal of Theology*, no. 2 (1995).

LIU, Xiaofeng. *The Sino-Christian Theology and Philosophy of History*. Hong Kong: Institute of Sino-Christian Studies, 2000.

LIU, Zongkun. "Phenomenon of Cultural Christian in the Modern Chinese Context." In *Cultural Christian: Phenomenon and Argument*. Hong Kong: Institute of Sino-Christian Studies, 1997.

Tang, Andres S. K., "Rethinking of Mahayana Theology: Focusing on the Mahakaruna and Prajna of Bodhisattva and Christ." *Logos & Pneuma: Chinese Journal of Theology*, no. 24 (2005): 124–46.

WANG, Xiaochao. "Methods and Paths for Understanding and Doubting Sino-Christian Theology." In *Preliminary Studies on Chinese Theology*, edited by YEUNG, Daniel H. N. Hong Kong: Institute of Sino-Christian Studies, 2000.

WANG, Xiaochao. "On the Characteristics and Boundary of Sino-Chiristian." In *Globalization, Values and Pluralism*, edited by Guo, Changgang, et al. Shanghai: Shanghai Sanlian Publishing House, 2010.

WANG, Xiaochao. "On the Influence of Sino-Christian Theology to the Chinese Academia and its Position." *Logos & Pneuma: Chinese Journal of Theology*, no. 32 (2010): 45–56.

WANG, Xiaochao. "On Three Characteristics of Sino-Christian Theological Studies." No pages. Online: http://www.iscs.org.hk/Common/Reader/News/ShowNews.jsp?Nid=770&Pid=9&Version=0&Cid=18&Charset=iso-8859-1.

WANG, Xiaochao. "Some Considerations of the Content of Sino-Christian Theology: Taking Account of the Delimitation Issue." *Logos & Pneuma: Chinese Journal of Theology*, no. 29 (2008): 167–81.

WANG, Xiaochao. "Understanding and Doubts: Reading Liu Xiaofeng's 'Sino-Christian Theology in the Modern Context.'" In *Modernity, Transformation of Tradition and Sino-Christian Theology*, edited by Qiuling, LI and YEUNG, Daniel H. N., 42–53. Shanghai: East China Normal University Publishing House, 2010.

WEN, Weiyao. *On the Transformation and Transcendence of Humanity a Sino-Christian Perspective*. Beijing: Religious Culture Publishing House, 2009.

XI, Wuyi. "The Fate of Christianality in Modern China." *Chinese Social Science Today*, 2008-04-03, 3.

XIE, Zhibin. "'Social' or 'Theological': Sino-Christian Theology and Chinese Society." *Logos & Pneuma: Chinese Journal of Theology*, no. 32 (2010): 71–84.
XIE, Zhibin. *Public Theology and Globalization: A Study in Max L. Stackhouse's Christian Ethics*. Beijing: Religious Culture Publishing House, 2008.
YANG, Huiling, and XIE, Zhibin. "Introduction to the Main Theme." *Logos & Pneuma: Chinese Journal of Theology*, no. 32 (2010): 19–26.
YANG, Huiling. "On Sino-Christian Theology: Its Unique Value from Linguistic Aspect." In *Modernity, Transformation of Tradition and Sino-Christian Theology*, edited by Qiuling, LI and YEUNG, Daniel H. N., 680–93. Shanghai: East China Normal University Publishing House, 2010.
YEUNG, Daniel H. N. et al., "Introduction." *Logos & Pneuma: Chinese Journal of Theology*, no. 29 (2008): 21–25.
YEUNG, Daniel H. N., ed. *Preliminary Studies on Chinese Theology*. Hong Kong: Institute of Sino-Christian Studies, 2000.
ZHANG Qinxiong, 'Between God and People' & 'Between Heaven and People': Reflection on Christian 'Creation' and 'Providence' from a Comparative Perspective with Chinese Culture." *Logos & Pneuma: Chinese Journal of Theology*, no. 15 (2001): 147–62.
ZHANG, Qingxiong. *Categories of Christian Theology: A Comparative Study from Historical and Cultural Perspective*. Shanghai: Shanghai People's Publishing House, 2003.
ZHUO, Xinping. "Academic Theology: A New Approach to Christian Studies in Contemporary China." In *Annual Report on China's Religions 2008*, edited by Jin, Ze and Qiu, Yonghui. Social Sciences Academic Press (China), 2008. 130–57.

Bibliography

Adamo, David Tuesday. *Africa and Africans in the New Testament*. Lanham, MD: University Press of America, 2006.

———. "Christ as the Anthropological Model." *Caribbean Journal of Religious Studies* 10 (1989) 23–25.

Ali, Abdullah Yusuf. *The Meaning of the Holy Quran*. Kuala Lumpur: Islamic Book Trust, 2005.

Al-Attas, Syed Muhammad Naguib. *The Mysticism of Hamzah Fansuri*. Kuala Lumpur: University of Malaya Press, 1970.

Al-Warraq, Abu 'Isá. *Against the Incarnation*. Cambridge: Cambridge University Press, 2002.

———. *Against the Trinity*. Cambridge: Cambridge University Press, 1992.

An, Ximeng. "Who is Cultural Christian?" *The Religious Cultures in the World* 1 (2000) 36–37.

Anderson, M. *The Trinity*. Caney, KS: Pioneer, 1994.

Anderson, Ray. *Historical Transcendence and the Reality of God*. Grand Rapids: Eerdmans, 1975.

Arberry, Arthur John. *The Koran Interpreted*. Oxford: Oxford University Press, 1964.

Armstrong, Karen. *The Case for God*. New York: Anchor, 2009.

Athanasius of Alexandria. *Athanasius: Select Works and Letters*. Nicene and Post-Nicene Fathers, vol. 4, Edited by Philip Schaff and Henry Wace. Peabody, Mass.: Hendrickson, 1994.

Atkinson, D. *The Message of Genesis 1–11*. Leicester, UK: IVP, 1990.

Aune, David. "The Prophetic Circle of John of Patmos and the Exegesis of Revelation 22:16." *Journal for the Study of the New Testament* 37 (1989) 103–16.

———. *Revelation 1–5*. Word Biblical Commentary. Dallas: Word, 1997.

———. *Revelation 6–16*. Word Biblical Commentary. Nashville: Thomas Nelson, 1998.

Badcock, Gary D. *Light of Truth and Fire of Love: A Theology of the Holy Spirit*. Grand Rapids: Eerdmans, 1997.

Bao, Limin. "The Trajectory and Types of Modem Public Theology: The Trajectory and Types of Modem Public Theology." *Logos & Pneuma: Chinese Journal of Theology* 32 (2010) 27–44.

Barth, Karl "Church and Culture." *Theology and Church.* Translated by L. P. Smith. London: SCM, 1962.
———. *Credo.* London: Hodder and Stoughton, 1964.
Bauckham, Richard. "The Conversion of the Nations." In *The Climax of Prophecy: Studies in the Book of Revelation,* 238–337. Edinburgh: T. & T. Clark, 1993.
Beale, Gregory K. *The Book of Revelation* The New International Greek Testament Commentary. Grand Rapids: Eerdmans, 1999.
Bediako, Kwame. *Christianity in Africa. The Renewal of a Non-Western Religion.* Edinburgh: Edinburgh University Press, 1995.
———. "Understanding African Theology in the 20th Century." In *Jesus in Africa,* 49–69. Yaoundé, Cameroon: Edition Clé, 2004.
———. *Jesus in Africa.* Yaounde, Cameroon. Editions Cle, 2004.
Berger, Renato. "Is Traditional Religion Still Relevant?" *Orita* 3.6 (1969) 15–18.
Berkhof, Hendrikus. *Christian Faith.* 2nd ed. Grand Rapids: Eerdmans, 1986.
Berryman, Phillip. *Liberation Theology: The Essential Facts about the Revolutionary Movement in Latin America and Beyond.* New York: Pantheon, 1987.
Bettenson, Henry., ed. *Documents of the Christian Church.* 2nd ed. New York: Oxford University Press, 1977.
Blount, Brian K. *Revelation.* The New Testament Library. Louisville: Westminster, 2009.
Boff, Leonardo. *Trinity and Society.* New York: Burns and Oates, 1985.
Bolaji, Idowu E. *Africa Traditional Religion: A Definition.* SCM, 1973.
Bonilla, Plutarco. "Viaje de ida y vuelta: Evangelización y misión. Apuntes sobre el pensamiento misionológico de Orlando E. Costas." *Orlando E. Costas: Un hombre en el Camino.* Rio Piedras, Puerto Rico: Cenetepa, 1995.
Bonino, José Míguez. *Faces of Latin American Protestantism.* Grand Rapids: Eerdmans, 1995.
Bousfield, John. "Islamic Philosophy in South-East Asia." In *Islam in South-East Asia,* edited by M. B. Hooker, 92–129. Leiden: Brill, 1983.
Boxall, Ian. *The Revelation of Saint John.* Black's New Testament Commentary. London: A. & C. Black, 2006.
Bruce, F. F. *The Real Jesus.* London: Hodder & Stoughton, 1985.
Brüeggemann, Walter. *The Message of the Psalms.* Minneapolis: Augsburg, 1984.
Brummer, Vincent. *Theology and Philosophical Inquiry.* London: MacMillan, 1981.
Chang, Carsun. *Development of Neo-Confucian Thought.* New York: Bookman Associates, 1962.
Chittick, William. *The Sufi Path of Love.* Albany, NY: SUNY, 1983.
———. *The Sufi Path of Knowledge.* Albany, NY: SUNY, 1989.
The Christian Post. No pages. Online: http://sg.christianpost.com/dbase/church/2422//1.htm.
Chun-I, Tang. *Zhong Guó Wen Hua Zhî Jing Shén Jiá zhí* (The Spiritual Values of the Chinese Culture). Taiwan: Cheng Chung Books, 1951.
Clarke, Peter. "New Religious Movements." In *Dictionary of Biblical Interpretation,* edited by R. J. Coggins, and J. L. Houlden, 493–94. London: SCM, 1994.
Comblin, José. *The Holy Spirit and Liberation.* Liberation and Theology 4. New York: Orbis, 1989.
Cone, James. *Black Theology and Black Power.* New York: Seabury, 1969.
Confucius, *The Great Learning.* Shangdong, China: Shandong Friendship, 2000.

Cook, Stephen L. "Eschatology in the Old Testament." In *The New Interpreter's Dictionary of the Bible*, Vol. 2, edited by Katharine Doob Sakenfeld, 299–308. Nashville: Abingdon, 2006.
Costas, Orlando E. *Christ Outside the Gate: Mission Beyond Christendom*. Maryknoll, NY: Orbis, 1982.
———. *The Church and Its Mission: A Shattering Critique from the Third World*. Wheaton, IL: Tyndale, 1974.
———. *The Integrity of Mission: The Inner Life and Outreach of the Church*. San Francisco: Harper & Row, 1979.
———. "La misión como discipulado." *Boletín Teológico*, March-April 1982.
———. "La vida en el Espiritu." *Boletín Teológico*, June 1986.
———. *Liberating News: A Theology of Contextual Evangelization*. Grand Rapids: Eerdmans, 1989.
———. "Pecado y salvación en América Latina." In *América Latina en la evangelización en los años 80: Un congreso auspiciado por la Fraternidad Teológica Latinoamericana, CLADE II*, ?–?. Buenos Aires: FTL, 1979.
———. "Proclaiming Christ in the Two Thirds World." In *Sharing Jesus in the Two Thirds World*, edited by Vinay Samuel and Chris Sugden, 1–15. Bangalore: Partner in Mission, 1983.
Cox, Harvey. *The Secular City: Secularization and Urbanization in Theological Perspective*. New York: Macmillan, 1966.
Cragg, Kenneth. *The Call of the Minaret*. Oxford: Oxford University Press, 1956.
———. *Jesus and the Muslim*. Victoria, Australia: Allen & Unwin, 1985.
———. *Muhammad and the Christian*. Oxford: Oneworld, 1999.
———. *The Christ and the Faiths*. London: SPCK, 1986.
The Declaration of Bangui. "The Future of Evangelical Theology in French Speaking Africa." Bangui Evangelical School of Theology, Bangui, Central African Republic, May 18–21, 2009.
Del Colle, Ralph. "The Triune God." In *Cambridge Comparison to Christian Doctrine*, edited by Colin Gunten, 121–40. Cambridge: Cambridge University Press, 1997.
Denegaar, Johan. "The Changed View of Man." *Journal of Theology for Southern Africa* 6 (1974) 41–64.
Dick, Devon. *The Cross and the Machete: Native Baptists in Jamaica: Identity, Ministry and Legacy*. Kingston: Randle, 2010.
Dickson, Kwesi. *Theology in Africa*. London: Darton, Longman and Todd, 1984.
Ding, Guangxun. "On the Development of Three-self Patriotic Movement of the Protestant Churches in China." *Tian Feng: the Magazine of the Protestant Churches in China* 1 (2000) 4–5.
Dopanu, Abiola T. "Secularization, Christianity and the African Religion in Yorubaland." *African Ecclesial Review* 48.3 (2006) 139–56.
Edmonds, Ennis B. *Rastafari: From Outcasts to Culture Bearers*. New York: Oxford, 2003.
Edwards, Joel. *The Jamaican Diaspora: A People of Pain and Purpose*. Kingston, Jamaica: Morgan Ministries International, 1998.
Ehrman, Bart D. *Misquoting Jesus: The Story Behind Who Changed the Bible and Why*. New York: HarperCollins, 2007.
The English Language Liturgical Commission. *Praying Together*. Nashville: Abington Press, 1988.

Erskine, Noel Leo. *From Garvey to Marley: Rastafari Theology*. Miami: University Press of Florida, 2007.

Escobar, Samuel. "Evangelical Theology in Latin America: The Development of a Missiological Christology." *Missiology: An International Review* XIX.3 (1991) 315–32.

———. *La Fe Evangélica y las Teologías de la Liberación*. El Paso: Casa Bautista de Publicaciones, 1987.

———. "Que significa ser evangélico hoy?" *Revista Misión* 1.1 (1982) 14–18, 35–39.

———. *Tiempo de Misión: América Latina y la misión cristiana hoy*. Santafé de Bogotá and Ciudad de Guatemala: Ediciones Clara-Semilla, 1999.

Fabien Eboussi Boulaga. *Christianisme sans fétiches*. Révélation et domination. Paris: Présence africaine, 1981.

Faruqi, Ismail. *Al Tawhid: Its Implications for Thought and Life*. Herndon, VA: International Institute of Islamic Thought, 1992.

Ferdinando, Keith. *The Triumph of Christ in African Perspective*. Paternoster Theological Monographs. Carlisle, UK: Paternoster, 1999.

Fiorenza, Elizabeth Schüssler. "Apocalypsis and Propheteia: Revelation in the Context of the Early Christian Prophecy." In *L'Apocalypse johannique et l'Apocalyptique dans le Nouveau Testament*, edited by J. Lambrecht, 105–28. BETL 53. Leuven: Leuven University Press, 1980.

France, R. T. *The Gospel of Mark*. New International Greek Testament Commentary. Grand Rapids: Eerdmans, 2002.

Friemuth, Maha El-Kaisy. "Al-Radd Al Jamil: Ghazali's or Pseudo-Ghazali." *The Bible and Arab Christianity*, edited by David Thomas. Leiden: Brill, 2007.

Gatje, Helmut. *The Quran and its Exegesis*. London: Routledge, 1971.

Gehman, Richard J. *African Religion in Biblical Perspective*. Rev. ed. Nairobi: East African Educational, 2005.

Gill, Jerry. *The Possibility of Religious Knowledge*. Grand Rapids: Eerdmans, 1971.

González, Justo. "Encarnación e historia." In *Fe cristiana y Latinoamérica hoy*, edited by René Padilla, 154–67. Buenos Aires: Certeza, 1974.

———. *Mañana: Christian Theology from a Hispanic Perspective*. Nashville: Abingdon, 1990.

———. *Revolución y encarnación*. Puerto Rico: Editorial Universitas, 1965.

Grayston, Kenneth. *The Epistle to the Romans*. Epworth Commentaries. London: Epworth, 1997.

A Guide to Churches & Christian Organizations in Singapore 2011–2012. Singapore: A Publication of the National Council of Churches of Singapore, 2011.

Gutierrez, Gustavo. *El Dios de la vida*. Lima: Instituto Bartolomé de las Casas, Centro de Estudios y Publicaciones, 1989.

———. *A Theology of Liberation*. Maryknoll, NY: Orbis, 1973.

Hannah, Barbara Mekeda Blake. *Rastafari: The New Creation*. Kingston, Jamaica: Jamaican Media, 2002.

Hansen, Guillermo. "El uso político de la cruz: Poder y contra-poder en la "theologia cruces" de Lutero." In *El silbo ecuménico del Espíritu: Homenaje a José Míguez Bonino en sus 80 años*. Buenos Aires: Instituto Universitario ISEDET, 2004.

Harris, Sam. *End of Faith: Religion, Terror, and The Future of Reason*. New York: Norton, 2009.

He, Guanghu. *He Guanghu's Self-selected Works*. Guilin, China: Guangxi Normal University Press, 1999.

———. "The Ground and Significance of the Chinese Language Theology." In *He Guanghu's Self-selected Works*, 85–97. Guilin, China: Guangxi Normal University Press, 1999.

———. "The Methods and Approaches to the Chinese Language Theology." In *He Guanghu's Self-selected Works*, 98–111. Guilin, China: Guangxi Normal University Press, 1999.

———. "The Present and Prospect of 'Christian Theology in Chinese' in the Academic Community in Mainland China." No pages. Online: http://www.iscs.org.hk/Common/Reader/News/ShowNews.jsp?Nid=806&Pid=3&Version=0&Cid=191&Charset=gb2312.

———. "Trends of Chinese Scholars in Christian Studies in the Turn of the Twentieth and Twenty-First Century." *Logos & Pneuma: Chinese Journal of Theology* 29 (2008) 53–75.

Hebblethwaite, Brian. *The Essence of Christianity: A Fresh Look at the Nicene Creed*. London: SPCK, 1996.

Heitzig, Skip. *When God Prays: Discovering the Heart of Jesus in His Prayers*. Wheaton, IL: Tyndale, 2003.

Heschel, Abraham. *The Insecurity of Freedom*. New York: Schoken, 1972.

———. *The Prophets*, vol. 2. New York: Harper, 1975.

Hoehner, Harold. *Ephesians*. Grand Rapids: Baker, 2002.

Hoekema, Anthony, et al. *Five Views on Sanctification*. Grand Rapids: Zondervan, 1996.

Hodgson, Marshall. *The Venture of Islam. Vol. 1: The Classical Age of Islam*. Chicago: University of Chicago Press, 1977.

Huai, Renlian. "Review on 'Cultural Christians.'" *The Religious Cultures in the World* 4 (2004) 51–52.

Huang, Ruicheng. "Modernity of Nationalism and Chinese Christian." In *Correlating Chinese and Western Culture*, edited by Xiaochao Wang and Xinan Yang. Guilin, China: Guangxi Normal University Press, 2006.

HoSang, David, and Roger Ringenberg. "Towards an Evangelical Caribbean Theology." *Evangelical Review of Theology* 7 (1983) 125–47.

Hultgren, Arland J. *Paul's Letter to the Romans: A Commentary*. Grand Rapids: Eerdmans, 2011.

Hughes, T. P. *Notes on Muhammadanism*. Victoria, Australia: Allen & Unwin, 1877.

Idowu Bolaji E. "The Study of Religion with Special Reference to Africa Traditional Religion," *Orita* 1.1 (1967) 1–8.

Ikenga-Metuth. *God and Man in African Religion: A Case Study of the Igbo of Nigeria*. London: Chapman, 1981.

Ilogu, Edmund. *Christianity and Igbo Culture: A Study of the Interaction of Christianity and Igbo Culture*. New York: NOK, 1974.

Internet World Stats. No pages. Online: http://www.internetworldstats.com/asia/sg.htm.

ISCS, ed. *Cultural Christian: Phenomenon and Argument*. Hong Kong: Institute of Sino-Christian Studies, 1997.

———. "On the Re-publication of Logos & Pneuma." *Logos & Pneuma: Chinese Journal of Theology* 1 (1994).

Isichei, Elisabeth. *A History of Christianity in Africa*. 1995.

Jüngel, Eberhard. *God as the Mystery of the World*. Edinburgh: T. & T. Clark, 1983.
Kapolyo, Joe M. *The Human Condition: Christian Perspectives through African Eyes*. Leicester, UK: IVP, 2005.
Kärkkäinen, Veli-Matti. "The Working of the Spirit of God in Creation and in the People of God: The Pneumatology of Wolfhart Pannenberg." *Pneuma* 26.1 (2004) 17–35.
Kasper, Walter. *The God of Jesus Christ*. New York: Crossroad, 1982.
Kato, Byang. *Theologial Pitfalls in Africa*. Kisumu, Kenya: Evangel, 1975.
Kostenberger, Andreas J. *A Theology of John's Gospel and Letters*. Grand Rapids: Zondervan, 2009.
Kraft, Charles H. "The Development of Contextualization Theory in Euroamerican Missiology." In *Appropriate Christianity*, edited by Charles H. Kraft, 15–34. Pasadena, CA: William Carey Library, 2005.
LaCugna, Catherine Mowry. *God for Us: The Trinity and Christian Life*. New York: Harper San Francisco, 1991.
Ladd, George E. *A Theology of the New Testament*. Grand Rapids: Eerdmans, 1993.
Lai, Pan Chiu. "Religious Studies, Theology and Sino-Christian Studies." *Shan Dao Journal* 12.2 (2009) 153–72.
———. "Types of Chinese Theology and Developing Paths." In *Preliminary Studies on Chinese Theology*, edited by Daniel H. N. Yeung. Hong Kong: Institute of Sino-Christian Studies, 2000.
Lampe, G. W. H. "The Testimony of Jesus is the Spirit of Prophecy (Rev 19:10)." In *The New Testament Age: Essays in Honor of Bo Reicke*. Vol 1, edited by William C. Weinrich, 245–58. Macon, GA: Mercer University Press, 1984.
Le Grys, Alan. *Preaching of the Nations: The Origins of Mission in the Early Church*. London: SPCK, 1998.
Li, Qiuling. "A Historical Reflection on Sino-Christian Theology." *Newsletters of Institute of Sino-Christian Studies* 2 (2005) 1–2.
Li, Xiangping. "Sino-Christian Theology: Invisible Church and Public Faith." *Logos & Pneuma: Chinese Journal of Theology* 32 (2010) 57–69.
Lin, Zichun. *A Polyphonic View on Sino-Christian Theology*. Beijing: Religious Culture, 2008.
Linton, Faith. *What the Preacher Forgot to Tell Me: Identity and Gospel in Jamaica*. Pickering, Ontario: Bay Ridge, 2009.
Liu, Xiaofeng. "Sino-Christian Theology in the Modern Context." *Logos & Pneuma: Chinese Journal of Theology* 2 (1995).
———. *The Sino-Christian Theology and Philosophy of History*. Hong Kong: Institute of Sino-Christian Studies, 2000.
Liu, Zongkun. "The Phenomenon of Cultural Christianity in the Modern Chinese Context." In *Cultural Christian: Phenomenon and Argument*. Hong Kong: Institute of Sino-Christian Studies, 1997.
Lubis, Mohammad Bukhari. *The Ocean of Unity: Waḥdat al-Wujūd in Persian, Turkish and Malay Poetry*. Kuala Lumpur: Dewan Bahasa dan Pustaka, 1993.
Lupieri, Edmondo F. *A Commentary on the Apocalypse of John*. Grand Rapids: Eerdmans, 2006.
Mackay, John. *The Other Spanish Christ*. New York: Macmillan, 1933.
Mahizhnan, Arun. "Networked Society in an Intelligent Nation." In *Impressions of the Goh Chok Tong Years in Singapore*, edited by Bridget Welsh, James Chin, Arun Mahizhnan, and Tan Tarn How, 409–21. Singapore: NUS Press, 2009.

Mandela, Nelson. *Long Walk to Freedom*. Boston: Bay Back, 1995.
Mantzaridis, Georgios I. *The Deification of Man*. New York: St. Vladimir Press, 1984.
Marley, Robert Nesta. *Bob Marley: In His Own Words*. Edited by Ian McCann. London: Omnibus, 1993.
Martin, R. P. *Philippians*. 2nd ed. Downers Grove, IL: IVP, 2004.
Matera, Frank J. *Romans*. Grand Rapids: Baker, 2010.
Mbiti, John. "African Indigenous Culture in Relation to Evangelism and Church Development." In *The Gospel and Frontier Peoples*, edited by R. Pierce Beaver, 79–95. Pasadena, CA: William Carey Library, 1973.
———. *Africa Religions and Philosophy*. London: SPCK, 1969.
———. *Concept of God in Africa*. London: SPCK, 1970
———. "Christianity and Africa Religion." In *Facing the New Challenges*, edited by Michael Cassidy and Luc Verlindin, 308–13. Nairobi: Kisumu Evangel, 1978.
———. "New Testament Eschatology and the Akamba of Kenya." In *African Initiatives in Religions*, edited by David B. Barrett, 17–28. Nairobi: East African, 1971.
———. "New Testament Eschatology in an African Background." In *Readings in Dynamic Indigeneity*, edited by Charles H. Kraft and Tom N. Wisley, 455–64. Pasadena, CA: William Carey Library, 1979.
———. *Religions et Philosophies Africaines*. Yaoundé, Cameroon: Clé, 1992.
McGrath, Alister E. *The Future of Christianity*. Oxford: Blackwell, 2002.
———. *Luther's Theology of the Cross*. Oxford: Blackwell, 1990.
———. "A Particularist View." In *Four Views on Salvation in Pluralistic World*, edited by D. L. Okholm and T. R. Phillips, 149–80. Grand Rapids: Zondervan, 1996.
Meier, John P. *Companions and Competitors: A Marginal Jew—Rethinking the Historical Jesus, vol. 3*. New York: Doubleday, 2001.
Migliore, Daniel. *Faith Seeking Understanding: An Introduction to Christian Theology*. 2nd ed. Grand Rapids: Eerdmans, 2004.
Miguez Bonino, José. *Rostros del Protestantismo Latinoamericano*. Buenos Aires: Nueva Creación, 1995.
Mnyandu, M. "Ubuntu as the Basis of Authentic Humanity: An African Perspective." *Journal of Constructive Theology* 3.1 (1997) 77–86.
Moltmann, Jürgen. *A Broad Place: An Autobiography*. Translated by Margaret Kohl. Minneapolis: Fortress. 2008.
———. *The Crucified God: The Cross of Christ as the Foundation and Criticism of Christian Theology*. Translated by Margaret Kohl. Minneapolis: Fortress, 1974.
———. *God in Creation: A New Theology of Creation and The Spirit of God: The Gifford Lectures 1984–1985*. Translated by Margaret Kohl. Minneapolis: Fortress, 1985.
———. *God for a Secular Society: The Public Relevance of Theology*. Translated by Margaret Kohl. Minneapolis: Fortress, 1997.
———. "On Latin American Theology." *Christianity and Crisis* 36 (1976) 57–63.
———. *Weiter Raum: Eine Lebensgeschichte*. Gütersloh: Gütersloher Verlagshaus, 2006.
Moser, Paul K. "Religious Skepticism." In *The Oxford Handbook of Skepticism*, edited by John Greco, 200–224. Oxford: Oxford University Press, 2008.
Mugabe, Henri J. "Salvation from African Perspective." *Evangelical Review of Theology* 23.3 (1999) 238–47.
Murrell, Nathaniel Samuel. *James Barr's Critique of Biblical Theology: A Critical Analysis*. Ann Arbor, MI: University of Michigan Press, 1988.

Musopole, Augustine C. *Being Human in Africa: Toward an African Christian Anthropology*. New York: Lang, 1994.
Mveng, Engelbert, and B. L. Lipawing. *Théologie, libération et cultures africaines*. Yaoundé, Cameroon: Clé, 1996.
Naphtali, Karl Philpotts. *The Testimony of His Imperial Majesty Emperor Haile Selassie I, Defender of the Faith*. Washington, DC: Zewd, 1999.
Nawawi, Razali. *Al Ghazali's Criticism of Christians' Theological Doctrines*. Kuala Lumpur: Muslim Youth Movement (ABIM), 1983.
Neill, Stephen, and Tom Wright. *The Interpretation of the New Testament: 1861–1986*. Oxford: Oxford University Press, 1988.
Netland, Harold A. "The Bible and Other World Religions." *English Standard Version (ESV)*. Wheaton: Crossway, 2008.
Ndjérareou, Abel. "Theology as the Hermeneutic of Identity: Understanding African Theology in the 20th Century. A Response to Dr Kwame Bediako." *Colloque des Amis de la Théologie*, 1–8. Abidjan, Ivory Coast: March, 1999.
Niebuhr, Richard H. *Christ and Culture*. San Francisco: Harper San Francisco, 2001.
Noelliste, Dieumeme. "The Church and Human Emancipation: A Critical Comparison of Liberation Theology and the Latin American Theological Fraternity." PhD diss., Northwestern University, 1987.
———. "Transcendent But Not Remote." In *The Global God: Multicultural Evangelical Views of God*, edited by A. B. Spencer and W. D. Spencer, 104–26. Grand Rapids: Baker, 1998.
Nolan, Albert. *Jesus Before Christianity*. Maryknoll, NY: Orbis, 1976.
Nunez, E. "The Theology of Liberation in Latin America." *The Evangelical Review Theology* 3 (1979) 37–49.
Ogunade, Raymond. "African Eschatology and the Future of the Cosmos." Online: www.unilorin.edu.ng/.../Journal%20of%20Arabic%20and%20Religious%20 Studies.h. [accessed July 29, 2011].
Opoku, Asare Kofi. *West African Traditional Religion*. Accra: FEF International, 1978.
Padilla, René. "Christology and Mission in the Two Thirds World." In *Sharing Jesus in the Two Thirds World: Evangelical Christology from the Context of Poverty, Powerlessness and Religious Pluralism*, edited by Vinay Samuel and Chris Sugden, 17–47. Bangalore: Partnership in Mission-Asia, 1983.
———. "Cristología y misión en los dos-terceros mundos." *Boletín Teológico* 8 (October–December, 1982) 58–59.
———. "El Espíritu Santo y la misión integral de la iglesia." In *El Trino Dios y la misión integral*, edited by Pedro Arana, Samuel Escobar, and C. Rene Padilla, 115–47. Buenos Aires: Ediciones Kairos, 2003.
———. "El Reino de Dios y la Iglesia." In *El Reino de Dios y América Latina*, edited by René Padilla, 43–68. El Paso, TX: Casa Bautista de Publicaciones, 1975.
———. "God's Word and Man's Words." *The Evangelical Quarterly* 53 (1981) 216–26.
———. "Jesús: ¿Mito o Historia?" *¿Quién es Cristo hoy?* Buenos Aires: Certeza, 1970.
———. "La nueva eclesiología en América Latina." *Boletín Teológico* (December 1986) 201–26.
———. "La autoridad de la Biblia en la teología latinoamericana." In *El debate contemporáneo sobre la Biblia*, edited by Peter Savage, 123–53. Barcelona: Evangélicas Europeas, 1972.

———. *Mission Between the Times: Essays on the Kingdom*. Grand Rapids: Eerdmans, 1985.

———. *Misión Integral: Ensayos sobre el reino y la iglesia*. Buenos Aires: Nueva Creación, 1986.

———. "¿Quién es Cristo Hoy?" *Misión: Revista internacional de orientación cristiana* 1.2 (1982) 24–25.

———. "Toward a Contextual Christology from Latin America." In *Conflict and Context: Hermeneutics in the Americas*, edited by Mark Lau Branson and René Padilla, 81–94. Grand Rapids: Eerdmans, 1986.

Parrinder, Geoffrey. *Africa's Three Religions*. London: Sheldon, 1969.

Packer, J. I. *Concise Theology: A Guide to Historic Christian Beliefs*. Wheaton, IL: Tyndale, 1991.

Palmer, D. V. *Messianic "I" and Rastafari in NT Dialogue: BioNarratives, the Apocalypse, and Paul's Letter to the Romans*. Plymouth, MA: University Press of America, 2010.

———. *Pronominal "I," Rastafari and the Lexicon of the New Testament*. Ann Arbor, MI: University of Michigan Press, 2008.

Pannenberg, Wolfhart. *Systematic Theology*, vol. 1. Grand Rapids: Eerdmans, 1988.

———. *Systematic Theology*, vol. 2. Grand Rapids: Eerdmans, 1994.

Pearson, David. "Excursus 1: Justification by Click." In *Romans in Context: A Theological Appreciation of Paul's Magnum Opus*, by Dalano Vincent Palmer, 55–57. Eugene, OR: Resource, 2011.

Petersen, David L. " Eschatology." In *The Anchor Bible Dictionary Vol. 2*, edited by David N. Freedman, 575–79. New York: Doubleday, 1992.

Peters, Ted. *God as Trinity: Relationality and Temporality in Divine Life*. Louisville: Westminster John Knox, 1993.

Prigent, Pierre. *Commentary on the Apocalypse of St. John*. Tübingen: Mohr Siebeck, 2004.

Rahman, Fazlur. *Major Themes of the Quran*. Kuala Lumpur: Islamic Book Trust, 1999.

Saracco, Norberto. "La Iglesia y el Espíritu." *Boletín Teológico* (January–June 1984) 70–83.

Schimmel, Annemarie. *Mystical Dimensions of Islam*. Chapel Hill, NC: University North Carolina Press, 1978.

Schnelle, Udo. *Theology of the New Testament*. Translated by M. E. Boring. Grand Rapids: Baker, 2009.

Schreiner, T. R. *New Testament Theology: Magnifying God in Christ*. Grand Rapids: Baker, 2008.

Schreiter, Robert J. *Constructing Local Theologies*. Maryknoll, NY: Orbis, 1985.

Selassie, Haile. "Building an Enduring Tower." In *One Race, One Gospel, One Task*, edited by C. F. H. Henry and W. S. Mooneyham. Minneapolis: WWP, 1967.

Shorter, Aylward. *Secularism in Africa: A Case Study of Nairobi City*. Nairobi: Paulines, 1997.

Siew, A. K. W. "The Identity of the Two Witnesses and the Two Beasts." In *The War between the Two Beasts and the Two Witnesses: A Chiastic Reading of Revelation 11:1—14:5*, 214–78. London: T. & T. Clark, 2005.

Singapore Department of Statistics. No pages. Online: http://www.singstat.gov.sg/.

Sitahal, Harold. "Caribbean Theology: Of the People/For the People." *Caribbean Journal of Religious Studies* 14 (1999) 41–48.

Slingerland, Edward. *Effortless Action—Wu Wei as Conceptual Metaphor and Spiritual Ideal in Early China*. Oxford: Oxford University Press, 2003.
Smalley, S. S. *The Revelation to John: A Commentary on the Greek Text of the Apocalypse*. Downers Grove, IL: IVP, 2005.
Shorter, Aylward, and Edwin Onyancha. *Secularism in Africa: A Case Study: Nairobi City*. Nairobi: Paulines, 1997.
Sobrino, Jon. *Cristología desde América Latina*. México: CRT, 1977.
———. *Christology at the Crossroads*. Maryknoll, NY: Orbis, 1978.
———. *Jesucristo liberador: Lectura histórico teológica de Jesús de Nazaret*. El Salvador: UCA Editores, 1991.
Stanton, H. U. Weitbrecht. *The Teaching of the Quran*. London: MacMillan, 1919.
Sweetman, James W. *Islam and Christian Theology*. 4 vols. Reprint. Cambridge: James Clark, 2002.
Sweet, J. "Maintaining the Testimony of Jesus: The Suffering of Christians in the Revelation of John." In *Suffering and Martyrdom in the New Testament: Studies presented to G. M. Styler by the Cambridge New Testament Seminar*, edited by W. Horbury and B. McNeil, 101–17. Cambridge: Cambridge University Press, 1981.
Tamiyyah, Ibn. *Al-Jawab Al-Sahih: A Muslim Theologian Response to Christianity*. Delmar, NY: Caravan, 1984.
Tano, R. D. "Towards an Evangelical Asian Theology." *The Evangelical Review of Theology* 7 (1985) 175–87.
Tan, Sri Joseph Pairin Kitingan. No pages. Online: http://www.pbs-sabah.org/pbs3/html/news/2011/291011-bernama.html.
Taylor, Burchell. "Engendering Theological Relevance." *Caribbean Journal of Religious Studies* 20 (1999) 24–30.
———. *The Church Taking Sides: A Contextual Reading of the Letters to the Seven Churches in the Book of Revelation*. Kingston, Jamaica: BBC, 1995.
Taylor, Burchell, and N. Samuel Murrel. "Messianic Ideology and Caribbean Theology of Liberation." In *Chanting Down Babylon: The Rastafari Reader*, edited by Nathaniel Samuel Murrell, 390–411. Philadelphia: Temple University Press. 1998.
Theodore de Bary, William. *The Unfolding of Neo-confucianism*. New York: Columbia University Press, 1975
Thielman, Frank. *Ephesians*. Grand Rapids: Baker, 2010.
Thoennes, Erik. "Biblical Doctrine: An Overview (Mankind)" *English Standard Version: Study Bible*, 2526–29. Wheaton, IL: Crossway, 2008.
Thomas, C. Adrian. *A Case for Mixed-Audience with Reference to the Warning Passages in the Book of Hebrews*. New York: Lang, 2008.
Thomas, Oral. *Biblical Resistance Hermeneutics within a Caribbean Context*. London: Equinox, 2010.
Thomas, R. *Revelation 8–22: An Exegetical Commentary*. Chicago: Moody, 1995.
Thompson, Leonard L. *Revelation*. Abingdon New Testament Commentaries. Nashville: Abingdon, 1998.
Torrance, Thomas F. *Reality and Evangelical Theology*. Downers Grove, IL: IVP, 1982.
Trites, Allison A. *The New Testament Concept of Witness*. Cambridge: Cambridge University Press, 1977.
Tsung-san, Mou. *History of Philosophy*. Taiwan: Student Press, 1976.
Tutu, Desmond. *No Future without Forgiveness*. New York: Doubleday, 1999.

Turaki, Yusufu. *Christianity and African Gods: A Methods in Theology.* Potchefstrom, SA: Potchefstrom University of Higher Education, 1999.

Turaki, Yusufu. *Foundations of African Traditional Religion and Worldview.* Nairobi: WordAlive, 2006.

Turaki, Yusufu. *Trinity of Sin.* Grand Rapids: Zondervan, 2011.

Van Der Walt, B. J. *The Liberating Message: A Christian Worldview for Africa.* Potchefstroom, SA: Potchefstroom University for Christian Higher Education, 1994.

Vanhoozer, Kevin J. "One Rule to Rule Them All? Theological Method in an Era of World Christianity." *Globalizing Theology: Belief and Practice in an Era of World Christianity*, edited by Craig Ott and Harold A. Netland, 85–126. Grand Rapids: Baker Academic, 2006.

Vassel, Sam. "Personal Purity." *The Evangelical Review Theology* 12 (1988) 359–68.

———. "Socio-political Concern of the Gospel of Luke." MA thesis, Wheaton Graduate School, 1982.

Vermes, Geza. *The Complete Dead Sea Scrolls in English.* London: Penguin, 1997.

———. *Jesus the Jew.* Philadelphia: Fortress, 1981.

Volf, Miroslav. *Exclusion and Embrace.* Nashville: Abingdon, 1966.

Wallis, Ian G. *The Faith of Jesus Christ in Early Christian Traditions.* SNTS Monograph Series 84. Cambridge: Cambridge University Press, 1995.

Waltke, Bruce. *Theology of the Old Testament.* Grand Rapids: Zondervan, 2007.

Wang, Xiaochao. "Methods and Paths for Understanding and Doubting Sino-Christian Theology." In *Preliminary Studies on Chinese Theology*, edited by Daniel H. N. Yeung. Hong Kong: Institute of Sino-Christian Studies, 2000.

———. "On the Characteristics and Boundary of Sino-Chiristian." In *Globalization, Values and Pluralism*, edited by Guo, Changgang et al. Shanghai: Shanghai Sanlian, 2010.

———. "On the Influence of Sino-Christian Theology to the Chinese Academia and Its Position." *Logos & Pneuma: Chinese Journal of Theology* 32 (2010) 45–56.

———. "On Three Characteristics of Sino-Christian Theological Studies." No pages. Online: http://www.iscs.org.hk/Common/Reader/News/ShowNews.jsp?Nid=770&Pid=9&Version=0&Cid=18&Charset=iso-8859-1.

———. "Some Considerations of the Content of Sino-Christian Theology: Taking Account of the Delimitation Issue." *Logos & Pneuma: Chinese Journal of Theology* 29 (2008) 167–81.

———. "Understanding and Doubts: Reading Liu Xiaofeng's 'Sino-Christian Theology in the Modern Context.'" In *Modernity, Transformation of Tradition and Sino-Christian Theology*, edited by Li Qiuling and Daniel H. N., Yeung, 42–53. Shanghai: East China Normal University, 2010.

Wen, Weiyao. *On the Transformation and Transcendence of Humanity a Sino-Christian Perspective.* Beijing: Religious Culture, 2009.

Watty, William W. "Jesus and the Temple: Cleansing or Cursing?" *Expository Times* 93 (May 1982) 235–39.

———. "The Significance of Anonymity in the Fourth Gospel." *Expository Times* 90 (April 1979) 209–12.

Weiss, Karl-Erich. "Die Rastari-Bewegung auf Jamaika." Hausarbeit zur Erlangung des Magister Grades, Westfälische Wilhelms-Universität, Munster, 1986.

West, Gerald. "Review of Oral Thomas, *Biblical Resistance Hermeneutics within a Caribbean Context*. London: Equinox, 2010." http://www.bookreviews.org/bookdetail.asp?TitleId=7658, 2011.

Williams, Lewin. *The Indigenization of Theology in the Caribbean*. Ann Arbor, MI: University of Michigan Press, 1989.

Williams, Lewin. *Caribbean Theology*. New York: Lang, 1994.

Wilhelm, Richard. *I-Ching (The Book of Change)*. London: Penguin, 1995.

Witherington, Ben. *Revelation*. New Cambridge Bible Commentary. Cambridge: Cambridge University Press, 2003.

Wong, Canon Terry. "The Church Ministry in a Digital Age." *Church + Society in Asia Today* 14.1 (2011) 53–59.

Xi, Wuyi. "The Fate of Christianality in Modern China." *Chinese Social Science Today* (2008).

Xie, Zhibin. "'Social' or 'Theological': Sino-Christian Theology and Chinese Society." *Logos & Pneuma: Chinese Journal of Theology* 32 (2010) 71–84.

———. *Public Theology and Globalization: A Study in Max L. Stackhouse's Christian Ethics*. Beijing: Religious Culture, 2008.

Yang, Huiling, and Zhibin Xie. "Introduction to the Main Theme." *Logos & Pneuma: Chinese Journal of Theology* 32 (2010) 19–26.

Yang, Huiling. "On Sino-Christian Theology: Its Unique Value from Linguistic Aspect." In *Modernity, Transformation of Tradition and Sino-Christian Theology*, edited by Li Qiuling and Daniel H. N. Yeung, 680–93. Shanghai: East China Normal University, 2010.

Yeung, Daniel H. N., ed. *Preliminary Studies on Chinese Theology*. Hong Kong: Institute of Sino-Christian Studies, 2000.

Yeo, Khiok-Khng. "Hope for the Persecuted, Cooperation with the State, and Meaning for the Dissatisfied: Three Readings of *Revelation* from a Chinese Context." In *From Every People and Nation: The Book of Revelation in Intercultural Perspective*, edited by David Rhoads, 200–221. Minneapolis: Fortress, 2005.

Yew, Lee Kuan. *My Lifelong Challenge: Singapore's Bilingual Journey*. Singapore: The Straits Times, 2012.

Yorke, Gosnell L. O. R. "The Bible and Africans in the Caribbean." In *The Africana Bible: Reading Israel's Scripture from Africa and the African Diaspora*, edited by Hugh Page et al., ?–?. Philadelphia: Fortress, 2009.

———. "Biblical Hermeneutics: An Afrocentric Perspective." *Journal of Religious Thought* 52 (1995) 1–13.

———. *The Church as the Body of the Christ in the Pauline Corpus: A Re-examination*. Lanham, MD: University Press of America, 1991.

Yoder, John Howard. *Jesús y la realidad política*. Buenos Aires: Ediciones Certeza, 1985.

Zhang, Qingxiong. *Categories of Christian Theology: A Comparative Study from Historical and Cultural Perspective*. Shanghai: Shanghai People's Publishing House, 2003.

Zhuo, Xinping. "Academic Theology: A New Approach to Christian Studies in Contemporary China." In *Annual Report on China's Religions 2008*, edited by Ze Jin and Yonghui Qiu, 130–57. China: Social Sciences Academic Press, 2008.

Index

African traditional religion (ATR), xx–xxiv, 3–23, 182, 191
African Church, Church in Africa, ix, 19–20, 158, 195
Allah, xx, 24–25, 26n1, 27–30, 32, 34–36, 41–42

Bediako, Kwame, 11, 18, 20
Boff, Leornardo, 57, 58n14, 105n12
Bonino, Miguez, 104–5, 171n10,
Buddhism, xxi, 72, 76, 79–80, 217, 227, 230

Calvin, John, 74
Christianity, xvii, xx–xxiv, 3–4, 14, 17–20, 22–23, 26, 28, 31, 35, 37, 40n21, 45, 47, 71, 103, 107–9, 185, 188, 192–93, 199n2, 212n28, 217, 219, 221–22, 225–28, 230–33
Christian atheism (New atheism), xxi, 49, 50–52
Christology, xii, xxi–xxii, 103–10, 112–13, 116–18, 120–22, 130, 139, 158, 226–27
    African Christology, 158
    Latin American Christology, xxi–xxii, 102n1, 103–6, 108, 110, 120
    Trinitarian Christology, 102n1, 105n12, 110n36, 112, 118, 121, 130, 139
Colonialism, xxi, 19, 69, 84

Church, the, xvii, xix, xxii, 22, 54, 58, 82–83, 92, 98, 103–4, 107, 113, 116–18, 120–27, 129–32, 133n128, 134n134, 136, 138–40, 143–47, 149–52, 154–58, 160–61, 163–66, 168–71, 174n16, 175–78, 182n2, 191–92, 193n48, 195, 198, 204n14, 205, 208, 211, 213–14, 217
Confucianism, xii, xxi, 76, 78, 217, 222, 227, 230
Costas, Orlando, xxi–xxii, 103–4, 106, 121–25, 126n90, 127–131, 132n123, 133–40, 174, 176
Creation, xx, 5–6, 8–9, 13–15, 23, 26, 28–33, 37, 48, 51–61, 63, 68, 72, 74–75, 93n12, 100, 112, 114, 116, 118–21, 124, 126–40, 147, 163, 166, 197, 204, 231
Cross, the, xxii, 17–23, 37, 41–42, 45–47, 61–62, 82, 94, 113, 115, 123, 126–30, 133, 135, 137, 147, 191, 197
Contextual theology, xviii, 102–3, 221–22, 139
Contextualization, 84, 103n2, 116, 122, 172, 197, 222, 224

Daoism, xxi, 79, 217

Escobar, Samuel, xiii, xvi, 104n6, 164, 165n3, 167,169n8, 170, 171n10, 171n11, 172–74

Ecclesiology, xxii, 143, 158
  The church as liberated and liberating community, xxii, 160–61, 164–65, 168–71, 177–78
  The church as pneumatic community, xxii, 158, 168
Enlightenment, the, 49, 62, 63, 223, 251
Eschatology, xix-xx, xxiii, 46, 98–99, 116–17, 119, 181–85, 190–91, 195–97
  African Eschatology, xix, xx, 181–85, 190, 195, 197
Evangelization, xxii, 103, 121, 125, 129, 133, 137–38, 153–54

Glorification, 42, 93, 98, 138, 215
Glorify, 42, 215
Globalization, 213–14, 233-33,
God, xi, xvi, xviii–xxiv, 3–63, 68, 75–83, 86n3, 87–88, 91–97, 99–101, 105–6, 107n19, 109–57, 160–78, 183–215, 227–31
  Attributes of, 25, 29, 58, 60–62
  Person of God, 33, 44, 56–57, 59, 83, 116, 118–20, 124–25, 129, 132n123, 135–36, 143
  Triune, xx, 37, 55, 56–60, 62–63, 121, 129–30, 132, 134–25, 137–38, 166
  Ultimate Self Revealing Subject, xxi, 52
  Will of God, 32–33, 41–42, 60, 166, 187, 190–91
  Works of God, 129n111, 134, 145, 165
Gospel, xii, xviii, xxi, xxiii, 7, 10, 13, 20, 22, 40, 67–69, 71, 73–74, 82–83, 85–89, 92, 93–95, 98, 102–3, 105–17, 119–21, 123–25, 130, 133, 137–38, 147, 153, 161, 163–66, 172n11, 173–75, 177, 192–93, 195, 197, 203–5, 207–11, 214–15, 226–27
  Eternal Gospel (Gospel of Eternal), xxiii, 20, 203–5, 208, 210, 215
  Gospel of Grace, 92, 94,
  Gospel of Liberation, xii, 69–71, 82, 85, 88, 93–94, 137
  Gospel of Redemption, xxi, 68, 71, 124, 215
  of Jesus Christ (Of God), xxi, 82, 107, 113, 125, 138
  Liberating Gospel, xii
  Pauline Gospel, 93
Gutierrez, Gustavo, 54, 100n28, 177n21

Historical Jesus, xxii, 54, 84n1, 106–10, 112, 115, 120, 122–23, 132, 135, 140
The Holy Spirit, xix, xxii, 55–56, 59, 83, 87–88, 111–13, 115–19, 124, 129–30, 133–34, 137, 143–76, 178, 191
The Paraclete, 148, 155
Human nature, 40, 72–74, 76–79, 194, 225
Humanity, xix–xxi, 3–6, 8–18, 21–24, 30, 33, 39, 46, 49, 57, 70, 73–79, 86, 88, 92, 93n12, 108, 110, 112, 116–20, 126, 128, 131, 136, 151, 165, 191, 225, 227, 229, 231

Idowu, Bolaji, 3n1, 9
Incarnation, 33–34, 38–41, 46, 54, 60, 68, 74–75, 86n2, 109, 112, 114, 119–20, 122–23, 126–28, 140, 156, 161, 193
Islam (Muslim), xxi, xx, 24–40, 42, 45–47, 185, 187–91, 210

Jesus Christ, xxi–xxii, 5–6, 12–13, 16–20, 22–23, 28, 32–33, 35–37, 39, 41–43, 51, 53–55, 60–61, 68, 77, 79, 82–88, 90–92, 98, 103, 106–20, 122–32, 135–40, 143–51, 154–57, 160–66, 170–78, 182, 185, 187, 192, 195–97, 199, 201, 206–7, 214–15, 221, 228
Justification, 68–69, 93–94, 96–97, 112, 211

Karl Barth, 52, 53n8, 68n1, 75n9, 229
Kato, Byang, xxiii, 181, 185, 191
Kingdom of God (Kingdom, The), 22, 53–54, 75, 110, 111–14, 116–21, 124–27, 132–39, 150, 160–71,

175–78, 191, 196–200, 204–5, 215, 230

Latin American Theological Fellowship, 104, 116n58
Latin American Theological Fraternity, xixn5, xxi, 105n5
Liberation, xxi, xviii, xxi, 57, 68–69, 79–80, 82, 85–86, 88–89, 91, 93–94, 98–101, 111, 113, 126, 137, 163, 166, 169, 177
Luther, Martin, 128n101

Mission, xii, xvi, xx–xxiv, 5, 42, 54, 71, 87–88, 90, 103, 107, 110–15, 117–22, 125–26, 129–34, 136–40, 145, 147, 149–50, 153–54, 157–75, 178, 182, 185, 191, 193, 195–97, 203, 208, 211–13, 215
 Christian mission in Africa, 182, 192, 195–96
 Christian mission in South East Asia, xxiii
 Eschatological mission, xxiii, 119, 133, 173
 Liberating mission, 132, 137, 160–63, 168
 of the Church of Africa, 19, 158, 182, 191, 195
 of the Church in South East Asia, xxiii, 198, 208, 212
 of Jesus, of the Messiah (of God), xxii, 5, 66, 54, 110n36, 112, 114–15, 118–20, 122, 125, 129–30, 132, 138, 160–63, 168–69
 Western mission, 192, 212n28
 Holistic mission, 174n16
Missiology, xix, xxiii, 103n2
Missional, xxii, xxiv
World Mission, xi, xvii, 5, 121–22, 125, 129, 136, 139, 158, 168, 213
Missionaries, xxiii, 8, 22, 71, 157, 164–65, 170, 171n10, 173, 175, 192, 196
 African missionaries, 22, 196
 Western missionaries, xxiii, 71, 192, 196

Moltmann, Jürgen, 48, 100n30, 127n100, 134n132, 229
Muhammad, 24, 32, 34–36, 42, 46
Mbiti, John, xxiii, 7n6, 9–11, 16–18, 20, 22–23, 181–85, 191

New Atheism, xxi, 50
New Age, 53, 98, 114, 116–17, 120
Neocolonialism, xxi, 84
Niebuhr, Richard, 72–73, 234

Padilla, Rene, xxi–xxii, 103–4, 106–13, 114n49, 114n50, 115–21, 139–40, 161, 167,
Pain and suffering, xx–xxi, 50, 61–63, 111
Pannenberg, Wolfhart, 107n19, 125n87, 229
Pentecostal Movement, the, 167
Poor and excluded, xxii, 162–63, 169–70, 172, 175
Predestination, xx, 27
Preferential option for the poor, 162
Pluralism, 193–95
Public theology, xxiv, 217, 226, 223, 234

The Quran, 25–28, 32, 35, 37, 42, 46, 186–89

Redemption, xxi, 17, 19, 56, 57, 59, 61, 68, 71, 115, 119, 121, 124, 126, 130, 134–35, 137, 139–40, 161

Salvation, xix, xxi, 5, 11, 14, 16–19, 22–23, 26, 42, 56–57, 68–69, 71, 73, 74–75, 78–81, 83–90, 93, 95, 97n18, 98–99, 105, 111, 126, 130, 135–38, 143–44, 147, 149, 152, 158, 162–63, 165, 184–85, 188–90, 194–95, 197, 199, 231
Saracco, Noberto, 166, 176
Secularism, xxiii, 21, 192–94
Soteriology, 100, 104–5

Theology of Liberation (Liberation Theology), xviii, 100

Tradition, xi, xxi, 20, 40–41, 45, 53, 69–71, 73, 75, 76–81, 83, 85–86, 93, 97, 106, 115, 122, 125–26, 134, 191, 218, 223, 225, 228–32

Trinity, The, 33–40, 47, 55–57, 62, 105, 110n36, 118, 121, 129–30, 133–34, 140, 143, 151, 155–56

Immanent Trinity, 37n17, 130, 133

Economic Trinity, 33, 133,

Turaki, Yusufu, 4, 8–11, 14, 22

Yoder, John Howard, 162

www.ingramcontent.com/pod-product-compliance
Lightning Source LLC
Chambersburg PA
CBHW071245230426
43668CB00011B/1595